Defoe's Perpetual Seekers

Defoe's Perpetual Seekers

A Study of the Major Fiction

Virginia Ogden Birdsall

Lewisburg
Bucknell University Press
London and Toronto: Associated University Presses

Associated University Presses
440 Forsgate Drive
Cranbury, NJ 08512

Associated University Presses
25 Sicilian Avenue
London WC1A 2QH, England

Associated University Presses
2133 Royal Windsor Drive
Unit 1
Mississauga, Ontario
Canada L5J 1K5

Library of Congress Cataloging in Publication Data

Birdsall, Virginia Ogden.
  Defoe's perpetual seekers.

  Bibliography: p.
  Includes index.
  1. Defoe, Daniel, 1661?–1731—Criticism and
interpretation.   I. Defoe, Daniel, 1661?–1731.
II. Title.
PR3407.B57   1985   823'.5   83-46154
ISBN 0-8387-5076-1

Printed in the United States of America

For Carolyn

Contents

Acknowledgments   9

1 Outward Bound: "terrify'd to the last Degree"   13

2 *Robinson Crusoe:* "a Miserable and almost Hopeless Condition"   24

3 *Captain Singleton:* "nothing but present Death"   50

4 *Moll Flanders:* "out of the Jaws of Destruction"   73

5 *A Journal of the Plague Year:* "Great were the Confusions"   101

6 *Colonel Jack:* "the grief of one absent Comfort"   121

7 *Roxana:* "Apparitions of Devils and Monsters"   143

8 Finis: "brought so low again"   171

   Notes   175

   Select Bibliography   196

   Index   200

Acknowledgments

The contributions that my friends, family, and colleagues have made to the various visions and revisions lying behind this study are beyond any easy acknowledgment, but I want to express, however inadequately, my special indebtedness to the following:

—to David A. Sonstroem, who supplied careful critical readings of the versions of the manuscript that I kept passing across his desk, and who contributed a detailed commentary far beyond what I had any right to expect of so busy a man.

—to Kim T. Phillips, who not only read portions of the manuscript about which I needed reassurance, but listened patiently to months and years of my mumblings and grumblings.

—to Caroline Birdsall, who gave me the benefit of both her enthusiasm and her editorial expertise when I turned to her in the final stages of my writing.

—to Richard D. Birdsall, who introduced me to the writings of Ernest Becker and Paul Hazard and lent me encouragement and support along the way.

—and, most important, to Carolyn O. Brotherton, who read and reread the entire manuscript, bringing to bear on my long sentences and longwindedness her clear legal mind and her lively sense of humor.

Defoe's Perpetual Seekers

1
Outward Bound
"terrify'd to the last Degree"

Robinson Crusoe describes the worst moments of the "terrible Storm" he encounters on his first sea voyage as "a time when every Body had his own Life to think of"; H. F. calls London's plague year "a Time when every one's private Safety lay so near them, that they had no Room to pity the distresses of others." And in one way or another, all of Daniel Defoe's fictional protagonists bear witness that personal survival in the midst of chaos was a subject that obsessed their creator. Defoe seems to have felt compelled to explore again and again the human condition at its starkest. It is as if, like his own heroes and heroines, he saw life from the point of view of a homeless orphan. It is as if for him all people were what his own Will Atkins calls "Aliens to bring Home."[1]

Defoe's fascination with man in a state of nature has been explored at length, as has the related question of the impact that Hobbes had on his thinking. But the full import of the Hobbesian influence on the fictions— and especially on those which followed *Robinson Crusoe*—has been obscured both early and late by critical preoccupation with other kinds of analyses. According to one well-known argument, the books are odysseys of *homo economicus:* the pursuit of money and status is at their center. And according to another widely held view, they are, on the contrary, spiritual autobiographies. Such viewpoints need not be regarded as irreconcilable. But reconciliation is only possible if, in effect, we step back a little and take a broader view—if, that is to say, we become aware of the elemental nature of not only Crusoe's experience but that of the other protagonists as well.

The point to be particularly emphasized is this: the experiences of Robinson Crusoe, Moll Flanders, and the rest involve both conversion to God and dedication to mammon. There can be no question that both themes are present. But placed within a Hobbesian scheme of things, they point to quite a different pattern in the fictions from what emerges when either is stressed to the exclusion or at the expense of the other. When the experiences of the protagonists are interpreted as secular ones involving personal expansion in materialistic terms, they are generally commented on pejoratively as indications of Defoe's advocacy of the virtues of economic man. When, on the other hand, they are interpreted as religious ones involving personal salvation as a result of awareness of sin and timely conversion, they are turned into proofs of Defoe's essentially Christian concerns—his determination to demonstrate the efficacy of religious conversion or to show the advisability of putting one's trust in the intervention of Providence. In a broader perspective, however, concern with personal salvation lies behind both the protagonists' dedication to materialistic expansion and their worries about timely conversion.

The fact is that if Defoe's heroes and heroines suffer, in the living of their lives, a clash within themselves between the demands of an old religion and those of a new one—between the traditional faith of their fathers and the capitalist faith—there are surely a great many details in the novels to indicate that such demands actually represent two different aspects of their more desperate battle: their struggle to discover a satisfactory *modus vivendi* in "a time of Warre, when every man is Enemy of every man."

Maximillian Novak, in his *Economics and the Fiction of Daniel Defoe*, cites Tawney's suggestion that poverty had, in the eighteenth century, become a sign not of salvation but of damnation;[2] and obviously, if to be poor was to be damned, then to be rich was to be at least likely to be saved. Thus, whether Robinson Crusoe, Moll Flanders, and Colonel Jack spend their time piling up earthly gains or heavenly credits—whether their stock-taking involves the concrete or the abstract—they may be seen as always pursuing, in some sense, the supernatural.[3] They will, in the last analysis, settle for anything that seems to work in providing an escape from, or at least a hedge against, the terror of their own mortality. Defoe's heroes never spend time, even in prayer, except in the effort to gain more time, just as they never spend money except in an effort to gain more money and the transcendent advantage related to that.[4]

Robbed of parents or mistrustful of them and facing a consequent emptiness, they also continually confront, albeit with varying degrees of awareness, the prospect of personal annihilation. Hence, appetitive creatures that they are, they keep trying to fill themselves up with food or with wealth or with knowledge in anticipation of a rainy day—to round themselves out into selves that will be complete and thus self-sufficient and all-powerful. But the clouds continue to lower and at times the storm actually strikes. And then they turn in their terror to the arms that they want to think are still held out to them.

The times in which Defoe lived, while exhilarating, were also disquieting and confusing, as watershed periods of history invariably are.[5] And perhaps no figure of the era represents more clearly than does Defoe a coming together of the old and the new in an uneasy juxtaposition. That Defoe eschewed the vocation of Dissenting clergyman and chose instead to become a tradesman may seem a resolute putting aside of the old in favor of the new. Yet, in view of the moralistic content of his voluminous nonfictional output, one concludes that his choice was neither easy nor in his own mind clear-cut. The speculator, the risk-taker, the individualist, whose faith lay in achievement of a secular kind, existed side by side with the Puritan preacher of morality and social order, whose faith lay in the past.

And when Defoe the essayist gives way to Defoe the creator of fictions, he abandons detachment and presents human experience in all its incongruity and confusion. Novak argues that in his fictions Defoe's "major concern was moral rather than psychological."[6] But it seems truer to say that Defoe's moral concerns actually turn out to be, at a deeper level, psychological ones—a fact that becomes especially evident in *Moll Flanders*. And here a comparison with Pope may be instructive. Defoe does not, like Pope, make of himself a disapproving audience of the human comedy or attack with some delight the follies all around him. He does recognize, along with Pope, man's dividedness. But Defoe posits no synthesis, no integration, for the "Chaos of thought and passion, all confused." He knows the human need for order, but fails of any true faith in the possibility. He never asks us to assume with him a godlike perspective upon little, erring man. Man for him may be the "riddle of the world," but he is neither its "jest" nor its "glory," and the world itself is possessed of no majestic and glorious mysteriousness.

For Defoe the novelist there is only the limited perspective of the first person singular. The world his heroes and heroines occupy is a peculiarly personal one. They exist, as it were, in an open boat. It is an odd but interesting fact, that in this connection, Defoe seems more closely akin to those remote heirs of Hobbes, the twentieth-century naturalists, than to most of his own contemporaries. We might well say of his protagonists what Stephen Crane says of his victims of the storm: "None of them knew the color of the sky." Not even such world travelers as Robinson Crusoe, Captain Singleton, and Colonel Jack reveal any sense of a "spacious firmament on high." Always they live at the survival level. The reason for Defoe's adoption of the Hobbesian viewpoint must, of course, remain speculative, and perhaps it does not matter. But one might guess that it has something to do with his middle-class, urban identity. The circumscribed and highly competitive environment of the London streets, along with his own tradesman mentality, would seem to have produced in him a feeling of aloneness and insecurity.

None of Defoe's most famous literary contemporaries belonged to the city in quite the same man-in-the-street way that he did. Rather, they were inhabitants of a belletristic scheme of things and of those two closely related social worlds, the country estate and the aristocratic drawing room. Whereas Pope, Addison, and Steele were urbane, Defoe was urban. To him civilization did not mean, as it meant to them, grace, decorum, and musical and artistic accomplishment. It meant upward mobility, competition, conquest. Whereas, for example, Addison and Steele adopted a tone of kindly benevolence in instructing women to better their education and broaden their intellectual tastes, Defoe—viewing the plight of women through the consciousness of Moll Flanders and Roxana—identified the basis of that plight as a struggle for power and dramatized the female determination to achieve economic independence.

There is a roughness, a harshness, about the world of Defoe's characters that puts it in sharp contrast with the refined and elevated, the sophisticated and serene world of Addison and Steele. The very difference in prose style makes the point. Moreover, there is no place in the London streets walked by Moll, Colonel Jack, and Roxana for the "softness of the heart" of which Steele speaks in his preface to *The Conscious Lovers.* The "comfortable sense of security" that C. S. Lewis ascribes to Addison remains always a dream for Defoe's protagonists.[7] And thoughts of chivalry, good taste, or gentlemanliness, when they occur to Defoe's characters at all, are heeded, not because such standards of behavior are good in themselves, but because their espousal can contribute something to the self-esteem of their advocates.

There seems, what is more, to have been nothing in Defoe's experience that would have prompted him to adopt the Shaftesburian view that man possesses an innate moral nature. To the extent (and it is a limited one) that Defoe as novelist can be called a moralist at all, his is largely a morality of self-protection. And here again he anticipates the twentieth-century naturalist's outlook. Had he been given to such pronouncements, he might well have said what Theodore Dreiser was to say on the subject in *Sister Carrie:* "The dullest specimen of humanity, when drawn by desire toward evil, is recalled by a sense of right, which is proportionate in power and strength to his evil tendency. We must remember that it may not be a knowledge of right, for no right is predicated of the animal's instinctive recoil at evil. Men are still led by instinct before they are regulated by knowledge. It is instinct which recalls the criminal—it is instinct (where highly organized reasoning is absent) which gives the criminal his feeling of danger, his fear of wrong."

Given Defoe's implicit, and occasionally explicit, view of man as motivated by animal instinct, we might expect his closest affinity among his contemporaries to be with Swift. In fact, however, it is in noting his differences from Swift, both in tone and in emphasis, that we can see with particular clarity Defoe's main preoccupations in his fictions. For one thing, we feel in him virtually none of the anger over human behavior that we associate with Swift. The "savage indignation" that Swift felt for all that was unclean and unworthy in man has no counterpart in the Defoe of the fictions. And the reasons are not far to seek. For Swift, the idealist, the true order was the moral one. As Louis Bredvold remarks, he possessed, as did all the Tory satirists, a "firm faith in the ultimate right order of things."[8] Defoe, on the other hand, inclining as he does in his "true stories" to the naturalistic position, reveals no confidence in the existence of a rational, ordered nature.

Hence his discontent with things as they are has quite a different focus. Whereas Swift sees the human condition as involving the difficulty man has in living up to his own potentiality, Defoe sees it as involving the difficulty he has in staying alive. For Swift, man must struggle to be good; for Defoe he must struggle to *be*. Both emphasize man's reasoning powers. But in Swift's view, to fail to use one's God-given reason—as do, say, the Lilliputians—or to misuse it—as do the Laputans—is to behave reprehensibly, whereas in Defoe, to do either is to put one's life in danger. Clearly, the two writers distrusted flights of fancy on wholly different grounds.

Thus, if Swift's world traveler represents everyman in search of the wisdom to discern and do what is good, Robinson Crusoe, Moll Flanders, and their confreres represent everyman seeking to maintain life itself—and risking death in the process. Defoe was no detached ironist, expressing disappointment in human behavior and holding it up to ridicule. Whereas Swift detested vanity, avarice, pretentiousness, and power drives, Defoe follows Hobbes in associating these characteristics with the human effort to survive in an inhospitable environment. Like many of the characters in Stephen Crane's naturalistic world, Defoe's protagonists experience fear almost continually as their dominant emotion: when they are not strutting, they are cowering in abject terror.

Hence it seems strange that Maximillian Novak, the chief scholar to have analyzed in detail Defoe's view of man in a state of nature, largely confines his consideration of the fictions to *Robinson Crusoe*. To be sure, his reasons for doing so are clear. Defoe, Novak insists, "never abandoned the ideals of Christianity and civilization. . . . For the most part, his picture of the savage represents the depths to which human nature can fall when deprived of the benefits of European religion and culture."[9] And Novak ends his chapter on the subject with a succinct summary of what he takes to be Defoe's underlying belief: "Without social intercourse, civilization and government, mankind cannot for long live comfortably, securely, or happily."[10]

A closer look at the experiences of characters like Moll Flanders, Colonel Jack, and Roxana, however, must raise some question as to whether, in Defoe's view as expressed in the fictions, men and women—even with the benefits of "social intercourse, civilization, and government"—can "for long live comfortably, securely, or happily." For surely the experience of each Defoe hero and heroine amounts, in the final analysis, to an elemental struggle in a world in which each confronts Hobbes's "continuall feare, and danger of violent death."[11]

Probably the most striking difference between Defoe and other eighteenth-century novelists lies precisely here. Defoe's central characters are not presented—as are those of Fielding or Smollett or even Richardson—against the background of a social scene whose values define them and whose challenges absorb them. We get in the Defoe fictions no sense of a life being comfortably carried on amidst inns and country estates and drawing rooms and coffee houses. Society, for Defoe, offers finally no buffer between the individual and chaotic, predatory nature. It is made up of wolves in sheep's clothing, and as a consequence it provides no place apart, no home. Indeed, a genuine sense of place is missing altogether in Defoe, despite the occasional mention of London parks and streets, American cities and rivers, African lakes, forests, and deserts. Defoe's characters—all of them inveterate travelers—seem always to be passing through one place or another on their way to someplace else.

It may seem that, in the course of his lifetime on his island, Robinson Crusoe does rise above that state of nature Hobbes describes.[12] But the fact is that civilization turns out to make very little difference for Crusoe—and apparently it made very little difference for Defoe. One might say that with each Defoe fiction we are moved, as it were, to a higher level of civilized existence. Robinson Crusoe's adventures on his island perhaps seem a far cry from Moll Flanders's adventures in the streets of London and farther still from Colonel Jack's enjoyment of upper-middle-class prosperity and Roxana's fraternization with princes of the realm. In whatever environment the central character finds himself, however, the peace he seeks—the sense of at-homeness—is for him invariably either illusory or elusive.

The protagonists' stories begin only when the solitary individual finds himself alone against the world. It is, in fact, his solitude that is the most notable indicator of the Defoe character's condition, whether he finds himself on an uninhabited island or on a populous London street.[13] The extent of that solitude becomes especially apparent when we view him side by side with Samuel Richardson's isolated heroines and hero. For is it even remotely thinkable that any of Defoe's protagonists could have presented themselves as letter writers in the Richardsonian vein? Pamela's and Clarissa's letters reveal not only trust but a capacity for intimacy that none of Defoe's characters can be said to possess. And to whom would any of them have written?

Novak's comment that for Defoe self-love was "the true key to human nature" would surely have come as no surprise to any reader already acquainted with Moll Flanders or Colonel Jack or even H. F.[14] Self-centeredness is at the heart of all the fictions. In each of them there is only one character deserving of much attention. Nearly all the other characters are doubles or projections of the protagonist. Or they function as protective parent-figures—the child-parent relationship being the only kind that matters in the survival game being played.

Moreover, any pursuit the heroes and heroines engage in—any social climbing, any accumulating of wealth, any human relationship—becomes for them a life-and-death matter. There may be various dramatis personae in the dramas of their lives, but for each of them there is only one antagonist that counts: that ultimate limiter of the precious self, death.

The characters' self-centeredness is everywhere manifest; and in this regard they illustrate one Hobbesian dictum after another: "of the voluntary acts of every man, the object is Good to himself"; "no man giveth, but with intention of Good to himself"; "man, whose Joy consisteth in comparing himselfe with other men, can relish nothing but what is eminent."[15]

What is more, the stories told by Defoe's heroes and heroines repeatedly attest to the endless nature of the pursuit of power to which their fears commit them. Again and again they call to mind that much-quoted Hobbesian dictum: "there is no such thing as perpetuall Tranquillity of mind, while we live here; because Life it selfe is but Motion, and can never be without Desire, nor without Feare, no more than without Sense." Again and again they reveal that "generall inclination of all mankind, a perpetuall and restlesse desire of Power after power, that ceaseth onely in Death." And for each of them "the cause of this, is not always that a man hopes for a more intensive delight, than he has already attained to or that he cannot be content with a moderate power; but because he cannot assure the power and means to live well, which he hath present without the acquisition of more."[16]

Implicitly, then, both Hobbes and Defoe recognize the pursuit of God and the pursuit of money and status as having the same root—namely, the "desire of Power," behind which lies the desire for peace and security, for freedom from fear. "Riches, Knowledge and Honour," writes Hobbes, "are but severall sorts of Power."[17] And finally it is to man's desire for knowledge that he traces belief in God:

> This perpetuall feare, alwayes accompanying mankind in the ignorance of causes, as it were in the Dark, must needs have for object something. And therefore when there is nothing to be seen, there is nothing to accuse, either of their good or evill fortune, but some *Power,* or Agent *Invisible:* In which sense perhaps it was, that some of the old Poets said, that the Gods were at first created by humane Feare. . . . But the acknowledging of one God Eternall, Infinite, and Omnipotent, may more easily be derived, from the desire men have to know the causes of naturall bodies, and their several vertues, and operations; than from the feare of what was to befall them in time to come.[18]

Although Hobbes does not here seem to have clearly in mind the equation that he himself has established between the desire for knowledge and the desire for power that is born of fear, certainly Defoe's fearful protagonists repeatedly demonstrate the connection. It may be true, as Novak says, that in his discursive writings Defoe attacks the savage "whose worship is merely the product of fear" and argues that only Christianity can save him.[19] It is demonstrable, however, that when Defoe's own fictional protagonists—all of them presumably good Christians—turn to their "one God Eternall, Infinite, and Omnipotent," that turning is always inspired, ultimately, by "the feare of what [is] to befall them in time to come." And what is more, they reveal at no time any lasting conviction that Providence can be counted on to save them.

"Ignorance is the Curse of God: Knowledge the wings wherewith we fly to Heaven" reads the motto on one eighteenth-century political pamphlet.[20] But no matter how desperately Defoe's heroes and heroines seek to escape the fact, they must invariably face—in the midst of the pride of power they feel as the result of their worldly successes—an awareness that the natural energies of their world defy both knowledge and control. Unable to know fully the reasons of things or to explore and exploit their universe fully, they acknowledge at last a higher reasoning power than their own. It is the will of Providence, they say. It becomes safer to be good children than prideful, defiant adults.

"What is glory without virtue?" Defoe demands, in an essay on Marlborough's funeral. "A great man without religion is no more than a great beast without a soul."[21] Here is precisely the thinking that leads all of Defoe's protagonists to grow concerned over their own wickedness and to look to God for help. But that decision does not really bring them the comfort they seek. Their uneasiness remains, and at times still becomes cold fear. If they are trying to turn dross into gold in their secular pursuits, they are trying to do exactly the same thing when they turn their faces to God. In either stance, they are looking upward. But as their narratives come to a close, we have no sense, even with the most successful of them, that they are entering the celestial city.

Although Defoe's characters seem to be acting purposefully in the world, they are always, in actuality, merely reacting to the terrors of their own finitude. When they seem to be the pursuers, they are really the pursued; what looks like running toward some elusive goal is, in reality, only a running away. And as they end their stories, they reveal themselves as in no sense visionaries; their point of view is a retrospective one.[22] They are all still looking over their shoulders—or all except Roxana, who has an awful sense that she has lost the battle. To put the matter another way, they are all looking upward in order not to look down beneath their feet at the gaping hole that may swallow them up at any moment.

There is a telling commentary on Crusoe's, Moll's, and Captain Singleton's kind of self-aggrandizing success in Defoe's account of the bankrupt tradesman bent on recouping his losses: "his Hand or Head is always at Work, or perhaps both; he rolls about the World like a Snowball, always gathering more, always increasing, till he comes to a Magnitude sufficient to exist of himself."[23] The irony is inescapable. Such an existence as he describes must at best have been precariously maintained and, one supposes, only in a very cold climate.

In the last analysis, Defoe parts company even with Hobbes. After all, Hobbes's Leviathan depends for its very existence on the ultimate supremacy of human reason. While certainly no believer in innate human virtue, Hobbes did believe in "that Rationall and most excellent worke of Nature, Man," and he described the commonwealth as an "Artificiall Man," with "Equity and Lawes, an artificiall *Reason* and *Will*. . . ."[24] Hobbes believed that man, possessed of reason, had not only the desire but the capacity to impose some order on the chaos of his life. Man may use reason to his own selfish ends, but at least he *can* make it dominate to the end of his being able to master his circumstances.

But another contemporary figure—namely, the Earl of Rochester—pursued the naturalistic element of Hobbes's view to its logical end. And a recent critic has argued convincingly that Rochester crucially influenced Defoe's thinking—more crucially than Novak's analysis might indicate.[25] Of Defoe's position on matters concerning the human possession of "reason, virtue and religion," John McVeagh says flatly: "one's suspicion of a subconscious attachment to the kind of thing Rochester was saying . . . is strengthened, despite his specific dissociation from parts of Rochester's philosophy, by moments in his own work in which his allegiance to reason and religion jostles with a cynical perception . . . that all spiritual effort is worthless"; that "reason, virtue and religion were sometimes—in practice—not very far from the nonentities which Rochester called them"; that "the workings of the reasoning faculty . . . are futilities"; and that "the religious believer, as well as being a failure, may . . . also be a fool."[26] And discussing *Jure Divino,* McVeagh insists that although Defoe wanted to believe in the supremacy of reason over the passions, he could not in all honesty do so. However reluctantly, he could see men only as "predatory, infected and monstrous." Not surprisingly, McVeagh uses the words *cynicism* and *nihilism* in the process of defining the Hobbes-Rochester aspect of Defoe's thought.

It is the purpose of the present study to argue that no one approaching Defoe as novelist can leave out of account the extent of the Hobbes-Rochester influence without neglecting a crucial aspect of Defoe's thinking. Whether those readers who see the fictions as success stories define that success as socioeconomic on the one hand or spiritual on the other, they can do so only by ignoring the cynical undercurrent almost altogether. For the experiences of Defoe's protagonists insistently attest to their creator's awareness that reason and religion work at best precariously—and in the last analysis not at all—in ordering and controlling the inner and outer irrationalities constantly encountered. The inconsistencies, the confusions, the self-contradictions of Crusoe, Moll, and the rest reflect Defoe's own. Perhaps the only certainty is that there can be none.

And here the matter of Defoe's ironic or satiric intent in the fictions must be addressed explicitly. First of all, there is surely some inconsistency and confusion in the minds of readers who see Moll Flanders, and to some extent Colonel Jack and Roxana but not the other protagonists, as objects of their creator's satiric commentary. A single author may of course be capable of ironic commentary in some cases and straightforward portraiture in others. But Defoe's central characters resemble one another so closely that it is hard to believe that he would have been critical of some but not of others.

Moreover, there is so little indication that any of them could have or should have handled things differently that one must ask what superior standard Defoe offers us by which to judge them. Are we asked to think that, given the circumstances they encounter, we could have handled things better?

It is no doubt tempting for any reader to disapprove of a character like Moll Flanders—and to think he is joining the author in so doing. Judgmental detachment, especially when shared with another, almost invariably carries with it a pleasing element of self-congratulation. The disengaged onlooker can feel outrage or contempt, secure in the knowledge that he knows the right, the good, the moral way. But what right way does Defoe posit for Moll Flanders, Roxana, or Colonel Jack? The satirist, as W. H. Auden has said, is an idealist. He believes that things can be better than they are, and his goal, in asking his readers to laugh at or despise his characters, is reform. In the case of Defoe, however, the flattering truth about human nature that he wanted to believe and the truth revealed by his own observations were, as McVeagh has persuasively argued, miles apart. And it is the latter truth that dominates in the fictions.

For purposes of clarity perhaps it should be noted that there are two sorts of irony in Defoe. First, there is that of the satirist, which is to be found in the poems and in some of the essays—the irony intended to expose human follies; second, there is the implicit irony of the realist, which is to be found from *Robinson Crusoe* to *Roxana*. But that irony is quite different from the other. It has to do with Defoe's perception of the terrible incongruity that exists in the very nature of things between what we ask of life and what we get. In Hobbesian terms, we want peace and we get war; we want stasis and we get perpetual motion.

Again and again Defoe explores in his novels that dark aspect of man's being which Rochester saw.[27] Repeatedly, we watch the ingenious machinations of a character engaged, both while living his life and while giving an account of it, in an effort to rise above his own creatureliness—his own irrationalities, limitations, finitude.

Defoe seems to have become less a disciple of Descartes and Locke with every passing fiction—and, however unwillingly, more a subscriber to the cynical view of Rochester. In the voices of Colonel Jack and Roxana we hear a tone of desperation, which is less audible in the earlier fictions. And in both the later novels, the protagonists' success stories are frequently reminiscent of familiar fairy-tale plots—a fact that surely suggests a growing lack of conviction on Defoe's part. Moreover, even in his worst moments on his "Island of Despaire," Crusoe does not face a world so dark as the nightmare world depicted in the closing pages of *Roxana*.

What lies at the heart of Defoe's fictions, then, is not the boy- or girl-makes-good element. And even less is it the fact that at some point each character undergoes a conversion of sorts. Always the Defoe protagonist is waging a battle against an enemy from whom there can be no escape. Behind the characters' Hobbesian "desire of Power," whatever form that desire may take, the fear of obliteration is always to be felt. That fear rules their lives, dictating every move they make and every word they utter. All they can do, as they struggle for control, is to create momentary stays against confusion—to take refuge in temporary hiding places.

Despite what Defoe says in his prefaces about "the religious and useful Inferences" to be drawn from the lives of his characters, in the fictions themselves his own two escapist identities—successful merchant-gentleman and puritan moralist—give way. It is Defoe the follower of Hobbes and Rochester who has the last word.

2

Robinson Crusoe

"a Miserable and almost Hopeless Condition"

Perhaps more than any other of Defoe's protagonists Robinson Crusoe suffers from a malaise that he himself is powerless to explain. At the outset of his adventures, it expresses itself as a strange but insistent desire to leave his father's house. Recalling that his "Head began to be fill'd very early with rambling Thoughts," he goes on to say rather bemusedly, "I would be satisfied with nothing but going to Sea" and can attribute that feeling only to some vague "Propension of Nature" (p. 3).[1] But just what is it that accounts for such a propensity? To attribute it simply to restlessness is to replace one question with another.

Crusoe himself seems to recognize the irrational character of his desires when he refers to his father's attempts at dissuasion as "serious and excellent Counsel" (p. 4). But just as Crusoe rebels against the career in law that his father has in mind for him—and hence against the traditional ordering and governing of things—so he rebels against the eminently logical arguments that his father sets forth. Like the original sinner, he cannot be content with the paradise that his father offers him—that "middle State, or what might be called the upper Station of *Low Life*" (p. 4).[2]

The "upper Station of *Low Life*." That is the condition in which Crusoe finds himself; and it is an apt characterization of the human condition as Hobbes saw it. Robinson Crusoe is man in all his self-contradictoriness. His father asks him to accept his human limitations in exchange for the "easy Circumstances" (p. 5) that such acceptance assures. But Crusoe has a "wandering Inclination," "rambling Thoughts," not to be satisfied if he remains earthbound, landlocked—if he accepts his position in the "middle Station of Life" (p. 5).[3]

Robinson Crusoe is indeed driven by the profit motive,[4] but only if we give that phrase its broadest possible application. He is driven by a desire for *self*-aggrandizement, which by its very nature involves the transcendence of those limits which the human condition imposes on the self. In these terms, what Robinson Crusoe is restlessly seeking is a wholly

24

fulfilling home—a structure of meaning, a scheme into which he can fit, a place that will insure not merely self-preservation but prosperity.

Logically, as Hobbes pointed out, no man will subordinate himself either to another man or to any power higher than himself unless he stands to gain thereby more life than he can gain on his own—and this, of course, includes his serving and worshiping any god. If he himself cannot feel supernatural—that is, feel himself to have power over the nature that dictates his own death—then he will turn to some supernatural other.

It follows that Crusoe's reason for leaving his father's house has to do with his youthful assumption that he can achieve on his own more life than is possible within the limitations imposed by his father and his consequent unwillingness to accept those limitations. Only in retrospect does he refer to the "evil Influence which carried me first away from my Father's House" (p. 16)—after he has encountered at sea such an awesome storm that his own continuing existence is threatened.

Crusoe does not of course—or not, at least, in a literal sense—ever return to his father's house—not even after a kind of proxy father figure in the person of the ship's captain on his first ill-fated voyage has talked to him in "a very grave and concern'd Tone," warning him again of the consequences of rebellion. He "exhorted me," says Crusoe, "to go back to my Father and not tempt Providence to my Ruine; told me I might see a visible Hand of Heaven against me . . ." (p. 15). Crusoe's dilemma in the early part of the novel is that if he faces sickness and death—those two fundamental threats to prosperity—outside his father's house, he also faces them inside. His father no longer has the power to protect him. Not only is he "very ancient," but he is "confined by the Gout" to his chamber (p. 4). Crusoe no longer believes in him as a supernatural being.

The father to whom Crusoe does finally "go home" is, of course, God the Father—who is also the God of his fathers. But he does so only after he has experienced being *ex patria* in both senses of the phrase—only after he has known first the radical isolation and exposure of the shipwreck and eventually his own helplessness to protect himself, to deliver himself from evil. Only when he experiences the "violent Motion" of earth and sea during the earthquake, the "violent Rain" of the hurricane, and a "violent ague— Difficulties to struggle with, too great for even Nature itself to support"— does he willingly subject himself to God (pp. 80, 81, 87, 91). Confronted with such chaos, the only way Crusoe can make sense out of the energies of the universe is to posit a final cause: "if God has made all these Things, He guides and governs them all, and all Things that concern them; for the Power that could make all Things, must certainly have Power to guide and direct them" (p. 92). And if God is both orderer and master, he is also savior and deliverer and feeder (he can "*spread a Table in the Wilderness*" [p. 94]).

But when Crusoe acknowledges his dependency, his limitedness, he does so, paradoxically, in order to insure limitlessness. He makes two sacrifices in serving God: a sacrifice of himself, his own autonomy ("resigning to the will of God"), and a sacrifice of his time, in that he "spends" it (several hours a day and sometimes whole days together) in prayer and thanksgiving. For Crusoe, religious observances become an expression of his will both to live and to matter in the universe—or in his terms, to be "saved."

The nagging question that arises here is just how comfortable and easy Crusoe feels in this particular home in which God is the father and he the son. Does the God of his fathers truly answer his needs any more effectively than does his own father? (Defoe invites us, as has often been pointed out, to make an association between Crusoe's father and God; and the association becomes virtually inescapable when Crusoe refers, late in the novel, to his "Original Sin.") Actually, Crusoe's God seems to be for him a failed immortality symbol—failed in that it does not prove effective for long in laying to rest his mortal fears.[5] Crusoe experiences his most overwhelming terrors not before his conversion but afterward. And he does not conquer those later fears by trusting in his God but rather by confronting them reasonably. He pins his hope of immortality on his own brainpower.

Robinson Crusoe would thus seem to be very much a man made in the Rochester mode, in that there is a definite skepticism at the core of his being; unquestioning trust in God is no part of his make-up. Crusoe seems to belong fundamentally to the self-help school. In the very midst of his peroration on God's "sole Power," he recognizes no contradiction in his taking steps to "refresh and support" himself in his illness nor in his devising his own cure of tobacco soaked in rum. He seems, indeed, to feel that when it comes to dealing with physical afflictions, the solution devised by his own ingenuity is the best one—or at least it constitutes a wise precautionary measure. Moreover, he takes similar precautions at the time of his "Deliverances," first from the island and later from the attacking wolves in the Pyrenees. He may afterward credit God with these deliverances and express his gratitude, but in both cases he lets us know that a substantial amount of credit goes to his own ingenious "stratagems."

If, as many influential critics have maintained, Crusoe is the man who first fails and then succeeds at being a good Christian to the end of procuring his own salvation, he is also the man defined by more recent critics: the man who survives and is saved by his own efforts. In such terms he is a hero, a triumphant defier of death. We experience with him his feelings of weakness and helplessness—and of terror—and as a result his triumphant survival becomes ours. That he seems to emerge as one of God's chosen—one of those blessed by Providence—is doubtless a part of the fascination he holds for us, since his survival against odds adds to his power. He creates for himself a home in which he at once serves and is served, is ordered and orders, is fed and feeds. And thus he continues in his "Original Sin," that sin which would seem to have been two-fold, involving both disobedience and ingratitude: disobedience to the human and divine sources of authority and wisdom, and ingratitude toward human and divine creators and protectors. Both merge in the sin of pride. Much of the time, in fact, Crusoe sets himself up as the possessor of sacred power, since he can escape his feelings of helplessness and insignificance only by casting himself in the role of the all-powerful and hence the all-controlling.

It may indeed be argued that Crusoe actually engages in a kind of power struggle involving careful manipulation in his dealings with God and Providence—that in some sense he seeks to control the controller or to make the God he serves serve him. If we look closely at Crusoe's reasoning process after his recovery from his illness, we can catch him in the act. "Have I not been deliver'd, and wonderfully, too, from Sickness?" he asks. ". . . And what Notice [had I] taken of it? Had I done my part? God had deliver'd me, but I had not glorify'd him; that is to say, I had not own'd and been thankful for that as a Deliverance, and how cou'd I expect greater Deliverance?" (p. 97). Here he is figuring out quite rationally what he needs to do to insure that God will take his side. After considering such a passage, one must conclude that Crusoe's future *mindfulness* of God is rather calculating. In applying day by day the lessons he learns from the Bible about how to please God, he alleviates his sense of helplessness and regains the illusion that he is capable of rationally controlling his fate.

Earlier, Crusoe has shown himself reluctant to ascribe to Providence anything that his mind can readily explain otherwise. When he sees barley growing near his fortification, he at first suggests, since the event seems to defy rational comprehension, that "God had miraculously caused this grain to grow and that it was so directed purely for my sustenance. . . ." But as soon as the naturalistic explanation occurs to him ("upon the Discovering that all this was nothing but what was common"), he confesses that his "religious Thankfulness to God's Providence began to abate" (p. 78). And only with the hindsight born of the dire experiences of succeeding days is he able to see that he "ought to have been . . . thankful," for—so the implication seems to be—*had* he been duly thankful, he might well have averted these afflictions.

Crusoe is always attempting to bring the wild, the threatening, the chaotic under rational control—that is, to subject it to his own mastery. Apropos of this, if we go back a step and look at the places where God comes to Crusoe's mind in the preconversion part of the novel, we find an instructive pattern. Invariably, it would seem, God is less an experience than an idea that emerges to explain the inexplicable.[6] "It would be absurd," says Crusoe in his *Serious Reflections,* "to conceive of God exerting infinite power to create a world, and not concerning His wisdom, which is His providence, in guiding the operations of Nature, so as to preserve the order of His creation, and the obedience and subordination of consequences and causes throughout the course of that nature. . . ."[7] Hence, just as divine wrath is a helpful explanation for those violences of nature otherwise apparently meaningless, so divine favor turns out to be a convincing explanation for those salutary events for which Crusoe cannot immediately find a cause. Once those explanations have become part of his consciousness, Crusoe must determine how to avert the wrath and assure the favor. In other words, Crusoe is concerned not really with final causes but with that kind of inquiry into causes which inspires both the scientific and the primitive mind—the kind that leads to a knowledge of how to predict and control events. The idea of a purposeful God is important because it makes the chaotic and threatening environment seem comprehensible and hence controllable. And the Bible, for Crusoe, proves a convenient book of instruction on the formulas one must follow if one is to control the Great Controller.

Defoe has, however, also supplied his hero with what may be regarded as subdeities or fairy godparents—products, perhaps, of Defoe's own wishful thinking. Clearly, it is one aspect of Crusoe's status as hero that he is able to command the service and fidelity of such figures as the Portugal captain, the captain of the mutineers' ship, and the "good ancient Widow." Having rebelled against his own home and parents, Crusoe creates for himself not only a more congenial home but more congenial parents. (Crusoe's attitude toward his natural mother is suggested by his recalling that he laid his case before her "at a time when I thought her a little pleasanter than ordinary" [p. 16].) It might at first appear to us, in considering such figures, that Defoe is implicitly conceding the inevitable limits to man's self-sufficiency—to his ability to take care of himself. And so he must be, to some extent. It is, after all, in Crusoe's moments of helplessness that a fairy godmother or godfather comes on the scene. To the Portugal captain, for example, he is indebted for his "Deliverance" from "a Miserable and almost Hopeless Condition" (p. 33); he becomes the beneficiary of the captain's charity and generosity at a time when he is wholly dependent on his good will. And to this same captain's fidelity (as well as to the "Justice and Honesty" of his two South American "Trustees") he owes the guardianship of his plantation interests during his twenty-eight-year absence.

Actually, though, Crusoe is able to have it both ways with such figures. For one thing, both the Portugal captain and the widow (and the English captain as well) serve him without wielding any authority over him. And for another, Crusoe finally emerges in these relationships as both beneficiary and benefactor. In the case of the Portugal captain, Crusoe expresses gratitude for his generosity at the time of the sea rescue, but later he himself secures the gratitude and hence the loyalty of the captain by foresightedly lining his pockets for him. And similarly he says of the widow that he "trusted her so entirely with everything that I was perfectly easy as to the

Security of my Effects" (p. 295), the reason being that he is confident she feels gratitude to him for the money he has sent her. We may be reminded here of Hobbes once again ("no man giveth, but with intention of Good to himselfe"). It is the same practice of buying trustworthiness with expressions of gratitude as that which obtains in Crusoe's dealings with God.

Much the same pattern reveals itself in the scenes involving the English captain. There Crusoe is both deliverer and delivered. He offers deliverance to the captain and his followers in exchange for their promise of future fidelity, and once the battle is won, the captain says to him: *"My dear Friend and Deliverer . . . there's your Ship, for she is all yours, and so are we and all that belong to her."* Whereupon Crusoe says of the captain, "I took my Turn and embrac'd him as my Deliverer; and we rejoyc'd together. I told him, I looked upon him as Man sent from Heaven to deliver me, and that the whole Transaction seemed to be a Chain of Wonders; that such things as these were the Testimonies we had of a secret Hand of Providence governing the World, and an Evidence, that the Eyes of an infinite Power could search into the remotest Corner of the World, and send Help to the Miserable whenever he pleased" (pp. 272, 273). But if the captain represents to Crusoe a visible sign of God's grace, Crusoe has been, nonetheless, extremely reluctant to trust him and has, in fact, largely taken matters into his own hands. In effect, it is Crusoe, not the captain, who is the "savior."[8]

A number of recent critics of Defoe have recognized that Crusoe takes on toward the end of the novel something approaching divine power.[9] Certainly he sees himself as the deliverer as often as the delivered. Of Friday he says, "I sav'd his Life" (p. 206); and thereafter he is to Friday what God has been to him at the time of his conversion—an "infinite Power." "When he espy'd me," writes Crusoe, "he came running to me, laying himself down again upon the Ground, with all the possible signs of an humble thankful Disposition, making a many antick Gestures to show it: At last he lays his Head flat upon the Ground, close to my Foot, and sets my other Foot upon his Head, as he had done before; and after this, made all the Signs to me of Subjection, Servitude, and Submission imaginable, to let me know, how he would serve me as long as he liv'd; I understood him in many Things, and let him know, I was very well pleas'd with him . . ." (p. 206).

Just as Crusoe himself has earlier acknowledged his powerlessness, his dependency on God, as a way of gaining a greater sense of power, so does Friday now willingly trade freedom for self-preservation. *"Me die, when you bid die, Master,"* he says to Crusoe (p. 231), because to him Crusoe represents supernatural power—the very source of life.

Crusoe describes Friday as "kneeling down every Ten or Twelve steps in token of acknowledgement for my saving his Life" (p. 203); and it is clear that Friday's self-abasement is directly related to the power he perceives Crusoe as wielding. Friday stands "like one amaz'd" (p. 204) as he looks at the bullet wound made by Crusoe's gun, and shortly thereafter Crusoe becomes Friday's nourisher: "I gave him Bread and a Bunch of Raisins to eat, and a Draught of Water . . . and having refresh'd him, I made Signs for him to go lie down and sleep . . ." (p. 205). Moreover, Crusoe makes it clear to Friday that the God whose favor he himself enjoys is far more powerful than Friday's pagan god: "he told me one Day, that if our God could hear us up beyond the Sun, he must needs be a greater God than their *Benamuckee,* who liv'd but a little way off, and yet could not hear, till they went up to the great Mountains where he dwelt, to speak to him . . ." (p. 217).

Yet it is not really Crusoe's Christian God that Friday worships, but Crusoe himself. "I believe if I would have let him," Crusoe says at one point, "he would have worshipp'd me and my Gun . . ." (p. 202). And the fact is that Crusoe often sees himself, or suggests that others see him, as a powerful and even a godlike figure, the center of a perfectly ordered and wholly nourishing life.

Is it not, after all, just such a life that Crusoe creates for himself on the island? More than one reader has commented on his rage for order. He devises a neat chart dividing the island year into rainy and dry seasons. He keeps a careful tally of the passing days. He draws up a balance sheet that sets "the Comforts I enjoy'd, against the Miseries I suffer'd" (p. 66). And he is forever preoccupied with setting his house in order. As a logical corollary of this characteristic, moreover, the only human relationship Crusoe can feel comfortable in is one in which he himself, either directly or indirectly, gives the orders. "I order'd *Friday* to take one of the Canoes and go and fetch our Muskets and other Fire-Arms," he writes in describing the aftermath of his victory over the cannibals, ". . . and the Next Day I order'd him to go and bury the dead Bodies of the Savages . . . and I also order'd him to bury the horrid Remains of their barbarous Feast" (p. 242). Crusoe is here behaving typically in that he is taking pleasure in ordering a servant to tidy things up. We later hear him stipulating to the English captain that "the Ship, if recover'd, should be wholly Directed and Commanded by me in every thing," and that the captain himself shall, while on the island, agree to be always "govern'd by my Orders" (pp. 255, 256).

In the course of the novel Crusoe asserts his authority—his ordering capacity—over more and more important and wider and wider areas. He arranges his possessions on shelves within his house; he plants fields; he pens in animals; and finally he presides first as "my majesty, the prince, and lord" over his "little Family" of animals (p. 148) and then as "King"— "absolute Lord and Law-giver"—over a "peopled" island (p. 241). And if he himself still professes gratitude to a benevolent, fatherly God, he is not only "Master" to his "faithful, loving, sincere Servant" Friday, but remarks that "his very Affections were ty'd to me, like those of a Child to a Father" (p. 209).

Nor is Friday the only beneficiary of Crusoe as feeder or nourisher. Just as Crusoe's God protects him from being eaten and later provides him with daily bread, so Crusoe has protected Xury and has provided food for him: "if the wild Mans come we will kill them, they shall Eat neither of us," he tells Xury, and then continues: "so I gave *Xury* a piece of Rusk-bread to Eat and a Dram out of our Patroon's Case of Bottles . . ." (p. 26). If God, moreover, has "laid a Table in the Wilderness" for Crusoe, he, Crusoe, presides over that table, with his faithful dog seated "at [his] Right Hand: and with his cats on either side "expecting now and then a bit from my Hand, as a Mark of special Favour" (p. 148).[10] Later he presides over another table at which humans rather than animals are his guests: "I set *Friday* to Work to boiling and stewing, and made them a very good Dish, I assure you, of Flesh and Broth . . . and as I cook'd it without Doors, for I made no Fire within my inner Wall, so I carry'd it all into the new Tent; and having set a Table there for them, I sat down and eat my own Dinner also with them . . ." (p. 242). He likes this role so well that he is still playing it and talking about it at the time of his *Farther Adventures:* the Spaniards, he says, "described how they were astonish'd at the Sight of the Relief I sent them, and at the Appearance of Loaves of Bread, Things they had not seen since their coming to that miserable Place; how often they cross'd it, and bless'd it, as Bread sent from Heaven. . . ."[11]

The delight Crusoe takes in acting the godlike benefactor to whom gratitude is owing is evidenced in other areas as well. Much earlier in the original *Adventures,* at the juncture when he kills a leopard on the African coast, he says, "I found quickly the *Negroes* were for eating the Flesh of this Creature, so I was willing to have them take it as a Favour from me, which when I made Signs to them that they might take him, they were very thankful for . . ." (p. 31). And when, at the end of his adventures, he has become a wealthy man, he frequently mentions instances of his own largess.

There can be little doubt, though, that the times that Crusoe feels the most powerful, the most invulnerable, are those times when he has at his command that most impressive of all tributes to human scientific ingenuity, gunpowder. Certainly he never feels so self-sufficient, so immune from the threats of a hostile world, as when he is armed with his musket. He often feels, in fact, omnipotent. The "Astonishment" and "Admiration" that the African natives show at "the Noise and the Fire" of Crusoe's gun recall Crusoe's own awed reactions to events that seem to defy rational explanation. And obviously Crusoe finds immense satisfaction in being regarded as a miracle worker. He dwells at length on what Friday's father says of the probable reaction of the savages to gunfire: "it was his Opinion that they were so dreadfully frighted with the Manner of their being attack'd, the Noise and the Fire, that he believed they would tell their People, they were all kill'd by Thunder and Lightning, not by the Hand of Man, and that the two which appear'd, (*viz.*) *Friday* and me, were two Heavenly Spirits or

Furies come down to destroy them. . . . And this old Savage was in the right; for . . . the Savages never attempted to go over to the Island afterwards; they were so terrified with the Accounts given . . . that they believ'd whoever went to that enchanted Island would be destroy'd with Fire from the Gods" (pp. 242, 243). In listening here to the echoes of earlier passages in the book, one may speculate that Crusoe makes his God in man's image, for in one of those earlier scenes, Crusoe, describing his "terrible Dream," writes: "I saw a Man descend from a great black Cloud, in a bright Flame of Fire. . . . He was all over as bright as a Flame . . . and all the Air look'd, to my Apprehension, as if it had been fill'd with Flashes of Fire. . . . I heard a Voice so terrible, that it is impossible to express the Terror of it . . ." (p. 87). The impression we get here is strikingly reminiscent of an earlier time when Crusoe says of the Africans that they were "ready to dye for fear, and fell down as Dead with the very Terror"—"frighted with the Flash of Fire" (p. 39). Crusoe, like God, can become "a consuming Fire to the Workers of Iniquity" (p. 28).

Thanks in large part to his gun, Crusoe moves in the course of his adventures from a position of utter defenselessness to one of almost total power. To be sure, from the moment he reaches the island he takes on a certain heroic stature. He is already the triumphant survivor. The crucial difference between the man who emerges alive from the shipwreck and the one who survives the battle with the cannibals has to do with his own feelings about himself. In the first instance he experiences exposure and powerlessness ("I had no Weapon either to hunt and kill any Creature for my Sustenance, or to defend my self against any other Creature that might desire to kill me for theirs" [p. 47]). And he expresses humble gratitude to a higher power. But in the second incident he has become a kind of god-king. His description of the battle even suggests that he regards it as something of a holy war: "Let fly then, says I, in the Name of God, and with that I fir'd again among the amaz'd Wretches . . ." (p. 234). And an earlier remark indicates that he takes a certain pleasure in having such wretches look upon his power as mysterious: "they knew not," he says, "from whence their Destruction came" (p. 234). Nor is there much question that his sense of the power he has to save his own life is increased by his sense of the power he wields over the lives and deaths of others—hence the body count in which he indulges after the battle with the cannibals and hence the satisfaction he derives later from assuring the English captain, with reference to the ship's crew, that "every Man of them that comes a-shore are our own, and shall die or live, as they behave to us" (p. 261).

Crusoe's sense of power, however, is not limited to his ability to inspire fear in inferior beings. It also includes his ability to evoke responses of awe. Just as Crusoe himself feels "surpriz'd and perfectly astonish'd" (p. 78) when he comes upon the barley, so does Friday feel "astonish'd and amaz'd" (p. 229) at what seems to him the magic of Crusoe's sailboat.

It is true that in one instance Crusoe modestly turns aside a tribute to his godlike power. When one of the stranded men from the English ship exclaims, *"Am I talking to God, or Man! Is it a real Man, or an Angel!"* Crusoe assures him that an angel "would have come better cloath'd" (p. 254). We may be allowed to wonder, however, what we are to make of the fact that Crusoe soon does become "better cloath'd." Furthermore, not only has he characterized himself only a few pages earlier as "absolute Lord and Law-giver," but in his dealings with the hostages late in the novel, he plays, in effect, a double role: he is "the Person the Governour had order'd to look after them" (p. 271), and he is also the governor himself, an invisible power.[12]

For Crusoe, then, guns and gunpowder bring to their possessor the godlike capacity to dominate the earth and its people. But behind them lies what is for Faustian man the truly significant power, namely, the power of the human brain. (At one point Crusoe seems to draw a clear distinction between Friday's physical prowess—"sure never Man or Horse run like him"—and his own mental agility—"I went to Work in my Thought" [pp. 240, 241].) Certainly, in the encounter with the mutineers and in the later one with the wolves, firepower alone is hardly enough to assure deliverance. It is Crusoe's powers of invention that in both cases carry the day. In fact, Crusoe's adventures as a whole comprise virtually an allegory of man's capacity to survive and prosper by means of his own intelligence. From his fashioning of his first crude shelter on the island to his governing of a colony, his story is a record of man's ability to triumph over nature by virtue of his brainpower—to impose his will on recalcitrant forces to the end of his own prosperity. Crusoe more than once admits that his physical strength or prowess proves inadequate. But although he may experience mental lapses, he rarely concedes mental helplessness. It is his lack of sufficient physical strength to which he attributes his failure to get his canoe into the water, but the real trouble is, he says, that in choosing "a vast Tree in the Woods," he allowed the "Eagerness of . . . Fancy" (p. 126) to outrun reason. Earlier he has affirmed his complete faith in the power of reason where such undertakings are concerned: "I must needs observe, that as Reason is the Substance and Original of the Mathematics, so by stating and squaring everything by Reason, and by making the most rational Judgment of things, every Man may be in time Master of every mechanick Art. I had never handled a Tool in my Life, and yet in time by Labour, Application, and Contrivance, I found at last that I wanted nothing but I could have made it, especially if I had any Tools; however, I made abundance of things, even without Tools . . ." (p. 68).

The latter qualification suggests, it is true, some limitation on the endeavors of individual men. Crusoe does obtain a great many tools and other necessities from the wrecked ship, and he also obtains the firearms and gunpowder without which he does not himself claim he could have survived. But both tools and arms are human inventions, and thus serve to reinforce the statement the novel seems to make about the human capacity to accumulate steadily the knowledge that leads to the conquest of nature and to expand steadily the extent of control.

Just as Crusoe enlarges his cave so that it can accommodate in an orderly way the "confus'd Heap of Goods, which as they lay in no Order . . . took up all my Place" (p. 67), so he enlarges his areas of knowledge to accommodate and hence reduce to order those confusions of thought, those terrors which, if not controlled by reason, dominate the consciousness. Crusoe's confusions of thought invariably occur when he encounters potentially destructive and thus terrifying forces. "Nothing can describe the Confusion of Thought which I felt when I sunk into the Water;" he recalls, as he tells of his struggle to gain the shore of the island. During the early moments of the ordeal, when he is carried "a vast Way on towards the Shore," he comments that he had enough "Presence of Mind" left to allow him to get to his feet and "make on towards the Land." But soon the sea overwhelms him once again and he knows himself "helpless, as to [his] own Deliverance" (pp. 44, 45). Confusion of thought carries with it a sense of impotence; presence of mind is associated with control and hence with power.

A similar sense of helplessness asserts itself again during Crusoe's illness. "Pray'd to GOD for the first Time since the Storm off of Hull," he writes in his journal for June 21, "but scarce knew what I said, or why; my Thoughts being all confused" (p. 86). And later, commenting again on this event in his life, he says much the same thing: "the dreadful Reproaches of my Conscience, extorted some Words from me, like praying to God, tho' I cannot say they were either a Prayer attended with Desires or with Hopes; it was rather the Voice of mere Fright and Distress; my Thoughts were confus'd . . ." (p. 90). His terrors abate only when he has reasoned things through—expanding his awareness to include what he calls "divine Knowledge."

Exploration as a means of expanding awareness or knowledge becomes, in fact, one of the central metaphors of the novel and is, as Eric Berne points out, closely tied in with Crusoe's "oral fixation," his eat-or-be-eaten preoccupation.[13] Ironically, exploration of the unknown is a fearful undertaking and yet is essential if a man is not to live perpetually in fear—in a virtually overwhelming sense of his own smallness and insignificance. Crusoe finds it terrifying to be "hurry'd out of [his] knowledge . . . by the Currents" (p. 153), and during his sea voyages he alternately fears being swallowed up by the sea and "starving for Hunger" (p. 139).[14] There is, he learns, no expansion without risk.

In these terms, Crusoe's adventures would seem to constitute a steady progression toward omniscience and thus toward self-sufficiency. The more Crusoe knows about his island, the less he is dominated by fear. "O what ridiculous Resolution Men take, when possess'd with Fear!" he exclaims after discovering the footprint. "It deprives them of the Use of those Means which Reason offers for their Relief" (p. 159). And recalling that time when "the Apprehensions which had so over-run my Mind were fresh upon me, and my Head was full of Vapours," he comments that the "Fear of Danger is ten thousand Times more terrifying than Danger it self, when apparent to the Eyes, and we find the Burthen of Anxiety greater by much, than the Evil which we are anxious about . . ." (p. 159).

Crusoe's sense of ease, comfort, safety, "at-homeness" obviously depends on his ability to master his own fears, to order his own confusions. And in the third climactic episode of the book, he does not, we may note, fall back on God but rather makes use of his own reasoning powers. "I did not now," he says, "take due Ways to compose my Mind, by crying to God in my Distress, and resting upon his Providence, as I had done before, for my Defence and Deliverance; which if I had done, I had, at least, been more cheerfully supported under this new Surprise, and perhaps carry'd through it with more Resolution" (pp. 159, 160). Surely there is a suggestion here that Crusoe now thinks of such "due Ways to compose my Mind" as illusory. The word *perhaps*, in any case, implies a certain dubiousness on his part, and the phrase *at least* hints at a sense of limited efficacy. How, then, does Crusoe manage to allay his fears? "This Confusion of my Thoughts," he tells us, "kept me waking all Night; but in the Morning I fell asleep, and . . . slept very soundly, and wak'd much better compos'd than I had ever been before; and now I began to think sedately; and upon the utmost Debate with my self, I concluded, That . . ." (p. 160). What follows is a closely reasoned series of "That" clauses, as Crusoe proceeds to "think sedately" about his predicament. In other words, a good sleep and his own rational powers allow him to "compose" his mind, to throw off his "burthen of Anxiety."

Throughout the novel, moreover, reason has come to Crusoe's rescue in moments of despair. In his early days on the island, for example, he tells us: "I would expostulate with my self, Why Providence should thus compleatly ruine its Creatures, and render them so absolutely miserable, so without help abandon'd, so entirely depress'd, that it could hardly be rational to be thankful for such a Life." But the voice of reason soon intervenes: "I was very pensive upon the Subject of my present Condition, when Reason as it were expostulated with me t'other Way, thus: Well, you are in a desolate Condition 'tis true, but pray remember, Where are the rest of you? Did not you come Eleven of you into the Boat, where are the Ten? Why were not they sav'd and you lost? Why were you singled out? Is it better to be here or there? and then I pointed to the Sea. All Evils are to be consider'd with the Good that is in them, and with what worse attends them" (pp. 62, 63). Only when his "reason" begins to "master [his] Despondency" is Crusoe able "to set the good against the Evil" (p. 65)—a process in which he engages several times during his adventures.

Both the fear and the despair are inner threats that Crusoe must conquer. Just as he tames outward nature by cultivating more and more land, domesticating more and more animals, exploring more and more widely the outlying areas of his island, so he tames inner energies by subjecting them to his powers of reason.[15] Symbolic of this conquest of inner space is Crusoe's exploration of the cave he comes upon one day during his island wanderings—a "natural Cave in the Earth, which went in a vast way, and where, I dare say, no Savage, had he been at the Mouth of it, would be so hardy as to venture in, nor indeed would any Man else, but one who like me, wanted nothing so much as a safe Retreat." Crusoe describes himself as "curious to look into it," and after "getting with Difficulty into the Mouth of it," he encounters an alarming sight: "two broad shining Eyes of some Creature, whether Devil or Man, I knew not. . . ." Having soon "recover'd" himself, however, he tells himself "that he that was afraid to see the Devil, was not fit to live twenty Years in an Island all alone; and that I durst to believe there was nothing in this Cave that was more frightful than my self . . ." (pp. 176, 177).

As with his earlier experience of the footprint, "Fear of Danger is ten thousand times more terrifying than Danger itself, when apparent to the Eyes," for what he discovers, once he enters the cave, is "a most monstrous frightful old He-goat, just making his Will, as we say, and gasping for Life, and dying indeed of mere old Age" (p. 178). Having once recognized the impotence of this force that lies in the way of inner exploration, Crusoe can go beyond it to probe the darkest inner recesses of the cave. Pat Rogers has suggested that the "safe Retreat" he finds ("a most delightful Cavity, or Grotto . . . though perfectly dark") is notably womblike.[16] Perhaps, then, what this symbolic exploration means for Crusoe is that, once known and hence mastered, irrational energies that have always threatened to swallow him up (just as the cave's "Mouth" threatens to do) can be put to life-supporting uses. Crusoe characterizes the inner space as "a Place of Security" (p. 179) where he can store his arms and ammunition—those weapons he counts on to defend him both from starvation and from hostile (potentially devouring) outside forces.

In all probability the old he-goat represents the devil Crusoe implicitly acknowledges as existing within himself. Not only does Crusoe later contemplate his own lying down and dying "like the old Goat in the Cave" (p. 180), but in one of the few passages in his narrative where he looks at himself from the outside, he describes himself as dressed in goatskins and as having mustachios "such as I had seen worn by some *Turks*," which "were of a Length and Shape monstrous enough, and such as in *England* would have pass'd for frightful" (p. 150). Moreover, we may recall that he has considered the possibility that the print of a naked foot may be his own. Thus he seems to know, subconsciously at least, that he carries death (that hostile alien force) within himself—that death which he is accustomed to thinking of as an outside threat of "wild Beasts and Men." In entering the cave he may indeed encounter "nothing . . . more frightful than my self." Daring to face this threat directly—to make it "apparent to the Eyes"—he manages to see it as essentially powerless and subject to the control of his conscious, rational self. And he can thus turn that inner self from a threat to a "Place of Security" in which he can hide, well-armed against any threat from without.

It is true that in working up the courage to penetrate the cave, Crusoe encourages himself "a little with considering that the Power and Presence of God was every where and was able to protect me" (p. 178); but in Crusoe's view, what really renders this particular devil impotent (powerless to inspire fear) is not so much "the Power and Presence of God" as the knowledge to which his own exploration leads. As with his response to the footprint ("I fancy'd it must be the Devil; and Reason joyn'd in with me upon this Supposition" [p. 154]), it is, in this case, the human imagination that conjures up devils; and once fancy is subjected to reason instead of the other way around, the sense of threat largely disappears. Looking back on the incident once again in his "Vision of the Angelic World," Crusoe emphasizes how, after suffering an "extreme of fright and amazement," he "afterwards conquered this childish beginning, and mustered up courage enough to go into the place with a firebrand for light and . . . was presently satisfied with seeing the creature whose condition made all the little accidental noises appear rational."[17] As for those later devils, the wolves of the Pyrenees, who threaten to devour Crusoe, that threat is undeniably real, but, as already mentioned, it is, in Crusoe's telling of the story, turned aside by brainpower and firepower, rather than by any reliance on providential care.

Crusoe's stay on the island is, in effect, a history of learning to do more and more things for himself and of extending his knowledge both outside and inside himself. As he makes his way on hands and knees into the cave, he acknowledges, "whither I went I knew not," and when he returns the following day with "six large Candles of my own making," he calls his "going into this low Place . . . a Venture bold enough, considering that I knew not how far it might go, nor what was beyond it" (p. 178). We may remember that Crusoe has mentioned earlier that he did not at first know how to make candles, and in fact the phrase *I knew not* echoes and reechoes through the first half of the novel. In a single paragraph describing his voyage with Xury, for example, he uses the phrase three times. As Berne says, it is an aspect of Crusoe's involvement in exploration that he always wants to place himself as precisely as possible both in space and in time.[18] And it might be added that he is frequently concerned with putting names

to the creatures he encounters. For him, to name is to know, and to know is
to feel in control.

The ultimate control that Crusoe imposes, the ultimate self-created
world in which he is both orderer and ordered, is his autobiography. The
extent to which, as narrator, he is conscious of exercising artistic control is
perhaps best attested to by the passage where he talks of beginning his
journal: "at first I was in too much hurry, and not only hurry as to labour,
but in too much Discomposure of Mind, and my Journal would ha' been
full of many dull things . . ." (p. 69). In other words, only when reason is in
control can one make one's experience seem anything but pointless or
meaningless.

Not only does Crusoe frequently keep accounts as a way of imposing a
sense of orderliness on his life, but he gives an account of his life that makes
it add up to something. Douglas Brooks has taken note of the "balance and
symmetry" of *Robinson Crusoe,* calling attention to "two structural schemes"
in the novel.[19] And of course Crusoe himself sees a meaningful pattern in
his life—"a strange Concurrence of Days, in the various Providences which
befel me. . . ." Constantly we have a sense of Crusoe as the ordering genius,
creating for us his adventures. Providence is not the only force to "order
and appoint." Crusoe repeatedly calls attention to his own powers in this
regard: "as I shall say afterwards in its order"; "of which more in its place";
"as I shall observe in its order"; "will be very diverting in its place." In short,
Crusoe as narrator becomes the controller, the master of time itself, making
it conform to his will. In his very naming of Friday, he may, on a subconscious level, be making time serve him. After all, one of the things he has
told his mother is that he would "never serve out my time" as an apprentice
and would "certainly run away from my Master before my Time was out"
(p. 6).

Thus—or so it would seem—*Robinson Crusoe* is indeed a success story of
the sort several recent critics have described. Crusoe becomes master of his
fate, bending even God or Providence to his will. He is a victorious rebel
against restriction. He controls his circumstances. But in thinking of our
actual experience of the adventures of Robinson Crusoe, we must surely
acknowledge something a little wrong about all this. For if we take Crusoe's
early and continuing defiance of his limitations to have a symbolic suggestiveness, we come abruptly to an inescapable realization about Crusoe's
pursuit of absolute power—namely, that it is destined always to remain a
pursuit. Defoe repeatedly tells us, in effect, that Crusoe can no more "run
away from [his] Master" before he has served his time than can any human
being; he cannot escape time or make time his servant. He can neither
count on Providence always to save him nor control his own fate by naming
it Providence and bowing down before it.

We cannot, if we read Defoe's novel attentively, ignore the fact that neither of the homes Crusoe creates for himself—neither the one in which he serves a higher master nor the one in which he is himself the master—proves wholly satisfactory. Crusoe at times discovers one to be as uncomfortable as the other.[20] In this regard, then, Crusoe is man as Hobbes and Rochester saw him: feeling powerless and futilely struggling to be or at least to feel all-powerful; experiencing almost constant fearfulness and struggling ineffectually to feel invincible.

Whatever his triumphs and conquests, Crusoe's sense of the precariousness of his existence and his own insufficiency never permanently leaves him from the time he is first thrown up, helpless and naked, on the island shore. He remains the vulnerable child, left all alone in the world without friends or protectors—always in need of father- and mother-figures on whom to rely and always feeling himself in peril of being "swallowed up," whether by the sea, by the earth, by beasts, or by cannibals. The oral fixation that Berne was the first to comment on remains characteristic of Crusoe throughout the novel and tends to undercut fatally any contention that his adventures truly involve a progressive mastery of his environment.

What they do involve are alternating periods of shelter and of exposure, and what Defoe implicitly concedes is that the choice Crusoe seems to have amounts, in reality, to no choice at all. For whether he chooses home or restless wandering, the underlying and inescapable reality is always death. He knows that he must leave the womb if he is to live, and that he is born to die—and that no power, whether human or divine, can change that deadly fact.

The dilemma receives its clearest symbolic expression at the point in Crusoe's island career when, having just constructed a "complete enclosure," he feels the earth shaking beneath him and flees from his cave "for Fear I shou'd be bury'd in it" (p. 80). Here Crusoe confronts the fact that there is no true safety to be found anywhere: "The fear of being swallow'd up alive, made me that I never slept in quiet, and yet the Apprehensions of lying abroad without any Fence was almost equal to it . . ." (p. 82). The scene is, in essence, a recapitulation of Crusoe's earlier experience of leaving home. Again he finds himself driven out of a secure habitation by subterranean rumblings beyond his power to understand or control, and again he discovers the state of things in the outside world to be even more threatening than that he has experienced inside. In the first crisis, he resolves that he will "like a true repenting Prodigal, go Home to my Father" (p. 8); and in the second he does, in fact, return to his cave to find shelter from the "violent Rain." On the whole, he decides, it is safer to be inside than outside: "when I look'd about and saw how every thing was put in order, how pleasantly conceal'd I was, and how safe from Danger, it made me very loath to remove" (p. 82).

Yet along with the comfort and security that Crusoe repeatedly associates with his "Father's House" in particular and with home in general, invariably goes a sense of imprisonment or confinement—of limitation—which Crusoe can never tolerate for long. "I broke loose," he says, in relating his first decision to go to sea (p. 7). It is the perversity of Crusoe—his "fate or fault"—that he is "not very easy and happy" in the "upper Station of *Low Life*." And indeed Crusoe's father's world, inhabited as it apparently is by models of passive acquiescence, has unmistakable suggestions of entrapment in death and decay.[21] The idyllic way of life that the senior Crusoe describes involves men who go "silently and smoothly thro' the World, and comfortably out of it" (p. 5). His father, in the younger Crusoe's view, has been just such a man: "how easy, how comfortably he had liv'd all his Days," Crusoe reflects, "and never had been expos'd to Tempests at Sea or Troubles on Shore . . ." (p. 8).

What Crusoe already seems to sense, however, and what he is later to learn firsthand, is that any such paradise, any such self-contained existence is actually a lie. In this connection, a modern-day Hobbesian has summed up the human condition in words that might well have been written with Crusoe in mind:

> There is . . . a true and a false way of evaluating the human situation. Of primary importance for the true way is the denudation of the spirit, the stripping away of all subterfuges, comforts, and evasions. Our true condition is one of *exposure:* in reality, we are defenseless, naked to the winds of chance and blind accident. There is an expressive German participle, *geborgen,* which translates into English as "secure" or "safe," but connotes the delightful feeling of protectedness, the comfort of being hidden away or concealed from lurking dangers. The little bird is *geborgen* in the nest, the infant in the womb, the beloved in the arms of a strong and tender lover. By exposure is meant just the opposite of this. Though the desire for protection and security, for *Geborgenheit,* is a characteristic and primary impulse of human creatures, it is also a profound illusion. Spiritually, we are all exposed to the yawning abyss, the primal night which originates all and to which we all return.[22]

In such terms, the action of *Robinson Crusoe* concerns not only the hero's search for a home, but his failure to find one. Clearly, Crusoe's "primary impulse" once he arrives on his island is "for protection and security." And so successful a homemaker does he prove to be that Pat Rogers has actually designated him *homo domesticus.* He points out that Crusoe calls his first night's resting place "my Apartment in the Tree," and he goes on to characterize his subsequent activities as "making a nest." Crusoe bakes bread; he "spends a fair portion of his time cooking and sewing"; he makes butter and cheese; he is the complete household manager—and "a good exemplar of that cherished Renaissance-to-Augustan ideal, the Happy Man."[23]

Yet as Rogers has also noted (though he does not pursue the implications of the fact), Crusoe's two homes turn out to be "easily employed as gaols" in which to incarcerate the mutineers.²⁴ They are, in other words, as effective as places of confinement for recalcitrant men as they are as fortifications against "wild beasts and men." But the recalcitrant aspect of Crusoe himself soon defies imprisonment and urges him forth to a free-ranging exploration of the island that lies beyond his self-constructed walls. However contented the conservative aspect of his nature may be with the domestic and civilized, the contradictory principle within him—the explorer and aspirer—chafes at the restriction and leads him more than once to refer to his being kept indoors as "this Confinement."

The frequent appearance of circle imagery in association with Crusoe's various efforts at domesticating his environment and thereby protecting himself is instructive. He is constantly preoccupied during his early years on the island either with surrounding (controlling) something or with being surrounded by (protected within) something. After getting two cargoes safely conveyed from ship to shore, for example, he tells of piling "all the empty Chests and Casks up in a Circle round the Tent, to fortify it from any sudden Attempt either from Man or Beast" (p. 59); and when, during the earthquake, the overhanging cave proves too threatening, he thinks of "building me some little Hut in an open Place which I might surround with a Wall as I had done here, and so make my self secure from wild Beasts or Men"—"I would go to work with all Speed to build me a Wall with Piles and Cables, &c. in a Circle as before . . ." (p. 82). The country bower that he does eventually devise lies within a "Circle or double Hedge" (p. 104). And he speaks later of the kid "which I had penn'd in within my little Circle" (p. 112).

Crusoe mentions repeatedly bringing projects "to Perfection": he has "brought to Perfection" the cave behind his tent (p. 69); he spends over three months *"working, finishing, and perfecting"* his wall *("being a half Circle from one Place in the Rock to another Place about eight Yards from it, the Door of the Cave being in the Center behind it"* [p. 76]); he achieves "an unexpected Perfection in [his] Earthen Ware," having devised a wheel with which he can make things "round and shapable" (p. 144).

Yet nothing is, apparently, quite perfect. Crusoe must extend half circles into whole circles; he must surround one half circle of trees with another; and he must, above all, make small circles into bigger circles. So persevering is he in "widening and deepening" his cave that he eventually makes it "spacious enough to accommodate me as a Warehouse or Magazin, a Kitchen, a Dining-room, and a Cellar" (p. 74).

What happens on at least three occasions, however, is that in enlarging or attempting to enlarge the area of his control, he exposes himself to those very fears and outside threats against which he has designed his walls. In speaking of one such occasion, he says, "I began now to think my Cave or Vault finished, when on a Sudden (it seems I had made it too large) a great

Quantity of Earth fell down from the Top and one Side, so much, that in short it frighted me . . ." (p. 74). Another time, after he has "work'd daily two or three Hours at enlarging my Cave," he succeeds in fashioning what amounts to a back door to his dwelling. But if his sense of confinement is thus lessened, so also is his peace of mind. "I was not perfectly easy at lying so open," he confesses, "for as I had manag'd my self before, I was in a perfect Enclosure, whereas now I thought I lay expos'd . . ." (p. 103). Most terrifying of all, though, in those early years, is his attempt "to make a Tour round the Island"—"to view the Circumference of my little Kingdom" (p. 137)—an attempt that brings him "a frightful Distance" from the shore and almost proves his undoing.

The world that Crusoe inhabits seems, invariably, either too big or not big enough. Effectually, the pattern of his adventures is one of a circularity involving alternating situations of expansion and contraction, exposure and protection. When, for example, after several months on the island, he makes his first "Journey . . . from Home"—prompted by a desire "to see the whole Island"—he is at first "exceedingly diverted" (pp. 108, 109). But after having lost himself in a valley and having "wandered about very uncomfortably," he finds himself "very impatient to be at Home," and his relief when he is at last back in his cave is plainly heartfelt:

> I cannot express what a Satisfaction it was to me to come into my old Hutch, and lye down in my Hamock-Bed: This little wandring journey, without settled Place of Abode, had been so unpleasant to me, that my own House, as I call'd it to my self, was a perfect Settlement to me, compar'd to that; and it rendred every Thing about me so comfortable, that I resolv'd I would never go a great Way from it again while it should be my Lot to stay on the Island. (P. 117)

Whenever Crusoe ventures far from any home, he encounters an alien world in which he feels at best lost and at worst utterly terrified. Crusoe, we may recall, refers to his years on the island as a "Life of Misery" and at one time names the place itself the "Island of Despaire." Still more to the point, however, the sea on which he suffers shipwreck functions archetypally as both tomb and womb. He emphasizes repeatedly his own helplessness to deliver himself from its grasp: "tho' I swam very well, yet I could not deliver my self from the Waves"; "the Sea, having hurried me along as before, landed me, or rather dash'd me, against a Piece of Rock, and that with such Force, it left me senseless, and indeed helpless, as to my own Deliverance." But at last the sea, having "buried" Crusoe "20 or 30 Foot deep in its own Body," deposits him on the shore and he is "sav'd . . . out of the very Grave." Yet "sav'd" though he may be, it is, as he says, "a dreadful Deliverance": "I was wet, had no Clothes to shift me, nor any thing either to eat or drink to comfort me, neither did I see any Prospect before me but that of perishing with Hunger, or being devour'd by wild Beasts . . ." (pp. 44–46).

There is no question that Crusoe's effort to tame the wild, to civilize the savage succeeds up to a point.[25] He does seem to become increasingly effective at imposing his will on the world he inhabits. He speaks of having become, in his "twenty third Year of Residence in this Island . . . naturalized to the Place, and to the Manner of Living" (p. 180). In actuality, however, it would be more accurate to say that he has "de-naturalized" his world in order to adapt it to himself and to make it serve him.

He never really succeeds in conquering his own terror, since he can never hide from himself the awareness that outside of himself lies a hostile universe.[26] By his twenty-third year he *seems* to be in control, to have a sense that he is someone to be reckoned with. He has taught three parrots to say "Robin Crusoe," has tamed several sea fowls and "cut their Wings," and keeps three household kids about him (p. 181). But while he has domesticated some of these wild creatures, some of the already domesticated animals who have come with him to the island—namely the cats—multiply so alarmingly that he is "oblig'd to shoot several of them at first, to keep them from devouring me, and all I had," and others have run "wild into the Woods" (p. 180). Moreover, he has discovered, in the process of fencing in his goats, that he "must keep the tame from the wild, or else they would always run wild when they grew up . . ." (p. 146). Crusoe cannot avoid knowing that in the natural world outside himself even the tamed can revert to wildness and become a danger. The awareness rather ironically calls into question his earlier characterization of himself as "Prince and Lord of the whole Island." It proves not to be altogether true that "I had the Lives of all my Subjects at my absolute Command. I could hang, draw, give Liberty, and take it away, and no Rebels among all my Subjects" (p. 148).

Furthermore, although his dog may have proved for sixteen years "a very pleasant and loving Companion" (p. 180), most of the animals he encounters on his adventures are part and parcel of the threatening outside environment in which solitary man walks fearfully and in which he must destroy or be destroyed. Whether Crusoe is confronted with "a dreadful Monster . . . a terrible great Lyon" (p. 27) on the Canaries shore or with "those ravenous Creatures" who, in a pursuit of "great Fury," at last "plung'd themselves into the Sea" (p. 30) near Cape Verde, his experiences never reassure him that the world in which he lives has been made for him. Strive though he may to build defenses, the threat remains. Indeed, in the last major adventure of the novel, as he pursues a seemingly safe overland route home, he faces once again some "ravenous Creatures"—this time a whole pack of them, from whom, after a night of stark terror, he barely escapes with his life. These creatures, he says, "came on like Devils." Still, wild animals play a relatively minor role in the hostile universe into which Crusoe ventures. Far more important to him—and far harder for him to defend himself against—are wind and weather. As he contrives his escape from the *Sallee Rover,* he notes: "The wind blew from the N.NE., which was contrary to my Desire" (p. 22). And the fact is that the winds of the world almost always blow for Crusoe "contrary to [his] Desire." The "dreadful Storm" that strands him on his island is only one of many that he experiences in the course of the novel, and he is never so aware of his own vulnerability as at such times. The rage and fury that he associates with the wild animals of shore and mountain are as nothing compared to the "raging Wave, Mountain-like" that, in the midst of the novel's major storm, "took us with such a Fury, that it overset the Boat at once" (p. 44).

For Crusoe natural forces are frequently "as furious as an Enemy" (p. 44). Even though he has, on the island, constructed his defenses so that "nothing could come at me from without, unless it could first mount my Wall" (p. 79), reasons for terror remain: an alien nature intrudes in the form of an earthquake that cracks the posts in the cave "in a frightful Manner." Crusoe does feel more "safe from Danger" within his cave than outside it, but he continues to pile fortification on fortification.[27] Shelter is always, for him, an overridingly important preoccupation, as it continues to be long after he has left the island. When beset by the wolf pack, he writes, "having nothing to shelter us, or retreat to, I gave myself over for lost . . ." (p. 302).

"Man," Heidegger has written, "shrinks back from losing himself in . . . the nightmarish, demonic frenzy in which nature has unleashed billions of individual organismic appetites of all kinds—not to mention earthquakes, meteors, and hurricanes, which seem to have their own hellish appetites. Each thing, in order to deliciously expand, is forever gobbling up others. Appetites may be innocent because they are naturally given, but any organism caught in the myriad cross-purposes of this planet is a potential victim of this very innocence—and it shrinks away from life lest it lose its own."[28]

Crusoe's dilemma—the human dilemma—is that in shutting himself in to preserve life, he must at the same time shut life out. His responses, while he is on the island, to the sun and the rain are cases in point. Having learned that direct exposure to the rain produces fevers, he finds that he must largely confine himself within his cave during the rainy season. And the sun too is at times an antagonist from which he must retreat: "it is to be considered that the middle of the Day when the Sun was in the Zenith, the Violence of the Heat was too great to stir out . . ." (p. 114).

Corresponding to the "complete Shade" provided by the trees surrounding his country bower ("sufficient to lodge under all the dry Season") are the hat and umbrella (again a piling-up of fortifications) with which Crusoe supplies himself as protection from sun and rain. In enumerating his articles of clothing, Crusoe refers to his umbrella as "the most necessary Thing I had about me, next to my Gun" (p. 150). That he never ventures abroad without both umbrella and gun strongly indicates that fear remains for him a constant companion all the while he remains on the island. At the time he discovers that deep inner cave in which he stores his weapons, he says, "I fancy'd my self now like one of the ancient Giants, which are said to live in Caves, and Holes, in the Rocks, where none could come at them; for I perswaded my self, while I was here, if five hundred Savages were to hunt me, they could never find me out; or if they did, they would not venture to attack me here." And two paragraphs later he comments about life on the island: "could I have but enjoy'd the Certainty that no Savages would come to the Place to disturb me, I could have been content to have capitulated for spending the rest of my Time there . . ." (p. 180). Hobbes could be describing Crusoe when he writes:

if one plant, sow, build, or possesse a convenient Seat, others may probably be expected to come prepared with forces united, to dispossesse, and deprive him, not only of the fruit of his labour, but also of his life, or liberty. And the Invader again is in the like danger of another.
    And from this diffidence of one another, there is no way for any man to secure himself, so reasonable, as Anticipation; that is, by force, or wiles, to master the persons of all men he can, so long, till he see no other power great enough to endanger him.

And later in *Leviathan* Hobbes again anticipates Crusoe's behavior in describing a London citizen: "when taking a journey, he arms himself, and seeks to go well accompanied; when going to sleep, he locks his doors; when even in his house he locks his chests; . . . what opinion he has of his fellow-subjects, when he rides armed; of his fellow citizens when he locks his doors; and of his children, and servants, when he locks his chests."[29] It is not, of course, human beings of flesh and blood who are usually the problem for Crusoe; rather, it is those imaginary figures his own apprehensions conjure up. Humans are, his mind tells him, all either savages or pirates or mutineers. They are attackers who kill and eat one another, prey on one another, or seize power from one another. Crusoe never registers a terror so abject as that he shows upon discovering "the Print of a Man's naked Foot on the Shore" (p. 153). He uses words like *Thunder-struck, perfectly confus'd and out of my self, terrify'd to the last Degree.* He speaks of his *affrighted Imagination,* of *wild Ideas,* of *terror of Mind* (pp. 153, 154). However successful Crusoe may be at defending himself against physical threats, he cannot escape his own mind. Immediately before relating his discovery of the footprint, he has spent two pages describing his plantations, and much of the detail has to do with order and security—keeping his land "duly cultivated and sow'd," keeping his surrounding hedges "in Repair," and so forth (pp. 152, 153). Yet not only is this description followed by the lengthy recording of his apprehensions about the footprint, but it is preceded by his recalling that fear he felt when he found his canoe being carried away from the island: "I had such a Terror upon my Spirits at the Remembrance of the Danger I had been in, that I could not think of it again with any Patience . . ." (p. 151). No matter how seemingly secure he is, he cannot shut out of his mind either the remembrance of dangers past or the antici-pation of dangers to come.

To Crusoe's way of thinking, primitive man is as much a part of "wild" nature as any animal. At one point he remarks: "to have fallen into the Hands of any of the Savages had been as bad as to have fallen into the Hands of Lyons and Tygers" (p. 25). Even of Friday, whom he calls a "faithful, loving, sincere Servant," he feels at times a profound mistrust. He arranges matters in his hutch "so that *Friday* could no way come at me in the inside of my innermost Wall, without making so much Noise in getting over, that it must needs waken me . . ." (p. 208). In a way, what he does with Friday is to tame him, as Friday himself suggests he should do for other savages: "*you teach wild Mans be good sober tame Mans* . . ." (p. 226). Yet he has spoken of being "not so easy about my new Man *Friday* as I was before," and although he at once admits to having "wronged the poor honest Creature," he has seriously imagined the possibility of Friday's betraying him and joining with the other members of his nation to "make a Feast upon me" (p. 224).

In fact, Crusoe proves himself in the two later volumes of his life story to be haunted by thoughts of cannibalism, and so does Defoe in his other writings. The subject comes up repeatedly not only in the *Farther Adventures* and the *Serious Reflections,* but in the *Review* and *Applebee's Journal* as well. And it is not, according to Defoe, only savages who experience cannibalistic impulses but civilized men, when the threat of starvation makes them des-perate enough. Of the incident involving a mother and her son and their maid, whom Crusoe meets early in his *Farther Adventures* on that "unhappy Ship" where all aboard have been brought to "the last Extremity of Hun-ger," the maid relates: "had my Mistress been dead, as much as I lov'd her, I am certain, I should have eaten a Piece of her Flesh with as much Relish, and as unconcern'd, as ever I did the Flesh of any Creature appointed for Food; and once or twice I was going to bite my own Arm"; and she goes on to tell of drinking her own blood. And when Defoe is telling of the "terrible Famine . . . in Thoulon," he writes: " 'Tis said that [the people] . . . have eaten the most loathsome and nauteous Things, such as Dogs, Cats, Rats, Mice, Leather, Starch, Soap, and, in a Word, that they are ready to prey even upon one another."[30]

Crusoe's concluding pages of his *Surprizing Adventures* are tantamount to a concession that neither human fears nor those forces in the universe that inspire such fears by threatening the survival of the self are ever quelled. In speaking of the shipwrecked Spaniards, he says, "I fear'd mostly their Treachery and ill-Usage of me, if I put my Life in their Hands" (p. 244). Moreover, though he has been victorious in his pitched battle with the cannibals, he voices apprehensions about a return engagement wherein he will have to cope with numbers that may prove overwhelming. And Crusoe's battles, as it turns out, are *not* over once he has defeated the savages. He must then face the mutineers, who, like his cats, are once-domesticated creatures now again given over to violence.

What is more, while Crusoe may have brought his tropical island largely under his control, he remains fearful of the sea, and in trying to avoid its perils (which, as he explains, prove again all too real), he finds himself—as he once more makes his way toward the supposed securities of home—facing the rigors of the Pyrenees, whose wintry barrenness has crazed the starving wolves. Crusoe's party have a guide to aid them in circumventing the worst of the snowy mountain terrain, but the guide's knowledge does not enable them to avoid the wolves, and Crusoe is again thrown back on his own resources, called upon again to devise a "stratagem" born of desperation in order to achieve mastery.

Crusoe does at last get home to England, but it is a "home" that represents only a stopping-off and stepping-off place. Remembering what he has told us about his early propensities—"though I had several times loud Calls from my Reason and my more composed Judgment to go Home, yet I had no Power to do it"—we can now see that the words constitute a kind of summary of Defoe's view of the human predicament. It is beyond the power of man truly to "go home." There is no hiding place, and he is fated to remain a restless seeker.

As might be expected, moreover, the circle pattern continues into the second volume of Crusoe's adventures. He speaks several times in the opening pages of the "strong Inclination" he felt "to go Abroad again," and then well along in this continuation of his story he admits, "When I was at Home, I was restless to go abroad; and now I was abroad, I was restless to be at Home." Unlike that Utopian figure the Muscovite prince, who "has got a Victory over his own exorbitant Desires, and has the absolute Dominion over himself, whose Reason entirely governs his Will," Crusoe is unable to remain a "happy Prisoner."[31] He continues to be, as it were, in thrall to the devil, who (as he has taught Friday long before) has "a secret access to our Passions, and to our Affections, to adapt his Snares so to our Inclinations, as to cause us even to be our own Tempters, and to run upon our Destruction by our own Choice" (p. 217).

In the *Farther Adventures* chaos comes again at every level. Crusoe tells, for example, of "a little Quarrel on board our Ship, which I was afraid once would have turned to a second Mutiny"; and on his voyage around the world he again fears mutiny. And earlier, in revisiting the island he discovers an alarming state of disorder to have existed there. Not only does he hear that there has been a new invasion of savages ("now they had, as I may say, a hundred Wolves upon the Island, which would devour every Thing they could come at, yet could very hardly be come at themselves"), but he learns that dissensions among the five Englishmen have led to repeated destruction of settled and ordered habitations.[32]

The destructive passions of men are everywhere in evidence. Perhaps it is no accident that the natural energy most often referred to is fire. Men are burned; a ship is burned; a house is burned; a whole settlement is burned. Again and again Crusoe encounters a world at war; and the "Peace" to whose existence he composes verses and of which he writes wistfully at the end of his *Farther Adventures* remains a future prospect.[33] The storms and tempests of his life have continued to rage within as well as without; the savagery within and without has not been left behind.[34]

Crusoe may have exchanged his goatskins for more civilized garments, but the change is more apparent than real.[35] His physical wanderings do finally end, but in the *Serious Reflections* his mind continues its restless seeking to impose some meaningful order upon the flux of things. And he is still looking over his shoulder. "It is a strange length that some people run in this madness of life," he observes in one passage; and a page later we find him calling himself "your fugitive friend, 'Robinson Crusoe.'"[36]

Even his confidence in an ordering Providence seems here at best a shaky one. "Providence," he affirms, "decrees that events shall attend upon causes in a direct chain, and by an evident necessity, and has doubtless left many powers of good and evil seemingly to ourselves, and as it were, in our hands, as the natural product of such causes and consequences, which we are not to limit and cannot expressly determine about, but which we are accountable for the good or evil application of; otherwise we were in vain exhorted and commanded to do any good thing, or to avoid any wicked one."[37] That is to say, all this *must* be so if the world is to make any sense; yet Crusoe's "seemingly" and "as it were" seriously undercut his "doubtless."

Crusoe-Defoe no more finds it possible to round off his *Surprizing Adventures* satisfactorily than Crusoe as protagonist finds it possible to end his travels and his speculations. Imagination breaks free from the captivity of reason to the extent that the novel concludes in syntactical confusion and leaves us with a sense of incompleteness:

> But all these things, with an Account how 300 Caribbees came and invaded them, and ruin'd their Plantations, and how they fought with that whole Number twice, and were at first defeated, and three of them kill'd; but at last a Storm destroying their Enemies Cannoes, they famish'd or destroy'd almost all the rest, and renew'd and recover'd the Possession of their Plantation, and still liv'd upon the Island.
>
> All these things, with some very surprizing Incidents in some new

Adventures of my own, for ten Years more, I may perhaps give a further Account of hereafter.

We put the book down feeling some bafflement as to the precise nature of the account Crusoe has given of what he tellingly calls his "unaccountable Life" (p. 181). Just what does Crusoe's experience add up to? Is it truly a spiritual autobiography? Or is the form of the spiritual autobiography merely a kind of wishful thinking—a construction within which Crusoe attempts to hide in order to avoid too much exposure?

Repeatedly, in the course of his narrative, Crusoe suggests that he is unable to capture in words the lived reality. "I cannot explain by any possible Energy of Words," he says at one point, "what a strange longing or hankering of Desires I felt in my Soul . . ." (p. 187). Moreover, he gives us three different accounts of his experience immediately following the shipwreck, each of which differs from the others in the details included and some of which actually contradict one another in certain particulars. Which is the true account? Can words capture reality at all, or do they *create* a reality, impose a meaning that does not, in the nature of things, exist?

And who is Robinson Crusoe? Is he all-conquering voyager or believing Christian? Is his name really Crusoe or is that simply what he is "called"?[38] Finally, we cannot as readers avoid some "Confusion of Thoughts"; and we may well end by crying, as Crusoe has taught his parrot to cry, *"Poor Robin Crusoe, Where are you? Where have you been? How come you here?"* (p. 143). We wait in vain for an answer.

3

Captain Singleton
"nothing but present Death"

Of all Defoe's homeless wanderers, none suffers that plight so uninterrupt-
edly from the opening pages almost to the closing as does the hero who is
called *"Bob Singleton, not Robert,* but plain *Bob."*[1] His life story is not, like
Robinson Crusoe's, a matter of a man's seeking to move upward in life by
leaving his existing home in order to find a more congenial one. Young Bob
is seeking to regain something that, through no fault of his own, he has lost
before ever having had any real sense of possessing it.[2] Moll Flanders at
least has some feeling of enjoying a "place" in the world, even if she thinks
of it as the wrong place. And she does know who her mother is. But
Captain Singleton, as his name suggests, finds himself, from the time of his
coming to consciousness, totally alone, unprotected and unguided. Both
the journeys he makes—the first by land and the second by sea—are journeys toward the home he can scarcely remember.[3] Both are, however devi-
ously pursued, journeys northward, and both involve steady accumulations
of power in the form of knowledge and wealth.

The one thing Singleton does know about his heritage at the outset (the
importance he attaches to the information being suggested by his reiterating it) is that at the time of his abduction at the age of two he was "very well
drest." The symbolism here is sufficiently obvious. His beginnings in the
world have entailed a fall from "the upper Stations of *Low Life*" as a result
of neglect on the part of a protector led astray by her appetites. (The
nursery maid "meets with a Fellow, her Sweet-heart" who "carries her into a
Publick-House, to give her a Pot and a Cake.") The consequence is that
while he is playing with, or rather being played with by a little girl "in the
Garden," he is kidnaped by some people whose "Hellish Trade" it is "to
Spirit Away little Children"—and specifically by a "Woman pretending to
take me up in her Arms and kiss me and play with me. . . ."

There is a good deal of sexual innuendo running through these opening
paragraphs, the full importance of which only becomes clear in the second
half of the novel. And along with the obvious Edenic allusions, the narrative introduces a theme that will prove basic in Defoe's writings. Young Bob

50

has been sold into slavery; he experiences subjection to an appetitive world represented by three women: first, his abductor (who bids his playmate report to his maid "that a Gentlewoman had taken a Fancy to the Child, and was kissing of it"), and then "a Beggar-Woman that wanted a pretty little Child to set out her Case," and finally "a Gypsey, under whose Government I continued till I was about Six Years old." This woman, he says, he "called . . . Mother."

The main characteristic that distinguishes the young Singleton from either Crusoe or Moll Flanders is his lack of any sense of upward mobility. He seems to accept his low condition without demur as long as he is protected and experiences no want. First "continually dragged about" by his "Gypsey Mother," who "never let me want for any thing," and then "frequently removed from one Town to another" by parish officials, he is, at the age of twelve, "carried . . . to Sea" by the Master of a Ship who "took a Fancy to me." But while this Master calls him "his own Boy," and young Bob "would have called him Father," this privilege is denied him ("he would not allow it, for he had Children of his own"). He continues to be treated as a helpless and isolated being, shut out of any stable human family.

Awareness of his plight, moreover, is slow in coming. Singleton as narrator emphasizes his difficulty in giving an accurate "Account" of his early years, for, as he says, "I kept no Journal" (p. 9). And when, on one of his first voyages, the ship on which he serves is taken by a Turkish man-of-war and his Master, already wounded by a "Splinter in the Head," is "very barbarously used by the Turks" (p. 3), Bob says twice within a few lines, "I was not much concerned." Here, as in *Robinson Crusoe,* the Turkish references are presumably intended to call to mind the irrational, the uncivilized, the chaotic. Hence Singleton's capture by these infidels suggests his domination by this aspect of the world and of the self. But it is a domination of which he is scarcely conscious.

Even when the Turkish Rover is in turn taken by two Portuguese men-of-war, Singleton acknowledges: "As I was not much concerned at my Captivity, not indeed understanding the Consequences of it, if it had continued: so I was not suitably sensible of any Deliverance. . . ." His mind has still not begun to function in bringing him to an awareness of his "primitive State." And that state is further underscored when he goes on to tell of his having been befriended by the pilot of the Portuguese ship:

> Whither must I go (said I?) Where you will, (said he). Home to your own Country, if you will. How must I go thither (said I?) Why have you no Friend (said he?) No, (said I) not in the World, but that Dog, pointing to the Ship's Dog, (who having stole a Piece of Meat just before, had brought it close by me, and I had taken it from him, and eat it) for he has been a good Friend, and brought me my Dinner. (Pp. 3, 4)

This pilot, having become Singleton's protector—supplying him with both food and shelter and thus with his first "home"—now also becomes the first pilot of his life journey. "I was too young in the Trade to keep any Journal of this Voyage," Singleton says in recounting his setting out as the pilot's "boy" on a Portuguese galleon, "tho' my Master, who was for a Portuguese a pretty good Artist, prompted me to it. . . ." He is still not ready, that is, to give an account of his life. But he does gain from the pilot "a little superficial Knowledge of Navigation, but not such as was likely to be sufficient to carry me thro' a Life of Adventure, as mine was to be" (p. 5).

That Defoe wants us to associate keeping a journal with knowledge-ableness is further attested to a few pages later: "I kept no Journal of this Voyage, nor indeed did I all this while understand any thing of Navigation, more than a common Business of a Fore-mast Man; so I can say nothing to the Latitudes or Distances of any Places we were at, how long we were going, or how far we sailed in a Day . . ." (p. 40).

But Singleton is now gradually coming to consciousness of where he is and where he is going; and a subsequent adventure produces a more concerned and knowledgeable teacher for him in the person of a Portuguese gunner:[4]

> This Gunner was an excellent Mathematician, a good Scholar, and a compleat Sailor; and it was in conversing intimately with him, that I learnt afterwards the Grounds of what Knowledge I have since had in all the Sciences useful for Navigation, and particularly in the Geographical Part of Knowledge.
>
> Even in our Conversation, finding me eager to understand and learn, he laid the Foundation of a general Knowledge of things in my Mind, gave me just Ideas of the Form of the Earth and of the Sea, the Situation of Countries, the Course of Rivers, the Doctrine of the Spheres, the Motion of the Stars; and, in a Word, taught me a kind of System of Astronomy, which I afterwards improv'd.
>
> In especial Manner, he filled my Head with aspiring Thoughts, and with an earnest Desire after learning every thing that could be taught me; convincing me, that nothing could qualify me for great Undertakings, but a Degree of Learning superior to what was usual in the Race of Seamen; he told me, that to be ignorant, was to be certain of a mean Station in the World, but that Knowledge was the first Step to Prefer-ment. He was always flattering me with my Capacity to Learn; and tho' that fed my Pride, yet on the other Hand, as I had a secret Ambition which just at that time fed it self in my Mind, it prompted in me an insatiable Thirst after Learning in general, and I resolved, if ever I came back to *Europe*, and had any thing left to purchase it, I would make my self Master of all the Parts of Learning needful to the making of me a compleat Sailor. (Pp. 55, 56)

This passage is clearly one of the key thematic statements of the novel, giving as it does both emphasis to and an interpretation of virtually all of Singleton's travels. Like Robinson Crusoe before him and Moll Flanders after him, Singleton is constantly on the move, and his story is peppered hereafter with references to his calculations as to the direction he is going.

When he enrolls himself as pupil to the Portuguese gunner—"with aspiring Thoughts, and with an earnest Desire after learning"—he also, it seems, takes charge of his own destiny and assumes what he regards as his rightful place in the world.

He has begun moving upward, however, as early as his first voyage on the Portuguese galleon. And he proves a quick learner, for not only does he commence his rise by stealing some of the ship's gold (calling this his "first Adventure") but he sees that, while passing for "a mighty, diligent Servant to my Master," he has "Opportunity particularly to take Care of my Master's Man." He uses his head, and in so doing, he is able to supply himself "with sufficient Provisions to make me live much better than the other People in the Ship" (pp. 5, 6). And soon he learns not to give himself away in still another sense, for when he is set ashore with his fellow mutineers on Madagascar, he takes care to keep secret the full extent of his wealth. He has already come to the point, thus early in his career, of feeling contempt for people's gullibility: "I was very far from honest," he says; "however, they thought me honest, which by the Way, was their very great Mistake . . ." (p. 5). Nor does it take him much longer to recognize the motives of self-interest that lie behind the seeming charity of others. Of the pilot who has befriended him, he writes: "He had taken me up as in Distress, and his Business was to keep me so, and make his Market of me as well as he could; which I began to think of after a different Manner than I did at first; for at first I thought he had entertained me in meer Charity, upon seeing my distrest Circumstances . . ." (p. 7).

Singleton's progress toward knowledge and hence, it might seem, toward freedom and self-government becomes, for the next fifty pages or so, a persistent if intermittent theme. He concedes that at the time he finds himself set ashore on Madagascar "to enter upon a Part of independent Life," he is "ill prepared to manage" such a challenge—being "perfectly loose and dissolute in my Behaviour, bold and wicked while I was under Government, and now perfectly unfit to be trusted with Liberty. . . ." And he goes on to describe himself as "a young Fellow that had no solid Thought ever placed in my Mind . . ." (p. 11). Indeed, the lack of "solid Thought" puts him in danger in two particular moments of crisis. The first results from his efforts to "deliver [him] self" from his cruel Portuguese master—efforts that lead him finally to the "Hellish Resolution" of doing murder ("the Devil prompting me very warmly to the Fact"). As is true for Moll Flanders, the devil for Singleton appears at moments of desperation and prompts him, supposedly in the interests of his own survival, to actions that can only bring about his own destruction. Had Singleton been better educated—had he had more "Sense of Virtue and Religion"—he would, it is suggested, have been able to recognize this temptation to do murder for the madness it was. Rashness has nearly been his undoing, as it is again in an early encounter between the mutineers and one of the Madagascar tribes. In both of these predicaments an open-eyed awareness of consequences has been the missing ingredient.

Yet a typical Defoe undercutting is already in evidence, for Singleton discovers quite early in his career the same thing that Crusoe learns at the time of seeing the footprint—namely, that knowledge can have its problems as well. In the two incidents just cited, the difficulty for Singleton is that he is too ignorant to be afraid. But knowing enough to be afraid can also lead to destruction. As Singleton expresses it,

> This thoughtless, unconcern'd Temper had one Felicity indeed in it; that it made me daring and ready for doing any Mischief, and kept off the Sorrow which otherwise ought to have attended me when I fell into any Mischief; that this Stupidity was instead of a Happiness to me, for it left my Thoughts free to act upon Means of Escape and Deliverance in my Distress, however great it might be; whereas my Companions in the Misery, were so sunk by their Fear and Grief, that they abandoned themselves to the Misery of their Condition, and gave over all Thought but of their perishing and starving, being devoured by wild Beasts, murdered, and perhaps eaten by *Cannibals, and the like.* (P. 12)

Defoe's handling of Singleton's early adventures presents us with human experience in all its frustrating contradictoriness. Whether free or enslaved, whether exposed or protected, whether knowledgeable or ignorant, human beings are always and inevitably limited by the "Cases of flesh and blood" (p. 48) within which they have their being. And Singleton's narrative exhibits a kind of point-counterpoint pattern.

One line of development undeniably has to do with young Bob Singleton's rise in the world from "English Dog" to the leadership of a newly formed society. What brings him to his position of supremacy is his superior mental capacity when it comes to survival. During the first "general Council" of his little group stranded on the Madagascan shore, Singleton is willing to offer no opinion at all as to either how they should get away or where they should go. He is wholly passive. And he manifests his ignorance still more plainly by proposing to take a short walk in the woods in search of provisions while the deliberations are going on and having to be told of the foolhardiness of exposing himself in this way. He is like the Tonquin natives Robinson Crusoe talks about, who are "fearless, because ignorant of their Danger."[5]

But once the group have finally made their way to Africa and are about to set out on their long overland journey, Singleton largely assumes command. It is he who comes up with an ingenious idea to solve their baggage problem: "this was to quarrel with some of the Negro Natives, take ten or twelve of them Prisoners, and binding them as Slaves, cause them to travel with us and make them carry our Baggage" (p. 51). The one-time slave has now become the enslaver. And by the time this matter is finally settled, Singleton has arrived at a new sense of himself: "I began to enter a little more seriously into the Circumstances I was in, and concern'd my self more in the Conduct of our Affairs; for, tho' my Comerades were all older Men, yet I began to find them void of Counsel, or, as I now call it, Presence of Mind, when, they came to the Execution of a thing" (p. 54).

Perhaps the chief event that has brought Singleton to this new self-satisfaction has been the role that, he now tells us, he has played in the recent battle with the natives. He has emerged as leader of the army, devising a military strategy and giving heart to his troops, so that they have not run away. It is logical that his men should now insist on calling him *"Captain* Bob" and that even the Gunner should turn to him "before them all" and say, "I think you must be our Leader." In the event, Singleton agrees to be only co-captain, deferring to his senior officer, but as the little band sets off across the African continent, there is no question as to who is in command. Not only does Singleton make the major contribution to the preliminary "Consultation," which involves "First, Which Way we should go, and Secondly, How to furnish our selves for the Voyage with Provisions" (p. 57), but he has, after all, acted as their savior. And in his dealings with the savages, he does not simply continue in this role but becomes in his turn mentor to a leader in the second rank—in this instance the man called the "Black Prince," of whom Singleton says approvingly, "he was very willing and apt to learn any thing I taught him" (p. 59). In his rapid rise to dominance Singleton has demonstrated that knowledge is power. And the first step in revealing that power—that sense of control and mastery—has been a change in social position.

Thereafter, Singleton takes measures to make sure that the lower orders remain under him—that is to say, under his control. At one point in particular, when the Negroes appear to have been disorderly and disobedient, he decides to show them that their gods can become wrathful. "We seem'd very angry at them," he says, ". . . and here we gave them the Law of Arms, *viz.* That if any Men appeared to assault them, or shoot at them, or offer any Violence to them, they might kill them; but that they should not offer to kill or hurt any that offer'd them Peace, or laid down their Weapons, nor any Women or Children, upon any Occasion whatsoever. These were our Articles of War" (p. 69). Singleton has taken on the role of law-giver.

One of the things he learns about the slaves, however, is that although he decrees that they be tied together, two by two, there is really no need for such a precaution. Theirs is a voluntary and thus quite Hobbesian submission to the victor.[6] The Europeans have retained exclusive control of the available guns, and as Singleton tells us, the Negroes "always believed our Guns had some heavenly Power in them, that they would send forth Fire and Smoke . . . whenever we bid them" (p. 70). The Negroes see the

Europeans as "People . . . who came from the Sun, and that could kill them all, and make them live again, if they pleased . . ." (p. 68).

The only trouble with all of this, of course, is that Singleton and his men obviously do *not* possess in any ultimate sense the powers ascribed to them. And their pretensions are frequently exposed for the sad frauds they are. No matter how much knowledge or power they gain, it is never enough. Singleton is, in the final analysis, "certain of a mean Station in the World" (p. 56) no matter what he does in his efforts to raise himself. He is, finally, no different from the rest of the mutineers as regards his situation, and they are no freer than the slaves they lord it over.

All the mutineers, Singleton included, having escaped one captivity, find themselves confronted with the necessity for making yet another escape as soon as they are put ashore. Their so-called freedom is, they discover, intolerable, involving as it does a terrifying exposure. It is simply another form of enslavement. They are driven first by their own physical necessities and then by a necessity of another kind, their need to return home—to seek the comfort and security that their own countries represent to them. Thus the entire first section of the book has to do with their repeated efforts to escape. Having once left behind the unwelcome authority they have rebelled against on shipboard, the mutineers must immediately turn their minds to devising ways "to get away from this cursed Place" (p. 23). And hundreds and hundreds of miles later in their travels, they are still trying to solve the same problem: "what to do to get out of this dreadful Place we were in . . ." (p. 113). More than once they are obliged to retrace their steps—to return to the point from which they set out. And when Singleton does at last succeed in getting to England, where is he but right back where he started from in the first place, comfortless and insecure?

Captain Singleton is plainly blood brother to Robinson Crusoe and Moll Flanders. But in neither of those other novels does Defoe dwell so mercilessly on the extent of man's helplessness in the face of nature—the extent to which the natural elements dominate his consciousness and control his being. Whether confronting earth or water, air or fire, as often as not the would-be controller becomes the controlled.

That Defoe knew what he was up to is persuasively suggested when he has Singleton underline, by a telling juxtaposition, the important role perspective plays in one's feelings of power or powerlessness. Describing an early attempt to escape from Madagascar, which has led to an encounter with a group of apparently friendly natives, Singleton comments:

It was as odd a Voyage as ever Men went: We were a little Fleet of three Ships, and an Army of between Twenty and Thirty as dangerous Fellows as ever they had among them; and had they known what we were they would have compounded to give us every thing we desired, to be rid of us.

On the other Hand, we were as miserable as Nature could well make us to be; for we were upon *a* Voyage and *no* Voyage; we were bound *some* where and *no* where; for tho' we knew what we intended to do, we did really not know what we were doing. (P. 32)

In some sense the entire novel rests on this kind of contradiction. Almost invariably, whether Singleton's feelings of power originate in the way he sees himself or the way other people see him, they give way sooner or later to an experience of impotence.

We see the contradiction most clearly perhaps in the incidents having to do with fire. The African savages may regard the little band of Europeans as coming "from the Sun" and may see their firearms as a manifestation of their "heavenly Power," but there are many occasions when the Europeans themselves know better. Their own actions are frequently determined by the energy which comes from the sun as fire and heat; they are themselves often controlled by it. Again and again, they must alter their plans in some way that involves their waiting upon the pleasure of the sun. And Singleton repeatedly uses words like *violent* and *intolerable* to characterize the equatorial heat from which the travelers must take care to protect themselves.

There are, to be sure, many ways in which they have tamed this energy and made it serve the cause of their survival, their firearms being only one. They use fire to cook their meat, to bake their bread, and to temper their tools. They use it as a way of signaling a potential rescuer. They use it as a defense to keep away the wild animals whose terror of it equals their own. They even use it as a means to knowledge, as when, Singleton says, "we had Reason enough to know the place was inhabited, because we several times saw Fires in the Night, and Smoke in the Day, every way at a Distance from us" (p. 46).

But if fire is associated with God, it is also associated, obviously enough, with the devil. We may recall that Singleton is unsure whether one of the first tribes of natives to be impressed by his men's firearms has taken them "for Gods or Devils." And he has depicted these savages as having "run screaming away as if they were bewitched." Singleton himself, in the second half of his narrative, finds himself similarly frightened during a storm at sea, and in this instance he feels anything but godlike.

The point need not be belabored, but it is plain that Singleton experiences either helplessness before or dependency on the other natural elements as well. He may feel able to harness and control the winds so that they take him where he wants to go on the waters of the planet, but he is really adapting himself to powers that are considerably greater than his own. As suggested earlier, one of the central metaphors of the novel has to do with man's navigational knowledge, his capacity to set his own course. The metaphor is made explicit when, after the terrifying storm, the pirates once again set sail: "so we hoisted our Topsails again, haul'd aft the Fore-sheet, brac'd the Yards, and went our Course as before: Nor can I deny but that we were all somewhat like the Ship, our first Astonishment being a little over, and that we found the Ship swam again, we were soon the same irreligious hardned Crew that we were before, and I among the rest" (p. 196).

It may be tempting, on the basis of this passage, to conclude that we are to read Singleton's entire story as a kind of pilgrim's progress.[7] After all, he has, subsequent to proclaiming "the Devil and a Portuguese equally [his] Aversion," cited "the English Proverb, He that is Shipp'd with the Devil must sail with the Devil" (p. 7). And at one time during their overland journey the Europeans are guided by what amounts to a pillar of smoke by day and a pillar of fire by night.[8] It would be a serious oversimplification of the novel, however, to conclude on the basis of these explicit and implicit biblical associations with the journey metaphor that Defoe's plan for Singleton has been all along to trace his route, with all its partial triumphs and momentary setbacks, until he at last leaves the devil behind and finds his way to God. Singleton's adventures can be read as a spiritual journey only if we take the word *spiritual* in its broadest possible sense, and even then the triumphant nature of that journey would have to be called into question.

Suffice it to say for the moment that for all of his pride in his own powers and his confidence that he knows where he is going and how he is going to get there, Singleton is forever being driven back, thrown off course, or forced to the expedient of time-consuming detours. His upward aspirations are forever being frustrated. A circular pattern, alternating a temporary shelter and security with a renewed setting out on a path that leads only to new exposure and fearfulness, repeats itself even more insistently in Captain Singleton's adventures than in Robinson Crusoe's.[9] And there is, in both novels, the same emphasis on the inability of the hero to remain comfortably where he is, however secure and well fed he may be.

And we witness time after time, in the passages concerning the travelers' numerous efforts to get away from Madagascar, lengthy debates as to means and ends followed by deliberate choices of some course of action—and then failure. While it may be a clear step upward in Singleton's rise to power when the Gunner concurs that recourse to piracy is "*our only Way now*," the problem is that, although Singleton may win the debate, his plan does not, in the event, work. The little group does manage to move "forward and forward by a Northerly Course" (p. 32), but after a voyage that involves miserable exposure ("without any Covering from Heat or Wet"), they experience, first, "the Discouragement and Melancholy" resulting from the unpleasant discovery that they are getting not closer but farther away from their destination, and second, the "Desperation" of being once more obliged to "run for the shore," having been "surprized with very bad

Weather, and especially violent Rains with Thunder and Lightning most unusually terrible to us" (p. 33).

Just at the point when Singleton is about to rise to a position of command (and just before the time that the Gunner, finding him "eager to understand and learn," teaches him among other things, "all the Sciences useful for Navigation"), he has experienced the basic helplessness of the Gunner and everyone else when it comes to the forces of nature. Paradoxically, in order to be free, man must learn what the laws of nature are and then obey them. But nature does not, any more than does man, always operate within the law. Hence it can prove too much for even the most intelligent and educated man. The point is made especially clear in the scene where Singleton's band arrives at what they call "the Golden River." The Gunner has, on this occasion, produced "his Carts and Maps, which by his Instruction," says Singleton, "I began to understand very well." And having established that the river before them is the Nile, the Gunner proposes building canoes and continuing the journey by water. But here a more rational head prevails—namely, that of the "Surgeon, who was himself a good Scholar, and a Man of Reading"—and this more rational head acknowledges that nature presents an insuperable barrier to such a plan:

> Some of his Reasons, I remember, were such as these; first, the Length of the Way, which both he and the Gunner allowed by the Course of the Water and Turnings of the River, would be at least 4000 Miles. Secondly, The innumerable Crocodiles in the River, which we should never be able to escape. Thirdly, the dreadful Desarts in the Way; and lastly, the approaching rainy Season, in which the Streams of the *Nile* would be so furious, and rise so high, spreading far and wide over all the plain Country, that we should never be able to know when we were in the Channel of the River, and when not, and should certainly be cast away, over-set, or run a-ground so often, that it would be impossible to proceed by a River so excessively dangerous. (P. 93)

In some sense this passage supplies an ironic commentary on the events immediately preceding it, for the little band of men has just triumphed over what has been the greatest obstacle yet confronted. They have stood at the edge of the Sahara Desert and quaked in their boots. The prospect was, recalls Singleton, "enough to astonish as stout a Heart as ever was created. It was a vast howling wilderness, not a Tree, a River, or a Green thing to be seen, for as far as the Eye could look . . ." (p. 79).

The travelers' journey across the desert proves to be one of the central symbolic episodes of the novel. It is, in little, the human story as Defoe sees it. We witness men in their confrontation with a hopelessly inhospitable, unsustaining world. They can choose, as many of them want to do, to turn back and refuse the challenge, thereby acknowledging their own inadequacies and remaining forever cut off from home: they can abandon themselves to despair. Or they can, as Singleton proposes, change their course. The Gunner—"our Guide to the Situation of Places"—knows that the choices before them are, in fact, severely limited—that they can avoid a present danger only at the risk of meeting a worse future one. He feels sure, though, that if they can but conquer the obstacle immediately before them, they can then "find Ways enough for [their] Escape Home" (p. 79). And sustained by this conviction (always, in Defoe, an illusory one), they proceed to what Singleton terms a "Regulation of Our Measures" (p. 80) and then set forth "without a Guide" (p. 81). Again Singleton finds himself ignorant and exposed—undirected and unprotected.

One of the multiplying ironies of this journey—a journey whose ending is at the same time the beginning of a still more arduous one—is that the man best equipped for survival and the one to whom the others must turn for help is not a civilized and knowledgeable European but the Black Prince, representative of the savages for whose ignorance Singleton has expressed such contempt. To him they must look for advice when, as Singleton says, it seems "as if all the Beasts of the Desart were assembled to devour us." ("We asked our Black Prince what we should do with them? *Me go*, says he, *fright them all* . . ." [p. 90].) The savage, in this crisis, is the one who knows how to make use of fire to strike terror into the hearts of inferior beings.

It would seem that there are times, in the struggle for survival, when the only knowledge worth having is that based on the experience born of risk and exposure. Here again Defoe has clearly gone to school to Hobbes ("by how much one man has more experience of things past, than another; by so much also he is more Prudent, and his expectations the seldomer faile him").[10] Robinson Crusoe makes the same point in his *Farther Adventures:* "it is impossible to make Mankind wise, but at their own Expence and their Experience seems to be always of most Use to them, when it is dearest bought."[11] When the travelers must depend on what Singleton terms "speculative Philosophy" (p. 110), as opposed to firsthand knowledge, they must base their course of action on guesses that do not always prove accurate.

Singleton's own experience tells us that whatever his godlike pretensions, he is always at bottom in a state of virtually total dependency. In turning the Black Prince and his men into slaves to serve him, Singleton does not finally free himself from his animal state so that his thoughts may soar unfettered. On the contrary, he abandons independence in favor of dependency to exactly the same extent as do the Negroes. The voluntary servitude works both ways. And indeed his self-delusion as to his own immunities may make his risk greater than theirs in that he is less able to feed himself and find his own way out of the wilderness.

It is thus especially apposite that before Singleton and his comrades can set out on their overland journey they must devise what are referred to as

"Gloves" for their feet out of goatskin. Where the leopard skin became a trophy symbolic of Singleton's power over nature, the goatskins are a countersymbol of his dependency and need for protection, his basic animality.

Man cannot free himself from the elements, either those which make up the world he lives in or those of which he himself is constituted. Once Singleton sets out on a sea adventure, if the wind does not drive him ashore, he can be sure that his own need for food will do so. Defoe never lets us forget this seemingly obvious fact. Over and over and over again, until we must begin to wonder why, Singleton tells us in impressively exhaustive detail about his provisions. Fresh water is always a problem for him. And next to that, as a matter always on his mind, comes meat. (How many times in the course of the novel do we hear about hogs and cows?)

Man may feel driven by spiritual hungers and thirsts, but he is always being distracted from pursuing their satisfaction by his more elemental demands. On his way toward his true home, he is constantly getting sidetracked by threats to his physical survival. Thus, we hear Singleton speaking one minute about his "insatiable Thirst after Learning in general" (p. 56), but not long afterward he is concerned with "Provisions" of a considerably more basic kind ("a great many cows, young Runts, about 16 Goats, and four young Bulls" [p. 61]), and his journey toward home is not many weeks old before he, along with his men, is "in a most dreadful Apprehension of being famished to Death"—so reduced that when at last they do hunt and kill some deer, Singleton relates: "we came to a full Stop to fill our Bellies, and never gave the Flesh time to cool before we eat it; nay 'twas much we could stay to kill it, and had not eaten it alive, for we were in short almost famished" (p. 106). Beside such a statement as this, Singleton's complacent expression of gratitude for his superiority to the "stupidly ignorant and barbarous" savages rings a bit false. In fact, on their journey across Africa, the dominant experience of the Europeans is one of terrified smallness and lostness when confronting the merciless hostility of uncharted, uncivilized nature.

What is more, Singleton rarely suggests much confidence on the travelers' part that they are heading in the right direction. The "best Guide" they have, namely the Gunner, proves at times to be mistaken, and in one instance actually sends the group off in the opposite direction from that they have set out to pursue, with the result, says Singleton, that "our men began to be uneasy, and said, we were now out of our Way for certain, for that we were going farther from home, and that we were indeed far enough already" (p. 109). Instead of moving upward and north, they are moving downward and south.

Nor does Singleton fare very differently after he has launched himself on his career of piracy. The world remains for him, even though not quite so insistently, an awe-inspiring and bafflingly extensive place. Again there is a certain irony in his rather pitying response to the ignorance of a group of savages, in this case some mutinying slaves who have taken over a Dutch ship: "they did not so much as know that it was the Sails that made the Ship go; or understand what they meant, or what to do with them." And he says further with regard to a conversation with one of their leaders: "When we asked him whither they were going, he said, they did not know, but believed they should go Home to their own Country again" (p. 163). They have, this same man acknowledges, felt "terribly frighted" at the approach of the pirates.

But Singleton himself is soon to experience a fright and confusion far greater than theirs. Of his reaction to the furies of the storm, he says, "I was all Amazement and Confusion. . . . My Soul was all Amazement and Surprize" (p. 195). Forcibly made aware of the enormous energies of the universe, he can only respond with abject "Terrour." And his feelings of impotence when he faces the prospect of crossing the "vast unknown Indian Ocean" (p. 205) are not very different from those he has experienced standing at the edge of the desert.

One of the things that Singleton learns even more unforgettably during his second experience of the world than during his first is how full of concealed rocks and shoals life is and how easily a man can be taken by surprise. The thematic focus of the second half of the memoirs, however, shifts markedly. If the first half recalls in many ways the adventures of Robinson Crusoe, the second half often anticipates those of Moll Flanders, involving as it does Singleton's criminal career—the part of his life given over to preying on his fellow man. The human appetites having to do with money and sex come to the fore in this half; and again the point-counterpoint pattern soon becomes evident.

Singleton's experience of money as power has actually begun quite early in his life. But as a boy, his knowledge of the power of wealth has been no more highly developed than his knowledge in other areas. Among the Portuguese travelers, the Surgeon and the Gunner—the leaders of the group and the ones always credited with superior knowledge and intelligence—are the ones who know the importance of gold. As for Singleton, we hear him admitting well along in the first half of his narrative—at the point when the travelers have discovered a vast amount of gold—his ignorance in this particular area. Soon, however, he finds yet another highly qualified teacher: in this case the Englishman for whose rescue he and his men have been responsible. And this new mentor delivers a lecture of some length, in the course of which he equates the African Gold Coast region with heaven, thereby establishing the accumulation of gold as a way to salvation.

Despite what certain readers have concluded about the "greed" and "avarice" of the Englishman,[12] it seems highly likely that Defoe (while no doubt

beset by some ambivalence) wants us to regard his advice as sound, especially in light of what a later mentor, Friend William, says to Singleton
toward the end of his adventures as a pirate. William, while not abetting
Singleton in his piracies, readily takes a hand in his trading transactions,
thus actively supporting him in adding to his wealth. And when Singleton
reveals his having higher aspirations than do his men in the matter of
accumulation, William stands firmly behind him: "almost all my Men said
we were rich enough, and desired to go back again to *Madagascar;* but I had
other things in my Head still, and when I came to talk to them, and set
Friend William to talk with them, we put such further Golden Hopes into
their Heads, that we soon prevailed with them to let us go on" (pp. 189,
190). And earlier it has been *"William's* Dream" of finding "a Mine of Gold"
that has led him and eventually Singleton and his crew to Captain Wilmot's
lost ship, which proves full of plunder. William is thus presented as a
dreamer, an aspirer, and it is only when he sees Singleton as "rich enough"
(p. 198), that he at last proposes going home to England and to God.

But Singleton, as a typical Defoe hero, is destined to learn a lesson similar
to that he learns in connection with his increase of knowledge. In the case
of the stockpiling of money he finds that self-aggrandizement does not
result in a greater sense of safety but quite the opposite. Man in society is
just as appetitive a creature as man in a state of nature. And when money
becomes power, it becomes something that everyone wants and that people
are willing to obtain at other people's expense. The Englishman learns this
lesson to his sorrow, "for he having sent a Thousand Pound Sterling over to
England by the Way of Holland, for his Refuge, at his Return to his
Friends, the Ship was taken by the *French,* and the Effects all lost" (p. 137).

As a pirate, Singleton knows all about such things, but he has shown
himself to be in possession of the knowledge much earlier. Recognizing the
discovery of gold as a threat to "the good Harmony and Friendship that
had been always kept among us, and which was so absolutely necessary to
our Safety," he makes with his comrades what he terms a "wholesom Agreement," the main points of which involve a mutual sharing of all the "Fruit
of their Labour" and the discouragement of "Wagering and Playing for
Money." The human appetites, he is well aware, require governing. (He is
in an especially good position to appreciate the truth about human greed,
since he decides to share the information about the gold with his comrades
only after the indiscretion of a colleague has unfortunately made it necessary.)

If Singleton has notable success in this instance, however, he is less successful in controlling the appetites of his men in another area. While carrying out their second search for gold, it happens that some of them "had
made something free with [the native] Women, which, had not our new
Guide made Peace for us with one of their Men, at the Price of seven fine
Bits of Silver, which our Artificer had cut out into the Shapes of Lions, and

Fishes, and Birds, and had punch'd Holes to hang them up by (an inestimable Treasure!) we must have gone to War with them and all their People"
(p. 130).[13]

The special irony here has to do with the lack of appetitive control
evinced by ostensibly civilized human beings in their relationships with
"uncivilized" ones. And this early incident of sexual misbehavior anticipates the much more fully developed one in the second half of the novel
when Singleton's ship encounters the Dutch-built ship whose slaves have
mutinied. The cause of the mutiny, Singleton's men eventually learn, has
been that "a White Man abused the Negro Man's Wife, and afterwards his
Daughter, which . . . made all the Negroe men mad; and . . . the Woman's
Husband was in a great Rage, at which the White Man was so provoked,
that he threaten'd to kill him . . ." (p. 161). In this case the white men *have*
"gone to War" with the Negroes, with the result that disorder has, in the
form of an uprising of the savages, taken over the ship. And the consequences for the ship itself have been disastrous.

Still another important incident relevant to this theme has similar consequences for Singleton himself, along with his crew. "We had," he recalls
about their first experience at Ceylon, "a little Skirmish on Shore here with
some of the People of the Island, some of our Men having been a little too
familiar with the *Homely Ladies* of the Country; for Homely indeed they
were, to such a Degree, that if our Men had not had good Stomachs in that
Way, they would scarce have touch'd any of them" (p. 218). Whatever
"barbarous thing they had done," he goes on, ". . . they had like to have
paid dear for it." The eleven offenders are in fact attacked by a large
number of resentful Ceylonese and barely escape with their lives. Of the
one who does not escape, Singleton emphasizes that he "rather died by
drinking some Arrack Punch, than of his Wound, the Excess of Drinking
throwing him into a Fever." Meanwhile, the ten spared offenders are still
not content. They become in their turn "mighty Warm upon their Revenge," and are only with difficulty dissuaded from it. Eventually, the affair
turns, metaphorically speaking, into a fire that burns out of control, for
after setting sail, the pirate ship is blown back ashore by "a violent Storm of
Wind from the South" (the direction has some significance) and must encounter these same natives again. Ultimately, that battle ensues in which the
two sides are equipped with firearms and fire-arrows respectively, and the
ship is in danger of catching fire. Not only is the air "full of Flame," but,
Singleton says, "it is impossible to express the Confusion and filthy vile
Noise, the Hurry and universal Disorder, that was among that vast Multitude of People . . ." (pp. 234, 235). We are given here, it seems plain from
both the juxtaposing of scenes and the insistent heat and storm imagery, a
view of the alienated human condition at all levels: man against himself,
man against his fellow man, and man against nature.

Singleton has by this time, of course, already discovered at first hand what dire consequences can follow from unwariness and from ungoverned self-indulgence. He has learned, after his return to England, that there is an alien, potentially destructive wildness within himself as well as without, for as the result partly of misplaced trust but largely of actions "to be conceal'd with Blushes"—"all Kinds of Folly and Wickedness"—he ends what he calls his "first Harvest of *Wild Oats*" in "Luxury," wasting the "glorious . . . Sum of Money" he has brought home with him. He has, that is to say, fallen from glory and having wholly forgotten the cautionary advice of the Gunner ("Have a Care!"), he has come to a point, he tells us, at which "I did not care where I went, having nothing to lose, and no Body to leave behind me" (p. 138). Lacking all sense of direction, he reverts to the aimlessness of his younger years, the outcome being that he eventually finds himself "entertained with a great deal of Joy by Captain *Wilmot* and his new Gang; and . . . well prepared for all manner of Roguery . . . without the least Checks of Conscience, for what I was entred upon, or for any Thing I might do, much less with any Apprehension of what might be the Consequence of it . . ." (p. 139). Not until some two years later does Friend William come into his life and a new pattern of upward motion begin.

If, as can be argued, "Captain *Wilmot*," with his recklessness and rejection of reasonableness, is to be associated historically with John Wilmot, Earl of Rochester, and "Friend *William*" (who enters Singleton's life in 1688) with William III of England, then the nature of Singleton's central conflict in the second half of the novel becomes quite clear, as does William's much-debated role.[14] In Defoe's own life, King William, as well as Rochester, was a key influence. And Defoe's ambivalent response to Rochester is mirrored by the response Singleton evinces toward Wilmot.[15] As Captain and eventually Admiral of the pirates, Wilmot—whom another of the pirates calls "a brave Fellow" (p. 139)—acts as the guiding spirit of the "irreligious" and "harden'd crew" in the early part of the pirate saga. But even before he and Singleton decide to pursue different courses, he has twice fallen sick and Singleton has turned to William for guidance. And at the time of the debate over a choice of direction, the pirate crew decide to follow Singleton, with his "forward, enterprizing Temper," and to have "nothing more to do with" Wilmot (pp. 184, 185), who has opted for a foolhardy journey to the Red Sea. Wilmot adamantly refuses to listen to rational advice as to "the Hazard" involved, and in fact he has become identified with the negative heat imagery that dominates this portion of the narrative. Not only does his illness take the form of a fever, but in describing their debate, Singleton remarks that "warm Heads are not easily cooled," and later tells of Wilmot's being in "a great Rage; so that he threaten'd if I came on Shore, he would cut my throat" (pp. 184, 185).

Novak has argued that one of the chief qualities Defoe demanded of a

"true Heroe" was the "ability to rule his passions";[16] and it is this ability that
Singleton seemingly learns from that "dry gibing Creature" William. (In his
chapter entitled "Friend of William," John Robert Moore says of Defoe:
"William's dry wit was congenial to him; he is almost the only observer who
has much to say about William's smiles."[17]) William is to the mature Singleton what the Gunner has been to young Captain Bob, acting throughout
their association as adviser and teacher. Or, if we choose to see him as a kind
of opposing voice within the hero, then he may be defined as the alienated
side of Singleton, the side that has been overruled as the second half of the
narrative commences but that, once it is allowed its rightful position of
dominance, will lead him back to the home from which he has been led
away by "the Masters of Mischief" to whom he has bound himself with all
"the most solemn Imprecations and Curses that the Devil and both of us
could invent" (p. 138). Singleton calls William at one point his "Privy-
Counsellour and Companion upon all Occasions" (p. 168) and at another
assigns him a role as "Plenipotentiary"—and he acknowledges him from
the outset as "fitter to be Captain than any of us" (p. 144). The secret of his
repeated successes, both in the actions he takes and in the debates he
carries on with Singleton and the other pirates, rests largely on the mental
agility he demonstrates in outguessing an enemy, whether that enemy be
within the men or outside them. Demonstrating the salutary uses to which
human brain power can be put, he repeatedly plays the role of savior or
deliverer from death, always in the process pursuing the path of sweet
reasonableness. He is "a wise and wary Man," to whom Singleton gives
credit for "all the Prudentials of my Conduct" (p. 265).[18]

The inner enemies with which he consistently deals are foolhardiness
and hotheadedness—emotions that he is able to expose as both unreasonable and self-destructive. He knows that moderation and self-interest go
hand in hand, and one of his first reassuring statements to the pirates is, "
shall be moderate" (p. 144). Thus he persuades the pirates to "be ruled by
Reason" (p. 153) in the matter of deciding what prizes to pursue, convincing them of the wisdom of eschewing men-of-war in favor of merchant
ships in order to avoid violence and death. And thus, on a later occasion, he
talks them out of their destructive impulses toward the "black Devils" who
have taken over the Dutch-built ship. Feeling "enraged," the men advocate
"cutting them all in Pieces." But William makes them see that the mutiny
"was nothing but what, if they were in the Negroes Condition, they would
do if they could" and that "the Negroes had really the highest Injustice
done them, to be sold for Slaves without their Consent; and that the Law of
Nature dictated it to them; that they ought not to kill them, and that it
would be wilful Murder to do it." In this way, says Singleton, William
"prevailed with them, and cooled their first Heat" (p. 157).

Singleton himself, however, at first responds with some heatedness to
William's well-intentioned counsel. "I think I swore at him," he says. *"Wha*

do you mean . . . what do you sneer at now? You have always one dry rub or another to give us" (p. 147). But he soon learns that William's repeated cautions to the pirates to keep cool and use their heads are sound.

Still, there are times, as William well knows, when reason tells us that our survival requires hand-to-hand combat—times when running away won't do. When, for example, Singleton's ship is being chased by a Portuguese man-of-war, William's advice is to turn and stand. "Will it be better for us to be taken further off than here?" he asks. And when Singleton protests, "he will talk to us in Powder and Ball," William, whom Singleton later praises for having "the Heart of a Lion" (p. 212), demonstrates that cowardice is no part of his reasonable nature by responding, "Very well then . . . if that be his Country Language, we must talk to him in the same, must we not? Or else how shall he understand us?" William clearly knows that pacifism has its limits. Even in battle, however, it doesn't work to lose one's head, and on this occasion William saves the day for the pirates by keeping his. Similarly, when the pirates are obliged to fight fire with fire in the hollow-tree affair, William remains cool and uses his head to devise stratagems. He knows that in countering violence and rage, brainpower in the form of outwitting techniques works better than fire power.

One cannot but wonder, however, in reading the conclusion of this affair, whether Rochester does not have the last word here, as at other points in the narrative,[19] for Singleton's voice of reason is not, in the event, heeded. Although William admits the justice of Singleton's contention that they have nothing to gain from conquering this enemy, whatever frustration they may feel over being "baulked by a few naked ignorant Fellows," he nonetheless sets about burning down the tree. And the Gunner then goes far beyond cool reason when he decides to "make a Mine of it" and with appalling results: "we saw what was become of the Garrison of *Indians* . . . who had given us all this Trouble; for some of them had no Arms, some no Legs, some no Head, some lay half buried in the Rubbish of the Mine, that is to say, in the loose Earth that fell in; and, in short, there was a miserable Havock made of them all . . ." (pp. 213, 214). We are reminded of Crusoe's violent response to the cannibals: disintegrate lest ye be disintegrated. Unleashed heat has here gotten so far out of control that no government seems possible. The pirates' "Curiosity" has been "gratify'd"; they have indeed "searched into the Thing," but at what Singleton admits is "a dear Price": "this was a losing Voyage, for we had two Men killed, one quite crippled, five more wounded; we spent two Barrels of Powder, and eleven Days Time, and all to get the Understanding how to make an *Indian* Mine, or how to keep Garrison in a hollow Tree . . ." (p. 214).

As for natural furies, a countering fire power obviously does not work at all. But man need not, it is suggested, stand helpless and terrified before the onslaught, for William demonstrates that even in the midst of such confusions and terrors, "presence of Mind" can bring salvation. Thus, at

the time of the terrible storm, as Singleton and his men respond in "Amazement and Confusion" to what sounds to them like "a Blast of a Hundred
Thousand Barrels of Gunpowder," none of them having "Presence of
Mind to apply to the proper Duty of a Sailor," Friend William saves the day:
"had not he run very nimbly, and with a Composure that I am sure I was
not Master of, to let go the Fore-sheet, set in the Weather Brace of the Fore-
yard, and haul'd down the Top-sails, we had certainly brought all our Masts
by the Board, and perhaps have been overwhelm'd in the Sea" (p. 195).

As a "most dexterous Surgeon" (p. 158), William once more illustrates
the point, again assuming the role of savior. When, in one instance, a Negro
on the Dutch ship is discovered to have a broken leg and is "in a miserable
Condition, the Flesh being mortified," all the Ships' surgeons declare that
the leg must be cut off. But William insists on looking further into the
matter and not only manages to save the leg but also takes steps to stop "the
spreading Contagion and to abate or prevent any feverish Temper that
might happen in the Blood," with the result that the Negro soon becomes
"a perfect sound Man" (pp. 159, 160). William is victorious over the
"spreading Mortification."

His healing powers are again called upon in the extended adventure with
the Malabars. In fact, it is interesting—in view of the heat imagery that
dominates this series of incidents—to find that the scene constitutes a sort
of summary statement of William's powers to assure survival whatever the
nature of the confrontation. When the wounded men have given themselves up for dead, it is William who has "cured them all but one." When
they have then been "mighty warm upon their Revenge," it is William—
arguing again from his knowledge of the "Laws of Nature"—who persuades them that in taking such action they would have nothing to gain and
everything to lose. And when the ship goes aground and Singleton, without
taking thought, wants to accept the Malabars' invitation to come ashore, it is
William who says to him, "if thou wilt go, I cannot help it. . . . Whether we
in the Ship may come off any better at last, I cannot resolve thee; but this I
will answer for, that we will not give up our Lives idly, and in cool Blood, as
thou art going to do; we will at least preserve our selves as long as we can,
and die at last like Men, not like Fools trepann'd by the Wiles of a few
Barbarians" (p. 223). And it is William who then devises a plan for dealing
with them. As Singleton says, "*William*, who was always useful to us, I
believe, was here again the Saving of all our Lives" (p. 222).

In reasonableness, in caution, in ingenuity salvation appears to lie. Thus
it is to be expected that William will finally be the one to advise repentance
as the way of steering clear of the ultimate fire toward which "this hellish
Condition" of piracy is leading. For Singleton, as for Robinson Crusoe and
Moll Flanders, repentance is a wise measure, a course that any thoughtful
person knows he ought to pursue. William suggests, with reference to
Singleton's piracy career, that he has behaved thoughtlessly long enough. It

is time now to take thought. And when Singleton does so, his new awareness leads to a new fear. He experiences himself again in all his finiteness; he feels exposed and defenseless. Contemplating the loot of his piracies, he writes: "I looked upon it as a Hoard of other Mens Goods, which I had robbed the innocent Owners of, and which I ought, in a Word, to be hanged for here, and damned for hereafter; and now indeed I began sincerely to hate my self for a Dog, a Wretch that had been a Thief, and a Murtherer; a Wretch, that was in a Condition which no Body was ever in . . ." (p. 267). Now only repentance seems to offer a way out.

At least one critic apparently sees Singleton's conversations with William on repentance as the climax toward which the novel has been moving from the first.[20] "Well," says Singleton to William, "I give you my Word, that as I have commanded you all along, from the Time I first took you on Board, so you shall command me from this Hour; and everything you direct me, I'll do." William, we are probably meant to note, has pointedly refused to act as guide to Singleton as long as the ship continues to sail south. "I would fain have had Friend William's Advice," Singleton has said in talking of his plans for sailing toward the Cape of Good Hope, "but he always put it off with some *Quaking* Quibble or other. In short, he did not care for directing us . . ." (p. 154). To continue to head south is, presumably, to remain in the "hellish Condition" of piracy, and William will not aid Singleton in his pursuit of his own destruction.

The problem that William knows Singleton must take care of now has to do not with his having devoted himself to the pursuit of money but rather with his having chosen piracy as the means. Novak observes that, unlike Moll, Singleton cannot in any way justify his thieving career on grounds of necessity, since it is his own "luxury" that has brought him to that state of poverty to which he has come as the second half of the narrative begins.[21] Thus he must turn to repentance and thoughts of restitution if he is to enjoy any "future Prospect of Living" (p. 255).

But to regard Singleton's contemplation of repentance as the climax of the novel is to be faced thereafter with a good deal of anticlimax, much of it taken up with William's and Singleton's fears not for their immortal souls but for the security of their "immense Treasure" (p. 198).[22] They spend considerably less time thinking of God than contriving various devious plans for protecting their lucre from a world full of predators. Again and again, in these concluding pages, Singleton sounds the note of suspicion and mistrust. Evidently, this is the chief consideration toward which taking thought has directed him. Again we are reminded that the smarter a person is, the more he knows enough to distrust his fellow man. The more money a person has, the more he has to lose.

In the course of his travels, the only group of people Singleton meets who are totally innocent in this respect are, ironically, those people who live so far inland from the African coast as never to have been exposed to "civilizing" influences.[23] They are described as being "stark naked without Shame, both Men and Women"—"a very frank, civil, and friendly sort of people" (p. 107). And Singleton says of them: "They came to our Negroes without any Suspition, nor did they give us any Reason to suspect them of any Villainy. . . ." We are also told that they value gold less than either silver or iron. Evidently, their lack of interest in gold and their trustingness are interrelated.

Such a state of innocence and serenity is forever denied Singleton. That he does not even dare speak his own language in his own country after his return points up the alienation and isolation he continues to feel. And the mistrust. He is as afraid as ever of giving himself away, of losing what he has gained.

Singleton's memoirs have been, in effect, an effort to define a meaningful self. His accumulated adventures, together with his accumulated wealth, are all he has to assure himself that he has had a significant existence. And it is true that in telling his story, the "famous Captain Singleton" is doing a little Hobbesian "glorying."

But if Singleton feels this way about himself, he also feels, at the end of his journeys, like the same helpless child in need of protection that he was when he started out. He refers to William on two occasions as his "Comfort"—in the second case writing, "he was my Ghostly Father, or Confessor, and he was all the Comfort I had" (p. 268). What God is to Robert Knox (whose interpolated story constitutes a kind of recapitulation of Singleton's African experience), William is to his friend. He is "the Father of the fatherless" (p. 241) and "a great Comfort to him in his Captivity" (p. 243)—and, as Singleton observes, "all the Methods for preserving our Effects, and even our selves lay upon him . . ." (p. 265).

When William is not cast as Singleton's father, he becomes his clone, his reassuring double. One has, at the end, a picture of the two men, with their "Mustachos or Beards" and their "long Vests," as identical stage actors who, in Singleton's words, "neither had or sought any separate Interest" (p. 272). It may well be the climactic event in Singleton's rise that he has now, in effect, merged with William and all he represents. But in pretending to be inseparably bound to reason he is, by implication, living a charade, and even his preoccupation with repentance constitutes a part of it: "we convers'd seriously and gravely, and upon the Subject of our Repentance continually; we never changed, that is to say, so as to leave off our *Armenian* Garbs, and we were called at *Venice* the two *Grecians*" (p. 272). It is hard to avoid the conclusion—especially given Singleton's "that is to say"— that talk of repentance tends to be as much a matter of self-protective play-acting as are the costumes he and William wear.

Singleton's feelings of dependency do not of course focus exclusively on William. They extend to William's sister as well—a woman whose "Tenderness and Kindness" (p. 273), not to mention her circumspection, are reassuring evidence that she "is fit to be trusted with Life or any thing" (p. 275). In her he sees, as Defoe himself saw in family life, "a Refuge for my self, and a kind of a Centre, to which I should tend in my future Actions . . ." (p. 276). She becomes his "faithful Protectress" at a time when he has felt "perfectly destitute of a Friend in the World to have the least Obligation or Assistance from" (pp. 276, 277).

The passage that includes the latter observation is one where we see quite clearly Singleton's contradictory feelings of self-importance on the one hand and fearfulness on the other, existing side by side. "You may think, perhaps," he comments, "that I was very prodigal of my ill-gotten Goods, thus to load a Stranger with my Bounty, and give a Gift like a Prince to one that had been able to merit nothing of me, or indeed know me: But my Condition ought to be considered in this Case; though I had Money to Profusion, yet I was perfectly destitute of a Friend in the World to have the least Obligation or Assistance from, or knew not either where to dispose or trust any Thing I had while I lived, or whom to give it to, if I died" (pp. 275, 276). Paradoxically, it is his wealth that has made him feel destitute. And his decision to "give a gift like a Prince" is hardly prompted by princely feelings. He must use the very money that makes him feel powerful to buy protection for himself.

Furthermore, for all that he has made William's sister "the Object of [his] Bounty" (p. 276) and for all his assurances of his and William's "maintaining an inviolable Friendship and Fidelity to one another," he does not completely trust either one of them. When William goes off to Bassora on a stockpiling mission and is gone for two months, Singleton recalls, "I began to be very uneasy about *William,* sometimes thinking he had abandoned me, and that he might have used the same Artifice to have engaged the other Men to comply with him and so they were gone away together . . ." (p. 260). And once he has made William's sister rich and stands on the verge of joining her in England, he tells us that "when it came to the Point, my Heart failed me, and I durst not venture . . ." (p. 275).

He does at last "go Home to England" (p. 277), but even then he is in it but not of it. He may see William's sister as "opening the very Door for us," but he and William nonetheless resolve "to keep our selves entirely concealed, both as to Name, and every other Circumstance . . ." (p. 275). He remains a homeless waif, without an identity and without a country—he and William having agreed to "pass for Grecians and Foreigners" as well as to "pass for Brothers." Having, in the course of his narrative, "boldly own'd what Life [he has] led abroad," he seems abruptly to feel he may, after all, have already given too much away and decides to "say no more for the present, lest some should be willing to inquire too nicely after" him (p. 277). He might well say of his condition now what he has said of his plight at the time he and his party were crossing the desert: "we . . . could see no End, no Change of our Prospect, but all looking as wild and dismal as at the Beginning" (p. 85). In his own mind, he is still on the run—seeking to escape some shadowy pursuer.

4

Moll Flanders
"out of the Jaws of Destruction"

Because Moll Flanders belongs almost exclusively to a city environment, the similarities between her experiences and those of Robinson Crusoe on his island and Captain Singleton on his land and sea journeys may not at first be obvious. Moll's is a social world—a world of competition, of buying and selling, of sexual encounters, of urban crime. Yet whatever the differences in form between Moll's adventures and those of Crusoe and Singleton, the essential content is much the same. Again, Defoe concerns himself with human psychology at its most elemental.[1] As with Crusoe and Singleton, life for Moll is a power game.[2] And the game, Defoe again recognizes, is in the final analysis a losing one.

But there is one way in which Moll resembles Crusoe not at all. If he is, at certain times on his island, *homo domesticus*, she is almost never *femina domestica*. She does, it is true, live briefly by her needle, but for the most part the background against which we view her is an outdoor one—the outdoors of the streets of London. The impression she leaves us with is one of virtually perpetual motion—seeking somewhere to go, moving toward some prey, running away from real or imagined pursuers. And even if her feet occasionally come to rest, her mind never does.[3] It is forever working ingeniously on stratagems for survival, whether those stratagems have to do with devising tricks to trap a husband or coming up with schemes for thievery or defending her behavior before judges and other potential punishers either human or divine. In fact, there are times when some devious escape route she describes is at once followed by an equally devious reasoning process, which she pursues with astonishing mental agility. In both kinds of peregrination necessity is the mother of invention.

To begin a discussion of Moll with perhaps the least debatable thing about her, however, is to begin with an area in which she resembles Crusoe closely. Like him she fears for her own physical survival with an intensity that rises many times to something close to animal terror. That Defoe himself understood this feeling well is amply attested to by something he once wrote in the *Review:* "I tell you all, gentlemen, in your poverty the best of you all will rob your neighbor; nay, to go farther . . . you will not only rob your neighbour, but if in distress you will EAT your neighbour, ay, and say grace to your meat too."[4] London is for Moll a jungle in which a person must struggle to eat and must take constant precautions against being eaten. The opening pages of the story she tells establish the pattern. At her birth in Newgate, she is as effectually alone in the world as is the "newly born" Crusoe on his island, and is "kept alive" she knows not how.[5] "I had no Parish to have Recourse to for my Nourishment in my Infancy," she writes (p. 8). But by the age of three she is already moving toward adeptness at surviving, and after a brief interlude with gypsies, she is "taken up by some of the parish officers of Colchester" and contrives "to be provided for"—albeit the "Provision" is only "a plain Diet" (p. 10).

Fewer than three years later, however, she is once again without "so much as Lodging to go to, or a bit of Bread to Eat" and is "frighted out of [her] Wits" (pp. 16, 17). And we witness the same fears at the time of her involvement with her Bath gentleman: "I was not without secret Reproaches of my own Conscience for the Life I had led . . . Yet I had the terrible prospect of Poverty and Starving, which lay on me as a frightful Spectre, so that there was no looking behind me . . ." (p. 120). Thereafter, her fear of starvation—in the literal sense at least—disappears from the forefront of her consciousness, only to reappear some forty years later, at the time of her banker husband's death. Then she finds her circumstances so "reduc'd" that she feels "desperate" and describes the "want of Friends and want of Bread" as "a desolate State" (p. 191). On the occasion of her first theft, she does give some "tormented" thought to her victim's possibly being "some poor Widow like me, that had pack'd up these Goods to go and sell them for a little Bread for herself and a poor Child," but she admits that soon "my Distresses silenced all these Reflections, and the prospect of my own Starving, which grew every Day more frightful to me, harden'd my Heart by degrees" (p. 193).

Moll can never be entirely "easy" unless she knows her present and future food supplies to be assured, and we find her still hounded by the same preoccupations about food as she arranges things on shipboard in preparation for being transported. The only details she mentions about the cabin are, significantly, that it had "very good Conveniences to set our Chest, and Boxes, and a table to eat on." And in anticipation of the voyage, she has, she says, "order'd . . . abundance of things for eating and drinking" (pp. 315, 316). What Eric Berne says of Robinson Crusoe is equally true of Moll: "The main problem is to have now all you want to eat and the indefinite assurance of future nourishment to avert the danger of starving to death."[6] Crusoe, in his *Serious Reflections,* defines eating and drinking as "the main end of life" for human beings. That is, he says, "their enjoyment, and to get food to eat is their employment," and sometimes the process includes "their eating and devouring one another."[7]

Moll, of course, knows all about this. When she remarks of the ship's captain that he was not a "Man craving and eager to make a Prey of us" (p. 316), we are reminded that she has, almost from the start, consciously inhabited a predatory world. Her experience with the older brother of the Colchester family has long since taught her how it feels to fall prey to someone. He had, she says, "known as well, how to catch a Woman in his Net, as a Patridge when he went a Setting"; he had "baited his Hook and found easily enough the Method how to lay it in my Way . . ." (pp. 19, 20). Thus it is that Moll learns how easily women can fall victim to masculine appetites. But she is also quick to learn that the fed can be turned into the fed upon.

Meanwhile, she has learned another truth the hard way—namely, that the preying male may lust not after a woman's body but after her bank account. She again finds herself "catched" in a "snare" at the time of her second marriage—having, she discovers, "sold" herself to a fortune-hunting tradesman. And again she learns her lesson well, for from this point on, whenever she must enter the marriage market—a market which, as she says, "runs very unhappily on the Men's side" (p. 67)—she arranges to become the victimizer before she becomes the victim. In fact, when she takes up thievery, preying becomes her primary means of livelihood. She has clearly subscribed, by this time, to Rochester's conviction that in a knavish world only fools are good.[8]

It is understandable, then, why Moll's tone, like Crusoe's, often hints at the self-glorying of the survivor and the controller, and why the cautionary advice she frequently hands out is almost always tinged with an undertone of condescension toward those who allow themselves to be taken advantage of. She insists, for example, that women seeking husbands have "Reason to be wary, and backward" and advises them to "act the wary Part" (p. 75). Self-protection is her motto, and she concludes by saying, "as for women that do not think their own safety worth their own thought . . . I can say nothing to them, but this, that they are a Sort of Ladies to be prayed for among the rest of distemper'd People; and they look like People that venture their whole Estates in a Lottery where there is a Hundred Thousand Blanks to one Prize" (p. 75). In Moll's view, only those who remain sharp-witted and are perpetually on their guard can expect to prosper.

And Moll has also learned, early in life, certain home truths about serving others. She tells us that the "service" her first lover renders his younger brother "was not indeed done to serve him, but to serve himself," and she concludes, "so naturally do Men give up Honour and Justice, Humanity, and even Christianity, to secure themselves" (p. 58).

Later, Moll recounts the story of her faithful nursing of her Bath gentleman during his serious illness—"hazarding my Life to save his." But it is significant that this way of characterizing her service is not hers but his; it is what "he called it." For Moll, the "service" she renders is simply a sound investment, for not only does it elicit from the gentleman a gift of fifty guineas, but it brings his "deep Protestations of a sincere inviolable Affection" (p. 114). In view of all this, it is difficult to see how any reader could regard Moll as "warm-hearted."[9]

Be that as it may, however, there can be little quarrel about what motivates her. We can say "greed." We can say "acquisitiveness." But from a Hobbesian point of view, Moll is simply looking out for herself in a typically human way; and if there is a certain boastfulness in her cautioning everyone else to do the same, there is also a substratum of wholly human fearfulness and insecurity.

In serving others, Moll is taking out insurance policies—like Robinson Crusoe before her. Consider, for example, her machinations on behalf of the captain's wife early in the novel. "My Dear and Faithful Friend, the Captain's Wife," she observes, "was so sensible of the Service I had done her in the Affair above that she was not only a steddy Friend to me but . . . she frequently made me Presents as Money came into her Hands, such as fully amounted to a Maintenance . . ." (p. 77). And when, toward the end of the story, she presents her son with a gold watch (a stolen one, of course), she reports that "He took it, kiss'd it, told me the Watch should be a Debt upon him, that he would be paying, as long as I liv'd" (p. 338).

With reference to the question of service, what she truly wants, it seems clear almost from the outset, is total self-sufficiency. Hence her outspoken resistance as a child to "going into service" represents an instinctive longing for independence. While Robinson Crusoe on his island has no choice but to live by his "Finger Ends" (p. 11), Moll actively makes that choice—the choice "to get my Bread by my own Work" (p. 13). The condition of servitude is anathema to her.[10] After all, any state of dependency includes a certain helplessness. Moll can understand perfectly Jemy's "apprehensions" about being transported to Virginia, where "he should be the most ignorant helpless Wretch alive." But she can offer him reassurance: "I TOLD him he frighted and terify'd himself with that which had no Terror in it; that if he had Money, as I was glad to hear he had, he might . . . avoid the Servitude supposed to be the Consequence of Transportation" (p. 303).

Moll, like Jemy, wants desperately to achieve and maintain a station in life above that of the "wretched Crew" of convicts. Jemy tells her "that Servitude and hard Labour were things Gentlemen could never stoop to" (p. 301), and Moll speaks later of their being "in the despicable Quality of Transported Convicts destin'd to be sold for Slaves" (p. 311). For them, to be a gentleman or a gentlewoman is to matter, to count in the world—to stand above the "ordinary Passengers, who Quarter'd in the Steerage" and even farther above their "old Fraternity" who "were kept under the Hatches . . . and came very little on the Deck" (p. 316).

Thus for Moll it is not enough simply to avoid servitude. She must "live great and high" as well. Not only is it important to her that Jemy be made to "appear, as he really was, a very fine Gentleman," but the outward trappings of a gentleman must include servants. Moll duly notes as part of the cargo sent from England both "a supply of all sorts of clothes" and "three Women Servants, lusty Wenches" (p. 340). Not content with feeling in control of her own life, she must feel that she controls the lives of others. She knows, with Hobbes, that servants are indices to the power of those they serve.

What is more, Moll loves making fools of people, proving them less clever and hence less powerful than she. And to recognize this is to see at once that her capacity for self-aggrandizement includes piling up not only money but triumphs in the game of power politics. There is no mistaking the relish with which she recounts every incident in which she succeeds in outwitting an adversary—and the worthier the better.

Moreover, it is a notable fact that the only two men in her life for whom she professes love are her first lover (the older brother of the Colchester family) and Jemy, both of whom prove a match for her in their talent for manipulation. Jemy—that man of "Vigour and Courage" whom she numbers among "the greatest Spirits" (pp. 313, 315)—is, for Moll, a power figure and thus a hero to be looked up to and at times served because he can save. ("'Tis something of a Relief," she says, "even to be undone by a man of Honour, rather than by a Scoundrel.")[11] He is, however, a power figure whom Moll ultimately outgrows, as she comes to learn the limitations of the power he wields. "I was," she says at the time of her reunion with her son, Humphry, "as if I had been in a new World, and began secretly now to wish that I had not brought my *Lancashire* Husband from *England* at all." But then she does a little knocking on wood, as she quickly adds, "that wish was not hearty either, for I lov'd my *Lancashire* Husband entirely, as indeed I had ever done from the beginning; and he merited from me as much as it was possible for a Man to do . . ." (p. 335).

What both the older Colchester brother and Jemy possess, like Moll herself, is the ability to think clearly—to be the masters rather than the victims of circumstances. Moll's contempt for those who allow their wits to become befuddled is obvious. Thus she calls the "poor unguarded Wretch" whom she meets at Bartholomew Fair "a Fop . . . blinded by his Appetite" and asserts: "There is nothing so absurd, so surfeiting, so ridiculous, as a Man heated by Wine in his Head and a wicked Gust in his Inclination together; he is in the possession of two Devils at once, and can no more govern himself by his Reason than a Mill can Grind without Water . . . nay, his very Sense is blinded by its own Rage. . . . Such a Man is worse than Lunatick . . ." (p. 226). And similarly, she tells later of stealing a gold watch from a lady "who was not only intollerably Merry, but as I thought a little Fuddled . . ." (p. 263).

But in losing one's head one stands to lose a good deal more than a gold watch. One stands to lose one's very self, as Moll has long before learned. "His words," she says of her Colchester lover when he first begins to pay her attention "fir'd my Blood; all my Spirits flew about my Heart, and put me into Disorder enough." And although, as she says, "I soon recover'd myself," the recovery is short-lived, for in the next paragraph she reports: "my Head run upon strange Things, and I may truly say, I was not myself" (p. 221). It is clear then why, when she falls into a "Distemper" and becomes "Delirious and light Headed" after her lover's rejection of her, the phrases *oppress'd my Mind, agonies of my Mind, distress'd in my Mind,* and *my Mind was oppress'd* follow one after another within the space of three paragraphs (p. 42).

For Moll as for Crusoe, moreover, devils of irrationality can threaten not only from without but from within, alienating one from one's true self. Moll, of course, ascribes her taking up and her continuing in her life of crime to her falling into a trap laid by the devil. "I am very sure," she protests, "I had no manner of Design in my Head, when I went out, I neither knew or considered where to go, or on what Business; but as the Devil carried me out and laid his Bait for me, so he brought me to be sure to the place, for I knew not whither I was going or what I did" (p. 191). Feelings of helplessness merge with feelings of confusion and lostness: "I cross'd and turn'd thro' so many ways and turnings that I could never tell which way it was, nor where I went . . . my Blood was all in a Fire; my Heart beat as if I was in a sudden Fright. . . . I still knew not whither I was a going, or what to do" (p. 192). Only when she ends up, at last, in Newgate, does she begin "to think." And as she goes on to remark, "to think is one real Advance from Hell to Heaven. All that Hellish harden'd state and temper of Soul, which I have said so much of before, is but a deprivation of Thought; he that is restor'd to his Power of thinking, is restor'd to himself" (p. 281).

Newgate is for Moll "an Emblem of Hell itself"; the "horrors of that dismal Place" fill her with such "terror" that, as she says, "I look'd on myself as lost" (pp. 273, 274). Speaking of "the hellish Noise, the Roaring, Swearing, and Clamour, the Stench and Nastiness," she associates such chaos with her own confusion of thought, which "left me overwhelm'd with Melancholy and Despair" (p. 274). Newgate is Moll's "Island of Despaire," and there, she tells us, her association with "a Crew of Hell-Hounds" brings it about that she "degenerated into Stone," turning "first Stupid and Senseless, then Brutish and Thoughtless, and at last raving Mad" (p. 278). The word *degenerated* or *degeneracy* appears three times here in as many paragraphs. She has, in her own view, become subhuman. She has, as John Richetti says, been "brought to accept death."[12] She has virtually lost "the Habit and Custom of good Breeding and Manners" (p. 279) which have defined her in her own self-regard as a "gentlewoman," as someone who counts. "I was, I may well say I know not how; my Senses, my Reason, nay, my Conscience were all a-sleep . . ." (p. 279). Degeneracy has "possessed" her to such an extent that all her "uneasiness" has disappeared—the fear of chaos, the sense of its horrors that has defined her humanity.[13]

Robinson Crusoe never sinks so low, but then he has not begun life in Newgate. He has occupied the "middle Station" to begin with, while Moll has had to climb out of the dirt and darkness of a world where people are more *bête* than *ange*. Robinson Crusoe's Muscovite prince, in defining human life, speaks of "the Jayl of Flesh and Blood" the human soul "is now enclos'd in" and of "the Dirt and Crime of human Affairs"; and for Moll Newgate is that "Jayl."[14] One of the things she commends in the "good Motherly Nurse" who first takes her in is that she is "Very Housewifly and Clean" and that she keeps ten-year-old Moll "very Neat" ("and if I had Rags on, I would always be Clean . . ." [p. 14]). And when, toward the end of her career as a thief, she once adopts the disguise of a beggar-woman, she calls it "the most uneasy Disguise to me that ever I put on," since, as she explains, "I naturally abhorr'd Dirt and Rags; I had been bred up Tite and Cleanly . . ." (p. 253). Moll likes things to be neat and clean in every sense of the phrase. She shares with Crusoe a passion for order. Dirt, confusion, disorder are all equally threatening to her sense of command. They are equated with hell, with evil, with death.[15] Thus, like Crusoe, she is easy and comfortable only when she feels she has life under control. Crusoe delights in being king on his island; Moll speaks of having "reigned" in the criminal world of London (p. 275). Crusoe savors his powers of largess in his dealings with the African savages, who have, only a little earlier, constituted a threat to his life; Moll speaks pleasurably of her queenly generosity toward the journeyman whose testimony has threatened to send her to Newgate. "I abated his Cringes," she says, "told him I forgave him, and desir'd he might withdraw, as if I did not care for the sight of him, tho' I had forgiven him" (p. 253).

Again like Crusoe, Moll has the artist's instinct for imposing form on the content of her life. She refers to picking pockets as an "Art" (pp. 201, 213) and earlier expresses distaste for the methods of some of her criminal confreres, making reference to their "Course and unhandy Robberies" and deploring the fact that they get "into the House by main Force" and remarking with disapproval that they "broke up the lock'd Place where the Watches were . . ." (p. 209). Not for Moll such lack of subtlety. She is an artist at her trade, and in recounting her successes, she implicitly compliments herself again and again on the ingenuity of her maneuvers. It is superiority of mind and not brute force that wins the day. People who use their heads come out ahead.

All of which leads us to recall that for Moll power is central. And if power resides in knowledge, it also resides in the money that a person of superior wit is able to accumulate. Here—at the money nexus—we can see many of the threads of Moll's seemingly complex personality coming together to form what is really quite a simple pattern. Moll's hatred of dirt and her love of money are the children of a single parent. Defoe seems to have known intuitively what Norman O. Brown was the first to articulate as an essential truth—that money, far from being, as Freud had argued, equated with feces, is a *"denial* of feces, of physicalness, of animality, of decay and death."[16]

No wonder that Moll is horrified by "the Stench and Nastiness of Newgate." It is, as she says, "the Place . . . where I was brought into the World" (p. 273) and the place that she has been seeking all her life to transcend. Commenting, as earlier noted, on having "scarce retained the Habit and Custom of good Manners," she goes on to bemoan the fact that "so thoro' a Degeneracy had possess'd me, that I was no more the same thing that I had been, *than if I had never been otherwise than what I was now"* (p. 279, italics added). She has sought to rise above her origins—to deny the immutable fact that she was born, to quote Swift, "in the place of excrement"—and that she was born to die. And thus it is that she is appalled to discover "how Hell should become by degrees so natural and not only tollerable but even agreeable . . ." (p. 276).

In the event, it is not God but money that is responsible for her being able to distinguish herself from the other Newgate wretches. "I had," she says, "obtained the Favour, by the help of Money, nothing being to be done in that Place without it, not to be kept in the Condemn'd Hole . . . among the rest of the Prisoners who were to die, but to have a little dirty Chamber to myself" (p. 290). And only money can raise her, once she arrives aboard the transport ship, above those "ordinary Passengers who Quartered in the Steerage" and her "old Fraternity . . . kept under the Hatches." As she has written long before, or rather etched on the window of her chamber, *"Money's Vertue; Gold is Fate"* (p. 79). Ostensibly, Moll is here acting the role of the cynical realist, but in fact she largely lives her life on this conviction. To be without money is indeed to be "reduc'd"—to be denied "a settled State of *Living"* (p. 128, italics added). "I knew," she says at one point, "that with Money in the Pocket one is at Home anywhere" (p. 178).[17]

Money is not for Moll an end in itself but a means to the end of ease and comfort in the most elemental sense—a means of achieving a feeling of at-homeness in the world and of freedom from fear. She is an accumulator because money is power and lack of it is weakness and vulnerability. Invariably, Moll's estimate of her own value at any given time relates directly to the value of her possessions. Thus, when she returns from her first journey to Virginia, she dwells insistently upon how "little" she owns: "what little I had in the World was all in Money, except as before, a little Plate, some Linnen, and my Cloaths; as for Houshold stuff I had little or none, for I had liv'd always in Lodgings; but I had not one Friend in the World with whom to trust that little I had . . ." (p. 130). Hence, in her own mind, she becomes a helpless prey. "If this Woman had known my real Circumstances," she says of her fellow lodger in London, "she would never have laid so many Snares and taken so many weary steps to catch a poor desolate Creature that was good for little when it was caught . . ." (p. 130).

Very seldom, however, does Moll find herself at so low a point as this. Obsessed with accumulating "stock," she devotes all her ingenuity to the piling-up process. And here we have come back, in a roundabout way, to Moll's primitive, eat-or-be-eaten outlook on life. What she does, in Ruskin's words, is to "take dust for deity," as men have ever done. She is the archetypal human creature who has, as Norman Brown says, "confused excrement with aliment" and who "draws no distinction between the necessary and the superfluous."[18] She insists, more than once, that whenever she behaves other than virtuously, "the Vice came in always at the Door of Necessity, not at the Door of Inclination" (pp. 128, 129). Knowing well the value of "a settled Life," Moll gives herself up to a pursuit of it, never seeing that "the Terror of approaching Poverty" will always lie "hard upon [her] Spirits" (p. 129).

But she does come close to a consciousness of her own drivenness when she is in the midst of her triumphs in the thieving line: "tho' by this jobb I was become considerably Richer than before, yet the Resolution I had formerly taken of leaving off this horrid Trade, when I had gotten a little more, did not return; but I must still get farther, and more . . . a little more, and a little more, was the Case still." She has kept hoping, she tells us, "that I might perhaps come to have one Booty more that might compleat my Desires; but tho' I certainly had that one Booty, yet every hit look'd towards another . . ." (p. 207).

Moll expands her stock as compulsively as Crusoe expands his fortifications; the accumulating instinct drives her on and on. Not only do we find her listing her assets at the beginning and the end of every adventure, but all her life she remains an obsessive counter and keeper of accounts. "I told the Guineas over and over a thousand times a Day," she says, after she receives her first substantial payoff from her Colchester lover (p. 26). And she refers to his "thousand protestations of . . . sincerity," "his thousand more preambles," "his many protestations," and tells us that he "kissed me a thousand times and more I believe and gave me money too."

Since it is Moll's accumulating tendencies that have drawn the most attention from critics of the novel, it is here that we must begin to come to grips with one aspect of that endlessly debated question as to Defoe's ironic intent in the novel. Of Defoe's treatment of Moll, Kenneth Rexroth writes: "He permits her to record her life only on the cash register, and in so doing he judges her without mercy."[19] In espousing such a reading of the novel and of Moll's character, Rexroth is following the lead of Dorothy Van Ghent, who has insisted that either we must see Defoe's characterization of

Moll as consciously ironic or we must regard Defoe's own value system as so corrupt as to invalidate his novel as a meaningful work of art.[20]

Even if we do, however, regard Moll as *femina economica*, Defoe's treatment of her experience need not be seen as either an indictment of capitalism or a broader condemnation of human materialism in general. Instead, the novel would seem to be, among other things, an examination of just what money has come to mean to civilized man. And therein lies the irony.

At this point in the argument, it is important to remember that what we may be tempted to see as Moll's propensity for hard-headed, rational calculation is actually motivated by her fears for her own survival, her desire to rise above her low origins. The irony of her situation is exactly that which Brown recognizes in Horace: he "sees poetry as a career, like all careers (trader, soldier, athlete, etc.) basically characterized by self-sacrifice and instinctual renunciation; it is nevertheless worth while if success will enable him 'to strike the stars with head sublime.'" But, says Brown, Horace's expressed hope that he "shall not altogether die" is "the hope of the man who has not lived, whose life has been spent conquering death. . . ." Horace's dedication to his work, to his "royal accumulation," has been ironically at once "death-defying and deadening."[21] If Moll has, as so many critics argue, betrayed her higher self, become subhuman in that she is a kind of money-making machine, the irony is that she has achieved that unhappy result in the effort to achieve its opposite—the effort, that is, to become superhuman.

The sacrificial nature of her dedication becomes especially clear in her erotic response to money. Van Ghent was among the first to point to the sexual suggestiveness implicit in Moll's financial transactions with her Bath gentleman:

> reaching in his Pocket, [he] pull'd out a Key, and bad me open a little Walnut-tree box he had upon the Table, and bring him such a Drawer, which I did, in which Drawer there was a great deal of Money in Gold, I believe near 200 Guineas, but I knew not how much: He took the Drawer, and taking my hand, made me put it in, and take a whole handful; I was backward at that, but he held my Hand hard in his Hand, and put it into the Drawer, and made me take out as many Guineas almost as I could well take up at once.
> When I had done so, he made me put them into my Lap. (P. 112)

We have earlier encountered an anticipation of this kind of thing when Moll's Colchester lover presents her with "a silk Purse, with an Hundred Guineas in it." "My Colour," Moll tells us, "came and went, at the Sight of the Purse, and with the fire of his Proposal together; so that I could not say a Word, and he easily perceiv'd it; so putting the Purse into my Bosom, I made no more Resistance to him . . ." (pp. 28, 29). And in the scene at the gambling house late in the novel, Moll's handling of the money belonging o "the gentleman who had the Box" possesses a similar suggestiveness: 'He . . . made me take the Box, which was a bold Venture: However, I held he Box so long that I had gain'd him his whole Money, and had a handful of Guineas in my Lap. . . . I understood the Game well enough, tho' I pretended I did not, and play'd cautiously; it was to keep a good Stock in my Lap, out of which I every now and then convey'd some into my Pocket; out in such a manner . . . as I was sure he cou'd not see it" (p. 261).

This is the game Moll has been playing all her life. For Moll, accumulating stock is tantamount to accumulating life, and thus she characterizes her "spending upon the main Stock," to which she is at one point reduced, as "but a certain kind of *bleeding to Death*" (p. 106). We hear the same phrase again when she reaches another low point in her career: "I LIV'D Two Years in this dismal Condition wasting that little I had, weeping continually over my dismal Circumstances, and as it were only bleeding to Death, without the least hope or prospect of help from God or Man; and now I had cried so long, and so often, that Tears were . . . exhausted, and I began to be Desperate, for I grew Poor apace" (p. 190).

There is, apropos of this, a notable irony in the nature of many of the things Moll steals, symbolically associated as they are with fertility: baby clothes, for example, and wedding rings and a horse (which, to add to the irony, she does not know what to do with once she has it). At one point too she steals from a pregnant woman.[22]

Moll is well aware that, as Brown puts it, "money *breeds*," and it is her desire, with reference to any money she has in hand, that "the Interest of it maintain me" (p. 129). In effect, she prefers devoting her reproductive capacities to producing money rather than children. Gold is the beloved offspring of her labor.

Understandably, then, Moll is always as concerned to have any children she produces "taken happily off of my Hands," as she is to retain any money she accrues "in my own Hands" (pp. 127, 129). And she sees to it that any of her children who are unhappily left on her hands will be as little expense as possible. The only child of hers of whom we hear in some detail is the son in Virginia, who proves to have become "a handsome comely young Gentleman in flourishing Circumstances" (p. 322), and hence an interest-bearing investment of time and energy. Just as Moll values her land—"very fertile and good"—in Virginia because it produces crops that produce income, so she values her own productiveness only if the product in turn reproduces satisfactorily. She speaks toward the end of her story of going "over the Bay to see my son and to receive another Year's Income of my Plantation." And she describes her son in this scene as "the same kind dutiful and obliging Creature as ever," and tells us that he "treated me now at his own House, paid me my hundred Pound, and sent me Home again loaded with Presents" (pp. 341, 342).

At this juncture it may seem that we have slipped back into something

resembling the familiar ironic reading of Moll's "adventures." But a point
that psychologist Ernest Becker makes, in explicating Norman Brown, may
provide a helpful clarification: "If we say that 'money is God,' this seems
like a simple and cynical observation on the corruptibility of men. But if we
say that 'money negotiates immortality and therefore is God,' this is a
scientific formula that is limpidly objective to any serious student of man."[2]
In these terms, the point being argued here is that in *Moll Flanders* Defoe
emerges as "a serious student of man" and is not, as has so often been
suggested, making "a simple and cynical observation on the corruptibility
of men."

Moll, in these terms, remains always an upward aspirer. What Van Ghent
calls "the spiritual dimension"[24] is, in fact, present. The distinction between
the sacred and the profane does not, in this context, exist. Perhaps a brief
consideration of Moll's preoccupation not simply with money but with gold
will clarify the point still further. The "prize" that she defines as her "greatest" consists of "a Gold Chain, an old fashion'd thing, the Locket of which
was broken, so that I suppose it had not been us'd some Years, but the Gold
was not the worse for that; also a little Box of burying Rings, the Lady's
Wedding-Ring, and some broken bits of old Lockets of Gold, a Gold Watch,
and a Purse with about 24£ value in old pieces of Gold Coin . . ." (p. 206).
But by this time we have already heard a great deal from Moll about gold
watches, gold rings, and gold coins—including those coins belonging to the
Bath gentleman that she sifts so lovingly through her fingers—and Jemy's
possessions—"ten Guineas, his Gold Watch, and two little Rings, one a small
Diamond Ring, worth only about six Pound, and the other a plain Gold
Ring"—which, she tells us, she "Sat . . . down and look'd upon . . . two
Hours together" (p. 153). Gold, Becker observes, is associated with both the
fire god Agni and the sun's disc. "Money," he goes on, "sums up the *causa
sui* project all in itself: how man, with the tremendous ingenuity of his mind
and the materials of his earth can contrive the dazzling glitter, the magical
ratios, the purchase of other men and their labors, to link his destiny with
the stars and live down his animal body."[25]

It is not, then, that Moll worships and hence serves money, unless we say
that here again it is a case of her serving in order to be served, for in her
view the money she possesses serves her—serves, that is, to raise her above
the lowly state into which she was born. One might say that she works
religiously toward that end. Her career, Defoe tells us in his preface, is
"fruitful of Instruction" that "no Case can be so low, so despicable, or so
empty of Prospect, but that an unwearied Industry will go a great way to
deliver us from it, will in time raise the meanest Creature to appear again in
the World, and give him a new Cast for his Life" (p. 4). Money brings
deliverance. And Moll can feel godlike in her powers of reproduction,
contemplating fondly the fruits of her labors. The irony lies in Defoe's
phrase *unwearied Industry,* since we see here again a situation that can only
be regarded as a sacrificing of self to the end of self-perpetuation. If Moll is

a self-made woman, she is so at the expense of her own energies, her own life force.

The fact is, moreover, that Moll is never truly able to go it alone; she is never able to rise above her state of dependency. Even more persistently than Crusoe's, her feelings of powerlessness and her need for protection continue to make themselves felt. She may at times believe that money is, as she tells Jemy in Newgate, "the only Friend in such a Condition" (p. 303), the only means of escape from servitude, but over and over she admits to the need for other friends as well: "to be Friendless," she says, "is the worst Condition, next to being in want, that a Woman can be reduc'd to" (p. 128).[26] For Moll, friendlessness and exposure are virtually synonymous, just as are poverty and exposure. She characterizes herself in her childhood as "a poor desolate Girl without Friends, without Cloaths, without Help or Helper" and hence "expos'd to very great Distresses" (p. 8), and at the time when she is faced with losing her Colchester lover, she imagines "being turn'd out to the wide World, a meer cast off Whore . . . and perhaps expos'd as such; with little to provide for myself; with no Friend, no Acquaintance in the whole World, out of that Town . . ." (p. 56). "To have friends, is power," says Hobbes.[27]

It is true that Moll has, as noted earlier, a great deal to say about the tendency of women not to take due precautions in the matter of husband-choosing: "'Tis nothing," she declares, "but lack of Courage, the fear of not being Marry'd at all, and of that frightful State of Life called *an Old Maid.*" But she is by no means advocating the single state, and she goes on, "would the Ladies once but get above that Fear, and manage rightly, they would more certainly avoid it by standing their Ground, in a Case so absolutely Necessary to their Felicity than by exposing themselves as they do; and if they did not Marry so soon as they may do otherwise, they would make themselves amends by Marrying safer" (p. 76).

Despite all of Moll's own ingenious machinations and painstaking precautions, however, she finds herself more than once exposed—left in a "dismal and disconsolate Case," "left perfectly Friendless and Helpless" (pp. 189, 190). After her return from Virginia, she complains of being "entirely without Friends, nay, even so much as without Acquaintance" (p. 105). And after the death of her banker husband, she says unhappily, "I had no Assistant, no Friend to comfort or advise me," and goes on to warn, "O let none read this part without seriously reflecting on the Circumstances of a desolate State, and how they would grapple with meer want of Friends and want of Bread" (pp. 190, 191). In Newgate, she cries, "Lord! what will become of me, I shall be cast to be sure, and there is nothing beyond that but Death! I have no Friends, what shall I do?" (p. 281). And finally, faced with crossing Chesapeake Bay some years later, she fears being "left naked and destitute, and in a wild, strange Place, not having one Friend or Acquaintance in all that part of the World." And she adds, "The very thought of it gives me some horror, even since the Danger is past" (p. 330).

Moll's fears of being "left alone in the World to shift for myself" (p. 57 are never allayed. Always she looks to her lovers and her husbands for protection. From the time she learns that the mother of the Colchester family is threatening "to turn me out-of-Doors" and finds reassurance in her lover's promise that "he would Protect me from all the World" (p. 32) she finds that world a terrifying place to face alone.

Moll's world, of course, is scarcely ever the natural one with which Robinson Crusoe must deal. But what little natural imagery she uses suggests that she too regards nature as unfriendly. "I saw the cloud, tho' I did not foresee the Storm" she says of her experience with her Colchester lover (p. 30). And when she has managed to secure her banker husband, she remarks, "I seem'd landed in a safe Harbour after the Stormy Voyage of Life was at an end" (p. 188).

And in some ways Moll's actual experiences of the natural world do resemble Crusoe's. She often sets out on sea voyages that prove to be "long and full of Dangers" (p. 85), after which she comes at last "safe to the Coast" (p. 319). Moll's voyages, while not exploratory and expansive in the same sense as Crusoe's, are undeniably expansive in another sense. She usually ventures forth onto the water when the land has become inhospitable. She undertakes her first trip to Virginia, for example—"a terrible passage," during which she and her husband are "frighted twice with dreadful Storms" (p. 85)—only when she finds herself with little cash in hand and when her husband has told her that he owns "a very good house there, well furnished." It is true that so long as she has "Possession" of "a House well furnished and a Husband in very good Circumstances' (p. 188), her fears remain largely in abeyance and she stays where she is. She feels momentarily protected and provided for.

But she can never be "easy" for long. There *are* times when God, or Providence, is on her side.[28] This she finds, though, is not always the case. When, she says of her Bath lover, he "abandon'd me and refus'd to see me any more," it was because he was "struck by the hand of God" (p. 188). And she is left as if "abandon'd by heaven" (p. 124). And she tells us that after living "in an uninterrupted course of Ease and Content for Five Years" with her banker husband, "a sudden Blow from an almost invisible Hand blasted all my Happiness, and turn'd me out into the World in a Condition the reverse of all that had been before it" (p. 189). The fear of abandonment haunts Moll all her life.

There is, in this connection, a telling passage about midway through the book, in which Moll holds forth at some length on the helplessness of children:

It is manifest to all that understand anything of Children, that we are born into the World helpless and uncapable, either to supply our own Wants, or so much as make them known; and that without help we must Perish; and this help requires not only an assisting Hand, whether of the

Mother or some Body else; but there are two Things necessary in that assisting Hand, that is, Care and Skill; without both which, half the Children that are born would die; nay, tho' they were not to be deny'd Food; and one half more of those that remain'd would be Cripples or Fools, loose their Limbs, and perhaps their Sense: I Question not but that these are partly the Reasons why Affection was plac'd by Nature in the Hearts of Mothers to their Children; without which they would never be able to give themselves up, as 'tis necessary they should, to the Care and waking Pains needful to the Support of their Children.

Since this Care is needful to the Life of Children, to neglect them is to Murther them; again to give them up to be Manag'd by those People, who have none of that needful Affection, plac'd by Nature in them, is to Neglect them in the highest Degree; nay, in some it goes farther, and is a Neglect in order to their being Lost; so that 'tis an intentional Murther, whether the Child lives or dies. (Pp. 173, 174)

Supposedly, Moll's concern here is with the fate of her own child. Yet it seems evident, from the ensuing paragraph, that she herself is, in her own mind, that helpless child whose welfare concerns her so deeply, for there she refers to "my Governess, who I had now learn'd to call Mother" and relates: "She ask'd me if she had not been Careful, and Tender of me in my Lying-In, as if I had been her own Child?" (p. 174). In fact, if all the men in Moll's life are essentially father-figures, most of the women are just as clearly mother-figures. The first—her "good old Nurse, Mother, I ought rather to call her" (p. 16), who "bred up the Children" in her school "with a great deal of Art, as well as with a great deal of Care" (p. 10)—is only one of a long series of women who look after Moll with "Care and Skill." There is her own mother in Virginia; there is "Mother Midnight," who arranges so competently for one of Moll's many lyings-in and who thereafter calls her "Child" and acts "a true Mother to [her]" until the transport ship leaves for Virginia. All these women are nurturers and comforters; all provide homes ("I came Home to my Governess," says Moll more than once after a thieving foray); and all give her instruction in the way she should go in the interest of her own prosperity.[29]

Moll may "reign" supreme in the kingdom of London thieves, but she needs authority figures nonetheless—friends and mothers to advise and direct her. "I was now a loose unguided Creature," she says of herself at forty-two, "and had no Help, no Assistance, no Guide for my Conduct . . ." (p. 128). And we may remember that she goes on to lament, "I had not one Friend in the World with whom to trust that little I had, or to direct me how to dispose of it . . ." (p. 130). And at an earlier stage of her career, she has told her "Dear and faithful Friend, the Captain's Wife" that "I would give up myself wholly to her Directions, and that I would have neither Tongue to speak, or Feet to step in that Affair, but as she should direct me; depending that she would Extricate me out of every Difficulty that she brought me into . . ." (p. 77). Clearly, Moll follows Hobbes in taking a wholly practical view of the mother-child relationship.[30]

Whatever her successes, Moll remains always a child in need of a gov
erness. Adept though she is at the power game, she continues to experienc
herself as powerless. Thus she comments, in recounting her actions afte
successfully making off with a silver tankard: "I came Home to my Gov
erness, and now I thought it was a time to try her, that if I might be put t
the Necessity of being expos'd, she might offer me some assistance
(p. 200). And thus we hear her, toward the end of her narrative, recallin
her need to secure from her mother in Virginia her means of indepen
dence from her brother/husband: "for my Mother had promis'd me ver
solemnly, that when she died, she would do something for me, and leave i
so, as that, if I was Living, I should one way or other come at it, without it
being in the Power of her Son, *my Brother and Husband* to prevent it . . .
(p. 323).

Her sense of powerlessness is compounded by her awareness that she ca
never fully depend on the people on whom she depends. Maximillia
Novak reminds us that the word *mother* is usually applied to the Madam of
brothel.[31] It seems that Moll must depend for protection on a fellow huma
being who is as inspired by the profit motive as she is herself and whos
"children" are her source of income. Moll knows, of course, that all peopl
live at the expense of other people, and at the time of the arrest of a fello
thief, she compliments herself on the canniness she possesses that has bee
born of that knowledge: "Here again my old Caution stood me in goo
stead; . . . I kept close a great while upon the Occasion of this Woman
disaster; I knew that if I should do any thing that should Miscarry, and
should be carried to Prison she would be there, and ready to Witnes
against me, and perhaps save her Life at my Expence . . ." (p. 222). Wha
Moll does is to save her own life at the expense of "this poor Woman"—a
fact which, as she says, "troubl'd me exceedingly." But, she continues, "m
own Life, which was so evidently in Danger, took off all my tenderness; and
seeing she was not put to Death, I was easy at her Transportation, because
she was then out of the way of doing me any Mischief . . ." (p. 223). And
"tenderness" has not even been a problem in the case of another of he
fellow thieves who winds up in Newgate. Fearing that he "might . . . have
bought his own Life at the Expence of mine," Moll expresses heartfelt
relief at "the joyful News that he was hang'd, which was the best News to
me that I had heard a great while" (pp. 219, 220). For Moll, a condition of
"dreadful Exigence" (p. 49) justifies anything;[32] and she assumes that everyone else holds the same view—hence her distrust of the foster parents her
governess proposes for her child. Even though she acknowledges that they
"want neither Care nor Skill," she still protests: "now we know Mother . . .
that those are poor People, and their Gain consists in being quit of the
Charge as soon as they can; how can I doubt but that, as it is best for them
to have the Child die, they are not over Solicitous about its Life?" But the
governess has an answer ready that largely satisfies her: "I tell you their

Credit depends upon the Child's Life, and they are as careful as any Mother of you all" (p. 175).

What Moll says she wants for her child—that it "be carefully look'd after and have Justice done it" (p. 175)—is what, in reality, she desperately wants for herself and yet trusts no one to provide. Rather, she is certain that even her friends will, if they can, live at her expense. Whatever Moll may say about trustworthy friends, "dear and faithful" friends, the predatory nature of her world is not to be gainsaid. She always, therefore, holds something back, never giving herself completely to anyone. Just as she withholds from Jemy a complete accounting of her assets—being "resolved . . . to keep what I had left . . . in Reserve" (p. 311), so she withholds from him a considerable stock of information about herself. When, for example, she first learns the truth about Jemy, she comments, "It was my happiness hitherto that I had not discovered myself, or my Circumstances at all; no not so much as my Name; and seeing there was nothing to be expected from him, however good Humoured, and however honest he seem'd to be, but to live on what I knew would soon be wasted, I resolv'd to conceal everything, but the *Bank Bill*, and the Eleven Guineas . . ." (p. 149). At the time of their first parting, moreover, she tells us, "I Gave him a Direction how to write to me, tho' still I reserv'd the grand Secret . . . which was not to let him know my true Name, who I was, or where to be found . . ." (p. 159). And when, many years later, she has come to Virginia with him, she notes, "I could never so much as think of breaking the Secret of my former Marriage to my new Husband; It was not a Story, as I thought would bear telling, nor could I tell what might be the Consequences of it . . ." (p. 324). She practices a similar reserve with the other person in her life in whom she professes to feel the greatest confidence, namely, Mother Midnight. At one point she indicates she is "frighted" at the thought that her governess knows more than she should about her past: "but reflecting that it cou'd not be possible for her to know anything about me, that Disorder went off, and I began to be easie, but it was not presently" (p. 175).

Here again what Moll fears is exposure. To tell anyone the real truth about oneself is a dangerous practice, and only "horrible Apprehensions" ever drive Moll to it. Such is the case when she is hiding out after her fellow thief has been sent to Newgate. "I had no Recourse, no Friend, no Confident but my old Governess," she says, "and I knew no Remedy but to put my Life into her Hands, and so I did, for I let her know where to send to me . . ." (p. 219). On an earlier occasion, however, she has taken care *not* to let this same friend know her whereabouts. Having declared that there was "no concealing any thing from her" (p. 172), she nonetheless concludes, as she contemplates a journey to West Chester, "at last it came as an Addition to my Design of going into the Country that it would be an excellent Blind to my old Governess, and would cover all my other affairs . . ." (p. 178).

From the time Moll, as a little girl, hides herself from the gypsies, she has been adept at concealment; and late in her story she remarks, "let them say what they please of our Sex not being able to keep a Secret; my Life is a plain Conviction to me of the Contrary. . . ." But she then goes on to add that "a Secret of Moment should always have a Confident, a bosom Friend, to whom we may Communicate the Joy of it, or the Grief of it . . ." (p. 325). She regards confiding her secrets to a friend as a kind of safety valve.

Moll's "account" of her life is, in fact, itself a kind of confession—a disclosure of secrets she might otherwise find oppressive. Yet as with the "relief" she gains from letting Jemy in on as much of her past as she thinks is necessary, she is, one supposes, telling us only as much as she must in order to gain relief from "the Oppression of this weight" (p. 326). Certainly, she does withhold information from her readers. If most of the people in her life do not know who she really is, neither do her readers ever really know. To tell us would be to take a chance on giving too much away. As her governess says to her in another context, "you would be Conceal'd and Discover'd both together" (p. 175).

But as we might expect, given Defoe's persistent awareness of the irony of things, if Moll's narrative is in some sense a confession, it is also an "account" of quite another kind, for it amounts to the sort of "stocktaking" she is forever doing at the end of every "adventure"—a kind of adding up of assets. Recalling here what Ernest Becker says about money, we can see that what Moll's story becomes is a *causa sui* project." Bringing the ingenuity of her mind to bear on the chaotic raw materials of her own existence, she has, like Robinson Crusoe before her, "made something" of her life. She has made sense out of it, made it add up to something. She has become the creator of a triumphant self, thereby rising above her earthbound Newgate origins.

In telling her story Moll has things all her own way. Or so it would seem. But there is always that insistently felt incongruity. The incongruity is not between Moll's professions and her practices (of which more in its place). It is between her pride in her own self-sufficiency on the one hand and her ultimate helplessness on the other. Defoe tells us in his preface something that seems, at first, to be quite gratuitous: "We cannot say indeed, that this History is carried on quite to the End of the Life of this famous *Moll Flanders* . . . for no Body can write their own Life to the full End of it, unless they can write it after they are dead . . ." (p. 5). Moll cannot, after all, transcend her own origins, cannot make of her life a *causa sui* project. Even after her release from Newgate, she remains imprisoned. She is never free from fear.

In effect, the character Moll sets before us is a lie. "It is enough to tell you," she insists, as she begins her story, "that as some of my worst Comrades . . . knew me by the Name of *Moll Flanders;* so you may give me leave to speak of myself, under that Name till I dare own who I have been, as well as who I am." Just as she survives in the criminal world of London—that is, stays out of Newgate—by adopting a series of disguises so that not even her closest associates know her true identity, so she survives psychologically in the world by hiding that identity from herself. After her second unfortunate marriage, she makes a resolution that contains within it the story of her life: "I resolv'd therefore, as to the State of my present Circumstances; that it was absolutely Necessary to change my Station, and make a new Appearance in some other Place where I was not known, and even to pass by another Name if I found Occasion" (p. 76). The thing she must conceal at this time is her poverty. And in some sense the guilty secret she keeps from her governess is this same one. It is the fact of her Newgate origins— the fact that she was born not high but low, not free but bound, not in light but in darkness. And the deceits she habitually practices on the men she seeks to "catch" always involve pretending to be better than she is, whether better means purer or wealthier or of higher social station. Thus it is that the one disguise she adopts during her thieving career that she cannot bear is that of a beggar-woman.

The clothes Moll wears are a crucial aspect of her self-esteem and of her aspirations toward higher status. "I was a Gentlewoman indeed, as I understood that word," she tells us early in her history, for at twelve years old, "I not only found myself Cloaths, and paid my Nurse for my keeping, but got Money in my Pocket too . . ." (p. 15). But thereafter clothes serve Moll not only as status symbols, but as a means of self-protection and a means of disguising herself as well—with all three coming, in the last analysis, to the same thing. When she returns from her first disappointing venture to Virginia and is afraid of having "all I had sav'd . . . taken away," she at once decides to "go quite out of my Knowledge, and go by another Name." Therefore, "I . . . drest me up in the Habit of a Widow, and call'd myself Mrs. *Flanders.*" And she continues, "I conceal'd myself, and . . . my new Acquaintance knew nothing of me . . ." (p. 64). And when, at the age of sixty-one, she takes ship once again for Virginia ("launched out into a new World"), she relates: "My Cloaths were poor and mean, but not ragged or dirty, and no one knew in the whole Ship that I had anything of value about me." But she at once goes on to assure us (and herself): "I had a great many very good Cloaths and Linnen in abundance . . . consign'd to my real Name in *Virginia* . . ." (p. 312). Ostensibly, "good Cloaths" are to be associated with the "real" Moll, but in fact they are as much a disguise as any other clothing she wears. There are at least two occasions in her thieving career where they quite literally save her from detection. On the first occasion, she has dressed up in a man's clothes and when her thieving is spotted and she is pursued and makes her way home, she has time, she says, "to throw off my Disguise and dress me in my own Cloths" (p. 216). And of course those clothes then serve as a means of concealment. Not long afterward she wears "good Cloaths," so that the Mercer from whom she seeks damages "might see I was something more than I seem'd to be that time they had me" (p. 250).

There is some question too as to whether the Moll of whom we read is, after all, the real one, for Defoe tells us in his preface that "the Pen employ'd in finishing her Story, and making it what you now see it to be, has had no little difficulty to put it into a Dress fit to be seen, and to make it speak Language fit to be read . . . to wrap it up so clean, as not to give room, especially for vitious Readers to turn it to his Disadvantage" (p. 1). In his "new dressing up this Story," he suggests that he has given it a "Beauty" which it does not really possess.

It is, perhaps, the ultimate irony of Moll's life that even when she seems to stand most firmly on her own base in all her pride of power, she remains disguised. "The Success I had," she tells us, as she recalls her triumphs in the thievery line, "made my Name as famous as any Thief of my sort had ever been. . . ." Yet immediately thereafter she goes on to recount, "generally I took up new Figures, and contrived to appear in new Shapes every time I went abroad" (p. 262). And of those people with whom she shares her profession, she has earlier said, "I never let them know who I was or where I Lodg'd; nor could they ever find out my Lodging, tho' they often endeavour'd to Watch me to it. They all knew me by the Name of *Moll Flanders,* tho' even some of them rather believ'd I was she than knew me to be so . . . and this wariness was my safety . . ." (p. 222).

Moll's whole history is at bottom a self-justification. She wants to "have Justice done" her; she wants us to know that in a chaotic and predatory world she has made it, has seized and held control of her own life. Yet we too know her only "by the Name of *Moll Flanders.*" She "would be Conceal'd and Discover'd both together." Self-denial goes hand in hand with self-assertion. Her memoirs themselves reveal her preoccupation with self-concealment at the very moment that self-revelation begins.

It is repeatedly the case with Moll that any new beginning carries with it fears of nakedness and exposure, since in psychological terms she is, on each occasion, beginning all over again her struggle to survive and prosper. The Moll whom we meet on page one of her self-revealing memoirs establishes at once her fearfulness.

Still, it might be argued that, unlike Robinson Crusoe's story, Moll's has a satisfactory sense of successful completion. Having had all their "Difficulties . . . made easy," Moll and Jemy have at last "come home" to England "in good Heart and Health" (p. 342). Yet while Moll talks a good deal at the end of her narrative about her feelings of ease and comfort, she nonetheless concludes by saying of herself and Jemy: "we resolve to spend the Remainder of our Years in sincere Penitence for the wicked Lives we have lived." Moll has remarked about herself at the time of her affair with her Colchester lover, "I had a most unbounded Stock of Vanity and Pride, and but a very little Stock of Virtue . . ." (p. 25), and what she seems to be looking toward now is increasing her stock of virtue. After all, in certain schemes of things, as she is well aware, one's virtue is one's value: "you may see how necessary it is, for all Women who *expect any thing in the World*, to preserve the Character of their Virtue, even when perhaps they may have sacrific'd the Thing itself" (p. 138, italics added).

There is really no irony in this, controversial though such a contention must inevitably be. The seeming incongruity between Moll's concern with morality and her patent self-interestedness is in reality none at all. Critics who have argued among themselves over the question of irony in the novel begin with a premise that is itself arguable—and is, indeed, at the root of the problem. Always they assume an incongruity, a conflict, a juxtaposition of contrarieties.[33] But if we consider Moll's motives, then there is no conflict, no incongruity between what she does and what she says about what she does. Her behavior is all of a piece, since invariably what motivates her is her concern for her own well-being. For Moll—and for Defoe—morality is a way of dealing with mortality: it is a matter of self-interest. We must include Defoe in this, or at least the voice of the preface, since the viewpoints in the preface and in the novel are virtually identical. Listen, for example, to what the voice that we take to be Defoe's has to say about "the good Uses of [this work], which the Story all along recommends to" its readers:

> There is in this Story abundance of delightful Incidents, and all of them usefully apply'd. There is an agreeable turn Artfully given them in the relating, that naturally Instructs the Reader, either one way, or other. The first part of her leud Life with the young Gentleman at Colchester, has so many happy Turns given it to expose the Crime, and warn all whose Circumstances are adapted to it of the ruinous End of such things, and the foolish Thoughtless and abhorr'd Conduct of both the Parties, that it abundantly attones for all the lively Description she gives of her Folly and Wickedness. (Pp. 2, 3)

More often than not, both Moll and her creator preach sermons of a let-that-be-a-lesson-to-you variety. When Defoe speaks of the "virtuous and religious Uses" to which Moll's story is applied, he seems himself to be speaking as an inhabitant of a predatory world in which people must be taught to know what's good for them. And it is in this same spirit that he goes on to insist: "Throughout the infinite variety of this Book, this Fundamental is most strictly adhered to; there is not a wicked Action in any Part of it, but is first or last rendered Unhappy and Unfortunate . . ." (p. 3). Defoe apparently regards his narrative as having moral uses in that it illustrates that even the cleverest of wrongdoers, such as Moll, wind up eventually in Newgate or feel the punishing hand of God in some other way. That is to say, both Defoe and Moll are basically concerned with the consequences of behavior: rewards for good behavior and punishments for bad. And it is in this sense that morality is in itself a means of survival. It is not a question of whether vanity is wrong. What is certain is that it can lead to a letting down of one's guard and hence to undue self-exposure and to the loss of those possessions so important to rising in the world. And the same is true of lust, of drunkenness, of avarice.

Moll's response to the gentleman whom she robs in a coach, which is often cited as an instance of her hypocrisy, is a clear case in point. She does, as mentioned earlier, feel contempt for his befuddlement. But she vacillates throughout her recounting of the incident between resentment and admiration; and we can take the tears she sheds for him as sincere as soon as we recognize what he symbolizes for her. As a consequence of drunkenness and lust ("in the possession of two Devils at once"), a "Gentleman" (she uses that designation insistently) has "expos'd" himself, has turned himself into a "poor unguarded Wretch." A "Man of Sense, and of a fine Behaviour; a comely handsome Person, a sober solid Countenance, a charming beautiful Face" (p. 227) has gone "*like an Ox to the slaughter*"—has fallen to a condition of bestiality. And the very things she steals from him are, fittingly, the symbols of his high station: "a silk Purse of Gold, his fine full bottom Perrewig, and silver fring'd Gloves, his Sword, and fine Snuff-box" (p. 225).

There is yet another point to be made in any discussion of what has often been seen as Moll's moral confusion. Novak writes convincingly of the relationship that Defoe saw between moral law and natural law. "Defoe does not believe," he states, "that anyone can resist using all his efforts to save his own life." And he adds that "Defoe was unable to believe that moral principle or even Christian virtue was strong enough to overrule the law of self-preservation," or that any "moral consideration will prevent a man from doing his utmost to survive."[34]

But Moll is not sure—how many human beings are?—precisely where the dividing line is to be drawn between the natural and the unnatural. There are times, of course, when she sees a clear distinction. She is appalled, for example, at discovering her participation, however inadvertent, in incest, which she calls "Unnatural in the highest degree" (p. 91). (For her, evidently, there are *degrees* of unnaturalness.) And earlier her awareness of the distinction has led her to say of the years she spends married to Robin: "I committed Adultery and Incest with him every Day in my Desires, which without doubt, was as effectually criminal in the Nature of the Guilt, as if I had actually done it" (p. 59). The paragraph that she ends with this acknowledgment, she has begun with the words *I confess;* and after all, as a "true Penitent," Moll is often in her memoirs engaged in confessing her sins. We hear her doing much the same thing after her theft during the fire. She calls her booty "the greatest and worst Prize that ever I was concern'd in," and thinking of "the poor disconsolate Gentlewoman who had lost so much by the Fire besides," she writes: "I confess the inhumanity of this Action mov'd me very much, and made me relent exceedingly, and Tears stood in my Eyes upon that Subject; But with all my Sense of its being cruel and inhuman, I cou'd never find in my Heart to make any Restitution: The Reflection wore off, and I began quickly to forget the Circumstances that attended the taking them" (p. 207). Again she is confessing a sin because she is well aware that her action cannot be justified by any appeal to natural law.

But Moll does not commit many crimes that qualify as "cruel and Inhuman"; and if the unnatural is to be defined, in Novak's words, as "doing evil to others where there is no excuse to be found in self-preservation or self-interest," then Moll is almost never guilty, since there is virtually always some excuse to be found. Defoe does fail "to distinguish between poverty and necessity," and so does Moll; but that is because neither of them sees a difference.[35]

Probably we ought to pause here a moment to deal with a related point having to do with what Novak views as Moll's "false speeches on poverty."[36] Such speeches can hardly be examples of Defoe's irony at Moll's expense when Moll herself knows them to be false. Thus to talk about her "perfunctory tone" at the time of her arrest and of the "false speech" she makes in her own defense is to forget whom she is addressing at this point. In effect, he acknowledges that she is acting a part here—pleading necessity in order to play on the sympathies of her apprehenders and get herself out of a tight place. And the method almost works: "I Gave the Master very good Words, told him the Door was open, and things were a Temptation to me, that I was poor, and distress'd, and Poverty was what many could not resist, and beg'd him with Tears to have pity on me; the Mistress of the House was mov'd with Compassion, and enclin'd to have let me go, and had almost perswaded her Husband to it also . . ." (pp. 272, 273). She attempts the same kind of thing again when she stands before the judges trying her for her life: "I spoke with more Courage than I thought I cou'd have done, and in such a moving Tone, and tho' with Tears, yet not so many Tears as to obstruct my Speech, that I cou'd see it mov'd others to Tears that heard me" (p. 286).

More important, however, Moll is often perfectly sincere in citing poverty or necessity as her excuse for a crime, even when the necessity seems by no means clear to us. And here we must return to Norman Brown's insight. The point is that Moll is typically human in that she "draws no distinction between the necessary and the superfluous."

It is, then, surely a misreading of Moll's character to emphasize a contradiction in her between the moral and the immoral. She has no "genuine abhorrence of evil" (if by that is meant that she is somehow innately moral);[37] and it even seems something of a misreading of her character to speak of her "taste for moral preachment."[38] When Moll refers to the

promptings of the devil and to the wickedness of her deeds and the horror
she feels at them, she is inspired not by her "natural impulse to be good" or
her "moral vision,"[39] but by her desire to avoid the punishment entailed.

In many of the passages concerning her thieving exploits, moreover, the
incongruity (and it is, it must be insisted, only a superficial one) is not
between her pride in her artistry and her detestation of the evil her crimes
involve, but between her pride and her fear. Such passages indicate a
profoundly human dilemma. Moll is at once proud of the success of her
ingenuity and fearful of its consequences. What is a gain in prosperity in
one frame of reference may lead to a loss in another, so she covers herself
just in case.

Far from having to do with "struggle," the passages usually cited as
containing ironic juxtapositions amount to Moll's taking care of herself in
at least two different ways. They are, as suggested at the beginning of this
chapter, instances of her mental agility—of the fact that necessity can be the
mother of invention in more ways than one. Consider first, for example,
that passage concerning her precriminal days, in which she talks of sharing
with her governess her "scruples about marrying" her London banker
when she is already married. The upshot of the conversation is, Moll tells
us, that her adviser "reason'd me out of my Reason;" and then she adds:
"not but that it was too by the help of my own Inclination" (p. 173). Here
Moll's fears of being alone in the world (hence her "necessities") incline her
to an action that her reason tells her may involve a breaking of divine law
and hence a threat of divine punishment. In this case, she can fall back on
her awareness that the natural law of self-preservation takes precedence
over the moral law.

A more complicated incident is that lengthy one in which she describes
her reactions during her first theft. "It is impossible to express the Horror
of my Soul all the while I did it," she writes. But this "Horror of . . . Soul," it
develops, is not shame or moral revulsion but sheer terror of being caught
in the act: "my Blood was all in a Fire; my Heart beat as if I was in a sudden
Fright." Having once made it safely home, however, she looks with undis-
guised satisfaction at her take. And then the passage continues:

All the while I was opening these things I was under such dreadful
Impressions of Fear, and in such Terror of mind, tho' I was perfectly
safe, that I cannot express the manner of it; I sat me down and cried
most vehemently; Lord, said I, what am I now? A Thief! why I shall be
taken next time and be carry'd to Newgate and be try'd for my Life! and
with that I cry'd again a long time, and I am sure, as poor as I was, if I
had durst for fear, I would certainly have carried the things back again;
but that went off after a while: Well, I went to Bed for that Night, but
slept little, the Horror of the Fact was upon my Mind, and I knew not
what I said or did all Night and all the next Day: Then I was impatient to
hear some News of the Loss; and would fain know how it was, whether
they were a Poor Bodies Goods, or a Rich; perhaps, said I, it may be some

poor Widow like me, that had pack'd up these Goods to go and sell them for a little Bread for herself and a poor Child, and are now starving and breaking their Hearts, for want of that little they would have fetch'd, and this Thought tormented me worse than all the rest, for three or four Days time.

But my own Distresses silenced all these Reflections, and the prospect of my own Starving, which grew every Day more frightful to me, harden'd my Heart by degrees; it was then particularly heavy upon my Mind, that I had been reform'd, and had, as I hop'd, repented of all my pass'd wickednesses; that I had liv'd a sober, grave, retir'd Life for several Years, but now I should be driven by the dreadful Necessity of my Circumstances to the Gates of Destruction, Soul and Body; and two or three times I fell upon my Knees, praying to God, as well as I could, for Deliverance; but I cannot but say my Prayers had no hope in them; I knew not what to do, it was all Fear without, and Dark within; and I reflected on my pass'd Life as not sincerely repented of, that Heaven was now beginning to punish me on this side the grave and would make me as miserable as I had been wicked.

Had I gone on here I had perhaps been a true Penitent; but I had an evil Counsellor within, and he was continually prompting me to relieve my self by the worst means; so one Evening he tempted me again by the same wicked Impulse that had said, *Take that Bundle,* to go out again and seek for what might happen. (Pp. 192, 193)

The passage has required quoting at some length because of the evidence it supplies first of Moll's constant preoccupation with her own survival and second of the reasoning methods she uses to assure it. There are three fears operating here: first, her fear of starving, which has prompted the theft (and which has, she hopes, justified it); second, her fear of being caught and "carry'd to *Newgate*"; and third, her fear of the consequences of her continuing in crime and of her increasingly hardened heart. The threatened consequences are of course finally the same in all three cases. And as she talks, her mind is busily seeking a way out of a frightening situation. If she does not steal—so the argument with herself goes—she will starve. If she does, she may either wind up in Newgate or eventually be driven . . . to the Gates of Destruction, Soul and Body." For Moll both moral goodness—"a sober, grave, retired Life"—and true penitence for past wickedness are ways of avoiding that destruction. And those she will pursue in due course. Meanwhile, it will have to suffice to register, prudently, her awareness of her sins, for at present starvation is the most immediate of the three punishments she stands to suffer.

One of the things Defoe recognizes again and again in the novel is what a wonderfully self-protective mechanism the human mind is. Just as Moll's mind works ingeniously to enable her to survive by committing thefts and getting away with them (thus avoiding both starvation and Newgate), so it works with equal ingenuity to enable her to survive in a different sense by justifying or otherwise covering herself for the thefts (thus avoiding damnation). Moll's "second Sally into the World" offers a still more complex

example of this same phenomenon. This is the incident perhaps cited most
often as an instance of ironic (and/or comic) juxtaposition. After stealing a
gold necklace from "a pretty little Child," "an innocent Creature," Moll has
a horrifying impulse: "the Devil put me upon killing the Child in the dark
Alley, that it might not Cry; but the very thought frighted me so that I was
ready to drop down. . . ." At this point she sends the child on its way
summing up the incident in these words:

> The thoughts of this Booty put out all the thoughts of the first, and
> the Reflections I had made wore quickly off; Poverty . . harden'd my
> Heart, and my own Necessities made me regardless of anything: The last
> Affair left no great Concern upon me, for as I did the poor Child no
> harm, I only said to myself, I had given the Parents a just Reproof for
> their negligence in leaving the poor Lamb to come home by it self, and it
> would teach them to take more Care of it another time.
> This String of Beads was worth about Twelve or Fourteen Pounds, I
> suppose it might have been formerly the Mother's, for it was too big for
> the Child's wear, but that, perhaps, the Vanity of the Mother to have her
> Child look Fine at the Dancing School, had made her let the Child wear
> it, and no doubt the Child had a Maid sent to take care of it, but she, like
> a careless Jade, was taken up perhaps with some Fellow that had met her
> by the way, and so the poor Baby wandred till it fell into my Hands;
> However, I did the Child no harm, I did not so much as fright it, for
> I had a great many tender Thoughts about me yet and did nothing but
> what, as I say, meer Necessity drove me to. (Pp. 194, 195)

The first thing to be mentioned here is that the self-justifications are
obviously myriad: "Poverty . . . harden'd my Heart"; "my own Necessities
made me regardless of any thing"; "meer Necessity drove me to it." Given
such valid reasons as these, Moll knows that God will understand. Indeed
we cannot but be reminded here of Moll's often-cited reference, a few
pages earlier, to "the wise Man's Prayer, *Give me not Poverty least I Steal*"
(p. 191).

There are other self-justifications as well. Moll draws the same moral
from the story that Defoe has drawn in the preface. She has, she says
taught the child's parents two valuable lessons: first, to take better care of it
hereafter, and second, to see what the consequences of vanity can be. Moll
virtually manages to make the good moral consequences of her theft out-
weigh any possible bad ones. It is almost as if she sees not the devil but God
as guiding her hand. Her discussion here and her memoirs as a whole
constitute not only a confession but an assurance that her life has been of
some use. "The Moral indeed of all my History," she writes in an ingenious
combining of the two motives, "is left to be gather'd by the Senses and
Judgment of the Reader; I am not Qualified to preach to them, let the
Experience of one Creature compleatly Wicked and compleatly Miserable
be a Storehouse of useful warning to those that read" (p. 268).

Moll's repeated expressions of fear may serve, however, as a reminder that if, in the two passages just discussed, Defoe reveals Moll's masterful capacity for self-justification to the end of looking out for herself, he also reveals the feelings of vulnerability that lie behind that need. For it is surely significant (although perhaps quite unconscious on Defoe's part) that in both passages the "poor Child" with whom we have so often watched Moll identify is again present. Moll's reference in the second instance to the "poor Lamb" who has been left "to come Home by it self" echoes her earlier thoughts concerning that child of her own with whom she has identified—the child who may be in danger of being "murthered, or starv'd by Neglect and Ill-usage."

Moll virtually never discusses any "poor Child" or "poor Lamb" without mentioning in the same breath a negligent or improvident parent or nurse, and it is hard to avoid the conclusion that she always tends to identify not with the parent, but with the child—that she sees herself not as the protector but as the one in need of protection. *She* is the "poor Lamb" whose negligent parent has exposed it to death. And her view of morality is essentially that of the child who hears himself cautioned about Santa Claus at Christmas time: "He knows when you've been bad or good/ So be good for goodness' sake." But of course it is not "for goodness' sake" that the child will be good but for the sake of the promised reward. To the good (including the penitent) God will be merciful; for the good, Providence will provide. Robinson Crusoe speaks in one passage of his *Serious Reflections* of the "care and concern of . . . Providence";[40] and at times too Moll Flanders casts Providence in the role of kindly parent. We are, in Christian terms, all God's children, and He is the ultimate protector and comforter whom we so desperately need. Thus Moll speaks, during her Newgate ordeal, of "casting my Soul entirely into the Arms of infinite Mercy as a Penitent" (p. 289) and shortly thereafter, she acknowledges "the merciful Providence that had as it were snatch'd me out of the Jaws of this Destruction" (p. 291).

Moll's thought processes during the time she spends in Newgate are, in other ways as well, exactly what we would expect on the basis of past practices. Just as she has seen poverty and the threat of starvation as having "harden'd" her before, so she sees her reduced circumstances as hardening her now. (She refers to the Newgate period as "this harden'd Part of my Life" p. 279.) And she repeats in essence if not quite word for word what she has said after her first theft: "I knew not what to do. . . ." But on this occasion, as she is "ingulph'd in the misery of Punishment" and with "an infamous Death just at the Door," she finds her mind momentarily failing her. She becomes "Brutish and thoughtless, and at last raving Mad . . ." (pp. 278, 279). The point at which she begins to think ("one real advance from Hell to Heaven"—that is to say, from punishment to reward, from death to life) occurs at the time when she sees Jemy led into Newgate as one of the three "brave topping Gentlemen" to suffer that fate. It is the thought of the fall of this "Gentleman" and her part in it which brings her to herself—moves her from being "Stupid and Senseless, then Brutish and thoughtless," and hence clearly more *bête* than *ange*, to a more proper sense of herself. It is as if she now has a role model other than the "Hell-Hounds of *Newgate*"—one who recalls her to herself.

Her ordeal in Newgate is not yet over at the time she becomes "another Body," but she has begun to take rational action again, and her eventual "conversion," like Robinson Crusoe's, makes, she is astute enough to see, a great deal of sense. Having "nothing before [her] but present Death," she sees it as "the greatest stupidity in Nature to lay any weight upon anything tho' the most valuable in this World," when "Eternity represented itself with all its incomprehensible Additions . . ." (pp. 286, 287).

Moll's penitence at Newgate precisely anticipates the "sincere Penitence" to which, she tells us, she and Jemy devote their old age. In fact she might use, with perfect appropriateness, exactly the words about her situation in her declining years that she has used to describe her Newgate change of heart: "I now began to look back upon my past Life with abhorrence, and having a kind of view into the other side of time, the things of life, as I believe they do with every Body at such a time, began to look with a different Aspect, and quite another Shape, than they did before" (p. 287). Defoe tells us in his preface that Moll "liv'd, it seems, to be very old; but was not so extraordinary a Penitent as she was at first; it seems only that indeed she always spoke with abhorrence of her former Life, and of every Part of it" (p. 5). The statement aptly summarizes the irony of Moll's existence: complacency, yes—but caution as well. She follows to the end the advice that, she has told us, her first lover gave her long before: "do not stand in the way of your own Safety and Prosperity" (p. 55).

5

A Journal of the Plague Year
"Great were the Confusions"

While Defoe chooses in all his fictions to concentrate on characters who find themselves *in extremis,* nowhere does he present the human preoccupation with sheer survival in quite so stark a form as in his *A Journal of the Plague Year.*[1] Just as cancer and death have become synonymous in our time, so plague and death were synonymous in Defoe's. As the narrator "H. F." tells us, in rounding out his tale, "it is not an ordinary Strength that cou'd support it; it was not like appearing in the Head of an Army, or charging a Body of Horse in the Field; but it was charging Death it self on his pale Horse. . . ."[2] It is an "Enemy" before which the populace feel themselves helpless. It moves inexorably from west to east like some destructive tidal wave.

When Albert Camus, some two-and-a-half centuries later, writes his story of a city under siege from an enemy within, he too chooses a first-person narrator to tell it—a man who participates in the ordeal and survives it. And he too keeps his narrator anonymous until the last chapter in the interest of objectivity. Even so, the two books are essentially dissimilar. Camus is concerned with the subjective states of his main characters—with their awakening to an awareness of injustice and radical limitation, with the ways in which they meet death, and with their compassionate reaching out beyond themselves.

Defoe's main character, by contrast, has very little in the way of an inner life, and it is his role to demonstrate not man's capacity to face death well but his struggle to avoid it. What is central are H. F.'s self-interested efforts to deal with chaos.[3] As J. H. Plumb says, we encounter in the world Defoe depicts "little affection and less love."[4] "The distress of the people," the narrator acknowledges, has "deserved the greatest Commiseration. But alas! this was a Time when every one's private Safety lay so near them, that they had no Room to pity the distresses of others; for every one had Death, as it were, at his Door, and many even in their Families. . . . This, I say, took

101

away all Compassion; self Preservation indeed appear'd here to be the first Law" (p. 115).[5]

Actually, for Defoe such a description does not apply only to a world in crisis. For him, as for Camus, man always lives under plague conditions; and in the *Journal* Defoe gives us again a narrator who is what he saw all men as being: a solitary soul—a lonely individual in a hostile world in which he inevitably finds himself the prey.

As with Camus's citizens of Oran, Defoe's Londoners can momentarily allay their "terrible Apprehensions" with hope (p. 4). (For a while, H. F. says, "we began to hope, that . . . it might go no farther; and . . . People began to be easy.") But, he goes on to say, it was not long before "all our Extenuations abated, and it was no more to be concealed, nay it quickly appeared that the Infection had spread itself beyond all Hopes of Abatement . . ." (p. 5).

Ostensibly, Defoe meant the *Journal* to constitute a warning—a piece of cautionary advice to the Londoners of another generation again threatened with plague. H. F. writes, recalling the time at which he had to decide whether or not to leave London: "I have set this particular down so fully, because I know not but it may be of Moment to those who come after me, if they come to be brought to the same Distress, and to the same Manner of making their Choice and therefore I desire this Account may pass with them, rather for a Direction to themselves to act by, than a History of my actings, seeing it may not be of one Farthing value to them to note what became of me" (p. 8). In short, as in *Moll Flanders,* both Defoe and his narrator offer the account of an experience, confident of its usefulness. We are given to understand that if we take to heart the lessons it teaches, we will be better equipped to win out in our own struggle for survival.

There are two assumptions implicit in H. F.'s statement: first, that we care about the history of others only to the extent that we can glean from it some guidance for our own "actings"; and second, that we *can* win out if only we will act sensibly and do the right thing. The first assumption is perhaps a valid one in Defoe's view, since it takes self-interest for granted as a basic human characteristic. But at once Defoe's familiar, though possibly unconscious, undercutting of the second begins. For just what is "this particular" that H. F. is about to "set . . . down so fully" as "a Direction" that his readers may later "act by"? (p. 8). H. F. is trying to decide at this point whether to run away from the threat of death or to stand and defy it. But what model does he really offer us that we may usefully follow? What lesson do we learn? What rational decision does he come to that we can emulate?

We are witness, for the space of several pages, to his mental efforts to deal with the pros and cons—to make a sensible decision on the basis of the evidence at hand. Common sense tells H. F. that he had better stay in London to look after his means of livelihood—his "Business and Shop . . .

in which was embark'd," as he says, "all my Effects in the World"—since to leave them behind "without any Overseer or Person fit to be trusted with them, had been to hazard the Loss not only of my Trade, but of my Goods, and indeed of all I had in the World." He can, he decides, "*trust God with my Safety and Health*" (pp. 8, 9). However, his elder brother, operating here as a kind of superior voice of reason, an opposing inner voice, insists that "the best Preparation for the Plague was to run away from it," and he goes on to argue: "Is it not as reasonable that you should trust God with the Chance or Risque of losing your Trade, as that you should stay in so imminent a Point of Danger, and trust him with your Life?" (p. 9). For the moment, these latter arguments carry the day, but then fresh "evidences" on the other side present themselves. Accidents keep occurring to prevent or delay H. F.'s departure—"these Disappointments being," he is convinced, "from Heaven" (p. 10).

At this juncture H. F. pauses in his narration to tell us again the lesson we are to learn from all this:

> I mention this Story also as the best Method I can advise any Person to take in such a Case, especially, if he be one that makes Conscience his Duty, and would be directed what to do in it, namely, that he should keep his Eye upon the particular Providences which occur at that Time, and look upon them complexly, as they regard one another, and as all together regard the Question before him, and then I think, he may safely take them for Intimations from Heaven of what is his unquestion'd Duty to do in such a Case; I mean as to going away from, or staying in the Place where we dwell, when visited with an infectious Distemper. (P. 10)[6]

Now he is determined to stay, he says, and "take my Lot in that Station in which God had placed me"; there having come "very warmly into my Mind, one Morning . . . that as nothing attended us without the Direction or Permission of Divine Power, so these Disappointments must have something in them extraordinary . . ." (pp. 10–11). But his brother scoffs at what he feels amounts to little more than a superstitious or pagan reading of portents, and H. F. finds himself once again "not knowing what to do" (p. 12). Still, he tells us of "the strong Impressions which I had on my Mind for staying," of "the Intimations which I thought I had from Heaven," and says that his "Mind seemed more and more encouraged to stay than ever" (p. 12). The clincher comes when, as he is leafing through the Bible, he finds his eye drawn to some verses in the 91st Psalm. It now becomes clear to H. F. that it is probably safe for him to stay in London, which is what he has really wanted to do all along. (He has acknowledged what he terms "a secret Satisfaction, that I should be kept" [p. 12].) And he is "confirmed in" his decision first by the illness of the woman in whose keeping he has planned to leave his house and then by his own illness. These occurrences, he says, "put off all my Thoughts of going into the Country" (p. 14).

Obviously, it is difficult to regard this "Resolution" finally taken by H. F. as one that it would be in our best interests or even possible to emulate. He reads the evidence as his instincts dictate, and far from exerting his own rationally directed powers over the circumstances in which he finds himself, he is moved by his own fears and finally sees himself as a child looked after by a protective father: "I resolv'd that I would stay in the Town, and casting my self entirely upon the Goodness and Protection of the Almighty, would not seek any other Shelter whatever; and that, as my Times were in his Hands, he was as able to keep me in a Time of the Infection as in a Time of Health . . ." (p. 13). What it comes down to, it seems, is that for H. F. it is more frightening to leave London than to stay. We have here what Erich Fromm describes as "the fear of emerging out of the family and into the world on one's own responsibility and powers."[7] For H. F., London is home and hence refuge.

As Robinson Crusoe discovers, however, the refuges that we find ourselves inhabiting or that we fashion for ourselves have a way of turning into places of entrapment; and it is not long before we hear H. F.—his head ringing with the "incessant Roarings," the "loud and lamentable Cries" of the dying—deploring his decision: "I cannot say, but that now I began to faint in my Resolutions; my Heart fail'd me very much, and sorely I repented of . . . my Rashness in venturing to abide in Town: I wished often, that I had not taken upon me to stay, but had gone away with my Brother and his Family" (p. 76).

It is little wonder that, "terrified by those frightful Objects," H. F. would withdraw into himself—"would retire Home sometimes, and resolve to go out no more"—nor is it surprising that he would spend his time "in the most serious Thankfulness for my Preservation and the Preservation of my Family, and the constant Confession of my Sins, giving myself up to God every Day, and applying to him with Fasting, Humiliation, and Meditation . . ." (p. 76). He can hardly fail to remember at this time those words of the 91st Psalm: *"Because thou hast made the Lord which is my refuge, even the most High, thy habitation: there shall no evil befal thee, neither shall any plague come nigh thy dwelling."*

H. F. needs to feel that he is special and hence merits special protection. But plainly, it is not out of feelings of power but out of those of impotence that he turns to God. It is important for him to distinguish himself from the wicked and to reassure himself that it is the wicked who die. In his own mind, his being among the protected of God makes him a part of a favored group. And he then comes to feel powerful by experiencing a kind of reflected glory.

We see this process occurring as frequently in H. F.'s account of his experiences as in Robinson Crusoe's. Consider, for example, his description of the scene in which he encounters the "dreadful Set of Fellows" whose "Mocks and Jeers," "profane and even blasphemous Expressions," "hellish, abominable Raillery," "devilish Language" fill him "with Horror, and a kind of Rage" (pp. 64–66). Defoe presents us in this scene with wickedness incarnate:

> These Men were guilty of many extravagances such as one would think, Human Nature should have trembled at the Thoughts of, at such a Time of general Terror, as was then upon us; and particularly scoffing and mocking at every thing which they happened to see, that was religious among the People, especially at their thronging zealously to the Place of publick Worship, to implore Mercy from Heaven in such a Time of Distress; and this Tavern, where they held their Club, being within View of the Church Door, they had the more particular Occasion for their Atheistical profane Mirth. (P. 67)

We have here an emblematic scene in which man's lower nature, associated with the tavern and thus with drunkenness and self-indulgence, insists on making itself heard and seeks to drag his rational, "controlling" nature downward. H. F. depicts himself as speaking to the blaspheming men with quiet self-control—with godlike detachment ("I gently reproved them"; "I took upon me to reprove them . . . with all the Calmness, Temper, and Good-Manners that I could" [pp. 65, 68]) and tells us that he was "grieved . . . rather than angered" and that he "went away, blessing God . . . that I had not spar'd them, tho' they had insulted me so much" (p. 66). And it was not long, H. F. reports, before "one of them . . . was struck from Heaven with the Plague, and died in a most deplorable Manner; and in a Word, they were every one of them carried into the great Pit" (pp. 66, 67). H. F.'s stance *vis-à-vis* the blasphemers is a victory of reason over passion, of order over chaos, of God over the devil. It is to be expected, therefore, that H. F. sees in the occasion and, by extension, in the entire visitation of the plague upon London, not meaninglessness but "Divine Vengeance" (p. 68). He becomes suddenly aware at this point, however, that while God's anger may be reasonable and just, his own may have been inspired by "private Passions and Resentment." "I had indeed," he concedes, "been in some Passion, at first, with them. . . ." And his fear of this, which brings him a sleepless night, is relieved only when he resumes the posture of prayer, "giving God most humble Thanks for my Preservation in the eminent Danger I had been in . . ." (p. 69).

But whatever his second thoughts about his own humble position, H. F. is, a good deal of the time, like Crusoe in bestowing largess on beings who stand reassuringly below him. If he tells us of his own thankfulness to God as his comforter and benefactor, he also tells us, at some length, of a waterman's thankfulness to him at the time when, as he says, "I could not . . . refrain my Charity for his Assistance" (p. 109). In such scenes as this one, he sees himself, apparently, as God's representative, and he even speaks in biblical language:

> *here*, says I, *go and call thy* Rachel *once more, and give her a little more Comfort from me. God will never forsake a Family that trust in him as thou dost;* so I gave him four other Shillings, and bad him go lay them on the Stone and call his Wife.
>   I have not Words to express the poor Man's thankfulness, neither could he express it himself; but by Tears running down his Face; he called his Wife, and told her God had mov'd the Heart of a Stranger, upon hearing their Condition, to give them all that Money; and a great deal more such as that, he said to her. The Woman too, made Signs of the like Thankfulness, as well to Heaven as to me, and joyfully pick'd it up; and I parted with no Money all that Year that I thought better bestowed. (Pp. 109–10)

Elsewhere in the *Journal*, the rich—among whom H. F. clearly counts himself—appear often in the role of saviors of the poor. It was, he tells us, thanks to "the Charity of the rich" that "a prodigious Number of People, who must otherwise inevitably have perished for want as well as Sickness, were supported and subsisted"; it was the God-inspired generosity of the rich that was instrumental "in preserving the Lives and recovering the Health of so many thousands, and keeping so many Thousands of Families from perishing and starving" (pp. 212, 213). Money is power, and here it gives to the rich power over life and death.

Moreover, because in a quite literal sense money can insure against death by starvation and by exposure, to possess it is to possess the means of one's own salvation. And we are repeatedly informed in the *Journal* that the rich had a far better chance of surviving the plague than did the poor. There is one clear instance of money's power relating to H. F. himself. Assigned to be an examiner in his precinct—that is, one of those who inspect infected people inside the closed-up houses—he is concerned that such a duty will "expose [him] to . . . Disaster," and is "greatly afflicted," trying every way he can think of to be let off (p. 159). As it turns out, he does have to serve two months of a four-month term in this "dangerous Office," but then he is able "for a little Money" to get someone else to take over the job (p. 169).

The poor have no such option. Indeed, they have an inferior chance of life from birth onward. (H. F. says that at the height of the plague, a poor woman about to give birth was unable to pay "the immoderate Price" required to get a competent midwife or sometimes any midwife at all.) It is the poor who, out of their need for a means of subsistence, are driven to take positions as guardians of plague-stricken houses and as drivers of the death-carts. And it is they who, when stricken, are unable to buy the assistance they need—"who being infected, had neither Food nor Physick;

neither Physician or Appothecary to assist them, or Nurse to attend them" and many of whom "died calling for help, and even for Sustenance . . ." (p. 85). Furthermore, many—as we are later told—"were the miserable Objects of Despair. . . . these might be said to perish, not by the Infection itself, but by the Consequence of it; indeed, namely, by Hunger and Distress, and the Want of all Things; being without Lodging, without Money, without Friends, without Means to get their Bread, or without any one to give it them . . ." (p. 96). These are the people who "ran about the Streets with the Distemper upon them without any control" and who threatened to "come out by force . . . to Plunder and Rob" (p. 155).

H. F.'s response to such people is especially revealing. When he moves beyond objective reporting of their situation, he expresses compassion less often than either fear or contempt.[8] We are reminded forcibly of Moll's reaction to the rabble of Newgate and the below-hatches mob on the transport ship—people whom, thanks to her having money in her purse, she can rise above. As with Moll, what frightens H. F., and wealthier Londoners in general, is the prospect of being dragged down to the brute level at which the "Mob" of the poor exist—the level at which death by starvation is as much a possibility as death by plague. No wonder that H. F. speaks of the "Apprehensions" felt by the Lord Mayor and Sheriffs, "that Desperation should push the People upon Tumults, and cause them to rifle the Houses of rich Men and plunder the Markets of Provisions; in which Case the Country People, who brought provisions very freely and boldly to Town, would ha' been terrified from coming any more, and the Town would ha' sunk under an unavoidable Famine" (pp. 96, 97). He repeats much the same point later when he observes that "the Lord Mayor and Justices did much to prevent the Rage and Desperation of the People from breaking out in Rabbles and Tumults, and in short, from the Poor plundering the Rich" (p. 129).

What becomes abundantly plain here is that the charity of the rich is by no means disinterested benevolence. It is a precautionary measure. In fact H. F. puts us on notice quite early in his narrative that he has good reason for dwelling at length on "the Case of the Poor at that Time, and what was apprehended from them"; it is a warning "from whence may be judg'd hereafter, what may be expected, if the like Distress should come upon the City" (p. 94). The rich, he implies, are using their heads when they use their money as, in effect, a bribe. Thus he points out that "the Prudence of my Lord Mayor and the Court of Aldermen within the City, and of the Justices of the Peace in the Out-parts, was such, and they were supported with Money from all Parts so well, that the poor People were kept quiet, and their Wants everywhere reliev'd, as far as was possible to be done" (p. 97). And it is a bribing of God as well as man, for, says H. F., in telling us of the "pious Ladies . . . distributing Alms to the Poor," "doubtless . . . *they that give to the poor lend to the Lord, and he will repay them* . . ." (p. 211).

There is an implicit parallel being drawn between the social world, in which law and order are threatened by lawlessness and confusion, and the little world of man, in which the passions threaten the reason—the danger in both cases being self-destruction. (We cannot but be reminded of Hobbes's calling a commonwealth an "Artificiall Man."[9]) Just as the individual is made vulnerable when his passions take over from his reason, so London is made vulnerable when its poor rebel against good government. The parallel seems inescapable when we note that the poor, as characterized by H. F., are less successful at surviving because they are, not to put too fine a point on it, the less intelligent part of the population. "It must be acknowledged," writes the saddler toward the end of the *Journal,* "that when People began to use these Cautions, they were less exposed to Danger. . . . But," he continues, "it was impossible to beat anything into the Heads of the Poor, they went on with the usual Impetuosity of their Tempers full of Outcries and Lamentations when taken, but madly careless of themselves, Fool-hardy and obstinate, while they were well. . . . This adventurous Conduct of the Poor was that which brought the Plague among them in a most furious manner, and this join'd to the Distress of their Circumstances, when taken, was the reason why they died so by Heaps; for I cannot say, I could observe one jot of better Husbandry among them, I mean the labouring Poor, while they were well and getting Money than there was before, but as lavish, as extravagant, and as thoughtless for tomorrow as ever . . ." (p. 210). In Hobbesian terms they represent "the most part of men"—those who make little or no use of reason in the day-to-day governing of their lives.[10]

H F.'s use of the phrase *thoughtless for to-morrow* makes it amply clear that in his view, as in Robinson Crusoe's and Moll Flanders's, the people who survive are the people who use the intelligence they were born with. It becomes more and more evident, the farther we read in the *Journal,* that its central focus is upon the mind's capacity for mastering experience, for exerting control over a recalcitrant world. And the problem with the poor is that they respond to the threat of death mindlessly. "It must be confest," says H. F., "that tho' the Plague was chiefly among the Poor; yet were the Poor the most Venturous and Fearless of it, and went about their Employment with a Sort of brutal Courage; I must call it so, for it was founded neither on Religion or Prudence; scarce did they use any Caution, but run into any Business, which they could get Employment in, tho' it was the most hazardous" (pp. 89, 90). *Caution* is H. F.'s favorite word.

There are, however, some people who just won't learn—a fact that H. F. takes note of again toward the end of the *Journal:* "I wish I cou'd say," he complains, "that as the City had a new Face, so the Manners of the People had a new Appearance: I doubt not but there were many that retain'd a sincere Sense of their Deliverance, and that were heartily thankful to that sovereign Hand, that had protected them in so dangerous a Time . . . but

. . . it must be acknowledg'd that the general Practice of the People was just as it was before. . . ." Indeed, some observers had even argued, although H. F. himself "will not carry it so far," that "the people, harden'd by the Danger they had been in, like Sea-men after a Storm is over, were more wicked and more stupid, more bold and hardened, in their Vices and Immoralities than they were before . . ." (p. 229). H. F. would advise anyone who knows what is good for him to show God the proper gratitude and thankfulness, and he is appalled by "the Unthankfulness and Return of all manner of Wickedness among us" (p. 248). He himself repeatedly expresses thankfulness for his own preservation, thereby setting a good example to the wise.

The cautionary advice here—and the morality as well— is virtually identical with that encountered in *Moll Flanders*—and so is what H. F. has to say about repentance. He hopes, he says, to "alarm the very Soul of the Reader" by the "moving Accents" he has used in relating "how many Warnings were . . . given by dying Penitents, to others not to put off and delay their Repentance to the Day of Distress . . ." (p. 104). The irony we keep seeing here is clear and is one we are coming to recognize as typical of Defoe. Again and again H. F. comments on the incautiousness, the thoughtlessness, the stupidity of the poor and asks us to admire his own enlightenment. There may be some people incapable of learning from experience, some people unable or unwilling to look after themselves in times of crisis, but he does not number himself among them. Yet the very cautions he gives regarding matters of thankfulness and repentance involve, ultimately, an acknowledgment of his own inadequacy. It is not simply the irony of a man's taking pride in his own humility—although that may be a related aspect. It is the irony of a man's having written an entire journal exhorting his readers to "be prepared" to combat—to "provide" themselves against—something that they are, in fact, powerless to avoid. There seems little or no evidence in the *Journal* of any concern on H. F.'s part with a life after death. Like others of Defoe's characters, he seeks "to be spared" his own mortality. Hence it is not really true for him that it is never too late to repent. For those who have waited until their distress is upon them, the implication is that it *is* too late. Only those intelligent enough to learn from the horrible example of the dying to repent earlier and thereby to earn the favor of God can hope to benefit. That, it would seem, stands to reason.

We see a related contradiction operating in those passages where H. F., with something not far from smugness, ridicules the superstitions of the unenlightened and counters them with his own rationality. He does concede, in relating the response of "old Women, and the Phlegmatic Hypochondriac part of the other Sex" to the comets that preceded first the plague and then the fire of London, that he himself "was apt to look upon them, as the Forerunners and Warnings of Gods Judgments; and . . . could not but say, God had not yet sufficiently scourg'd the City." But he at once goes on to qualify this: "I cou'd not at the same Time carry these Things to the height that others did, knowing too, that natural Causes are assigned by the Astronomers for such Things . . ." (p. 20).

Eventually H. F. has a good deal to say about natural causes. He has already roundly condemned people who regard the plague as "an immediate Stroke from Heaven . . . which I look upon with Contempt, as the Effect of manifest Ignorance . . ." (p. 75). And now he deplores the conduct of those misguided people who, having adopted "a kind of a Turkish Predestinarianism," have thrown caution to the winds; and he goes on to argue his point at some length. We are witness to H. F.'s familiar effort to explain experience rationally. It is just as Hobbes says: "Anxiety for the future time disposeth men to enquire into the causes of things; because the knowledge of them, maketh men the better able to order the present to their best advantage."[11] And however questionable H. F.'s reasoning, he does have a perfectly rational end in view. All the evidence before him makes him doubt the efficacy of putting oneself completely in the hands of God and trusting in His mercy. If the plague is attributable to natural causes, then one can take commonsense measures to avoid it. The only trouble with this eminently reasonable argument is that H. F. has introduced the entire passage with the statement: "It is impossible in a Visitation to prevent the spreading of the Plague by the utmost human Vigilance . . ." (p. 191).

What is to be done? How can human beings deal with their fears under plague conditions? Following his discussion of the comets, H. F. has carried on for several pages on the subject of the superstitious poor, often making fun of their credulity. He sounds, in fact, very much as Robinson Crusoe sounds in explaining to the benighted Friday the inferiority of the pagan god he worships. The "common People," according to H. F., have moved from being "brutishly wicked and thoughtless" to being "ignorant and stupid in their reflections" (p. 29). In their efforts to explain and on that basis to cope with the infection, they are led by their "Terrors and Apprehensions . . . into a Thousand weak, foolish, and wicked Things" (p. 26). In following "Oracles of the Devil" ("blind, absurd, and ridiculous Stuff"), they fall victim to "a horrid Delusion"; they turn to the "wicked Practices" of wizards, which "the most sober and judicious People despis'd and abhor'd . . ." (pp. 27, 28). In short, the ignorant poor, in thinking to calm their own fears and to bring the madness of the plague under control, are actually making things worse. They are "kept in a Fright" (p. 27); they are "led by their Fright to extreams of Folly" (p. 29); the "Conjurers and Witches" to whom they run have "fed their Fears, and kept them always alarm'd. . . ." And they are equally "as mad, upon their running after Quacks, and Mountebanks" and thereby have "even poison'd themselves before-hand, for fear of the Poison of the Infection . . ." (p. 30). And H. F. goes on to tell of "still another Madness. . . . which may serve to give an Idea of the distracted humour of the poor People," namely, that of "wearing Charms, Philtres, Exorcisms, Amulets, and I know not what Preparations, to fortify the Body with them against the Plague . . ." (p. 32).

H. F. contrasts his own "*steady Eyes*" with the "*Hypochondriac Fancy's*" of the poor and reflects "how the poor People were terrified by the Force of their own Imagination" (pp. 22, 23). And similarly he contrasts the "foolish Humour of the People" with the "sober and religious" behavior of the Lord Mayor in appointing "Physicians and Surgeons for Relief of the poor . . ." (p. 35). Yet if the poor soon discover the futility of their efforts, the "sober and religious" fare no better. The madness is, H. F. has to admit, not to be contained: "the Violence of the Distemper, when it came to its Extremity, was like the Fire the next Year; the Fire which consumed what the Plague could not touch, defy'd all the Application of Remedies; the Fire Engines were broken, the Buckets thrown away, and the Power of Man was baffled and brought to an End so the Plague defied all Medicine. . . ." And he goes on: "we were not to expect, that the Physicians could stop God's Judgments, or prevent a Distemper eminently armed from Heaven, from executing the Errand it was sent about" (pp. 35, 36).

H. F. has the same problem with God that Moll Flanders has with the authority figures in her life. He looks to Him as a giver of life—as a provider and protector—and yet does not and cannot trust Him not to rob him of that very life He has promised to cherish. But the God we encounter in the *Journal* is of violent rather than pacific tendencies, and H. F. repeatedly justifies the plague—a God-sent phenomenon described not only as "a Distemper eminently armed from Heaven" but as "a Formidable Enemy . . . arm'd with Terrors" (p. 235)—as a punishment for man's sins and a call to repentance.[12] Moreover, the *Journal* itself is a kind of sermon, calling man to repentance "by Terror and Amazement" (p. 25). Thus, struggle though he may to make sense of things, H. F. only manages to embroil himself in confusions and contradictions;[13] and his rational mind is, finally, no more successful at controlling his fears than are the physicians at controlling the plague.

He does keep trying, though, and because he clearly does not think it works to put oneself completely in God's hands, a good deal of his cautionary advice involves a do-it-yourself program—the *Journal* being a "how-to" book where the project is one's own survival. If Providence cannot be counted on to provide protection, then you had best provide for yourself, and in that area H. F. suggests that future generations of men can profit from his mistakes. (And Defoe, in writing the *Journal,* implicitly suggests that the London of 1721 can profit from the mistakes made by its government in 1665.) H. F. deplores, for example, the failure of most people to heed timely warnings of the plague and to supply themselves with enough provisions so that they need not leave their houses. Those who did so, he reports, "were in a great Measure preserv'd by that Caution" (p. 75). He himself, he admits, "was one of those thoughtless Ones"—although he did, he says, become "wise" in the nick of time.

And, says H. F., the public negligence has been equally reprehensible—to the extent that "the whole Body of the People" is, "at the first coming of this Calamity," left in an "unprovided Condition" (p. 122). H. F.'s constant preoccupation with "the whole Body of the People," and especially with London's poor, may at first seem to be evidence of a selflessness not to be expected of a typical Defoe protagonist. It has been argued that we hear from H. F. far less about his personal struggle for survival than we do about the struggle of the London populace. In fact, Novak maintains that the *Journal* is "a novel with a collective hero—the London poor."[14] Actually, however, it is understandable that H. F. will be as much concerned with the survival of London itself as with his own personal survival once we recognize that the first is an aspect of the second.[15]

Perhaps H. F.'s worries about communal survival go some way toward explaining why the lengthiest installment having to do with advice on "how to survive" is the story not of one man but of three and has an applicability not only on the individual level but on the communal one as well. It is a story that, says H. F., "will be a very good Pattern for any poor Man to follow" and one that, whether or not another plague strikes, "may have its Uses so many Ways that it will . . . never be said, that the relating has been unprofitable" (p. 58). It "has a Moral in every Part of it"; and H. F. says of the three men, "their whole Conduct, and that of some who they join'd with, is a Pattern for all poor Men to follow . . ." (p. 122).[16] The men constitute the beginnings of a community: they are John, once a soldier and now a biscuit-maker; Thomas, a lame sailor who is now a sailmaker; and Richard, a carpenter; and their experiences are essentially those of Robinson Crusoe and Moll Flanders rolled into one.

The man named John might be expressing Moll's feelings about Newgate or Crusoe's about his earthquake-threatened shelter when he says of London, *"If I am once out of this dreadful Place I care not where I go."* Tom, meanwhile, is facing the terror of being "turn'd out of [his] lodging"—a terror familiar to Moll. London for both men has become a thoroughly inhospitable place, for as John remarks, *"People are so afraid of one another now, there's no getting a Lodging any where."* They face a dilemma that Crusoe knew well: "if we stay here we are sure to die, and *if we go away* we can but die." The question is "where to go." "Any where to save our Lives," says John (pp. 125–27).

The prospect that has frightened them most is that of starvation, but John has insisted that *"for any Town upon the Road to . . . deny me Provisions for my Money, is to say the Town has a Right to starve me to Death, which cannot be true*" (p. 123). Soon, however, the situation in London becomes desperate: there is no work to be had and by staying they risk starving to death. As John later says, "the dreadful Plague . . . devours thousands every Week" (p. 138). Resolving, therefore, to be "as good Husbands as they could," they provide themselves for their journey, first putting all their money "into one publick Stock." And, as practical-minded as Crusoe, they make sure that their provisions include "a small Bag of Tools, such as might be useful . . . for their Subsistence" and a gun—"for the Soldier would not go without Arms" (pp. 125–27).

Once on the road, they contrive to live by their wits. Because they know that people in the countryside are terrified of all Londoners as possible plague-carriers, "it came into their Heads to say . . . they came out of Essex"—a "little Fraud" that serves them well (p. 129). And later, when the people of Walthamstow, who have "good Reason" to be "very cautious," refuse to allow them even to pass through town and are "not to be per-swaded by Reason," John devises a ruse that is fully worthy of the ingenious Crusoe. The three men have, by this time, joined forces with another group of "poor distress'd People . . . seeking Shelter and Safety" (p. 131), and John arranges things in such a way that the townspeople are deceived into thinking that the little group of refugees is a numerous and well-armed company. Feeling "Alarm'd and terribly Frighted," the country people are intimidated not only into allowing the group free passage through their town but into selling them food. It is notable that the group succeeds by recognizing the fears of their real or potential opponents and knowing how to play on them.

The group now becomes a little community in its own right, with John, by virtue of his superior ingenuity and his superior powers of insuring survival, their "captain" ("they now willingly made him their Leader" and "all referred themselves to his Direction" [p. 140]). For a time the little band settles in Epping forest, where they manage to make themselves "com-pletely close and warm" (p. 140); but again their presence arouses the fears of the nearby community, and again John's ingenuity is called for. This time he succeeds by arguing "very calmly with them" (p. 142)—"talking . . . rationally and smoothly to them" (p. 144)—but it is instructive to note the nature of his argument:

[He] told them, "That *London* was the Place by which they, that is, the Townsmen of *Epping* and all the Country round them, subsisted; to whom they sold the produce of their Lands, and out of whom they made their Rent of their Farms; and to be so cruel to the Inhabitants of *London*, or to any of those by whom they gain'd so much was very hard, and they would be loth to have it remembered hereafter, and have it told how barbarous, how inhospitable and how unkind they were to the People of *London*, when they fled from the Face of the most terrible Enemy in the

World; that it would be enough to make the Name of an *Epping*-Man hateful thro' all the City, and to have the Rabble Stone them in the very Streets, whenever they came so much as to Market; that they were not yet secure from being Visited themselves, and that as he heard, *Waltham* was already; that they would think it very hard that when any of them fled for Fear before they were touch'd, they should be deny'd the Liberty of lying so much as in the open Fields." (P. 142)

But, John continues, " 'if you will shut up all Bowels of Compassion and not relieve us at all, we shall not extort anything by Violence, or steal from any one; but when what little we have is spent, if we perish for want, God's Will be done' " (pp. 143, 144). In this way, John, with brilliant insight into elemental human psychology, uses both of the methods that have already worked so well for his little group. Out of one side of his mouth he intimidates his opponents by arousing their fears for their own survival, and out of the other he allays the fears that he knows they are already experiencing.

From this point on, the group's alternating feelings of security and insecurity, of self-sufficiency and dependency occur in a manner that parallels the experiences of both Crusoe and Moll Flanders. They manage, now and again, to achieve some protection and comfort as the result of their own technical ingenuity. (H. F. refers to "the ingenious Carpenter," "the ingenious Joyner" [pp. 147, 149]). But they have not been long at Epping before he is speaking of them as "these new Inmates" and is telling us that the infection has spread through the countryside to such an extent that "they began to be afraid to trust one another so much as to go abroad for such things as they wanted. . . ." In short, their plight has become exactly what it was in London, and they find themselves "obliged to quit the Place" out of "Necessity, and the hazard of Life." And their leader, being, as it were, at his wit's end, must himself turn to a kind of father-figure—to "that gentleman who was their principal Benefactor, with the Distress they were in . . . to crave his Assistance and Advice" (pp. 146, 147). Following the familiar Defoe pattern, feelings of power have evaporated, and the refugees have once more become "terrified" outcasts adrift in a predatory world. They must struggle for their existence among people even more desperate than themselves, wandering hordes who rob and plunder.

At last, like Moll and Crusoe, the three men go "home to the City again" (p. 150), but it is not a city in which anyone can subsist for long without taking precautions, for in one sense or another people will always find themselves in a struggle to survive under plague conditions.

The fact is that what has happened to the people of Wapping in 1665 can happen to anyone. They are the ones who, H. F. tells us, in their "Sleepiness and Security" not only did "not shift for themselves as others did" but "boasted of being safe" (p. 121). And as both Defoe and his narrator know, that way lies disaster. In the *Journal*, the sick—the carriers of disease—bear a striking resemblance to the criminals of Moll Flanders's London, since both groups threaten to rob one of the means of subsistence: health in one case and money in the other. But neither group is easy to recognize, and hence one must be constantly on one's guard against them.

Just as criminals like Moll are hard to recognize when they appear in the guise of gentlewomen, so are carriers of plague when they are "seemingly sound." "People were only shye," H. F. says, "of those that were really sick, a man with a Cap upon his Head, or with Cloths round his Neck, *which was the Case of those that had Swellings there;* such was indeed frightful; but when we saw a Gentleman dress'd, with his Band on and his Gloves in his Hand, his Hat upon his Head, and his Hair comb'd, of such we had not the least Apprehensions . . ." (p. 209).

While H. F. maintains that people who took precautionary measures "were less exposed to Danger" (p. 210), he has to keep coming back to the inescapable conclusion that it "was impossible to know" who was infected and who was not. "And this is the Reason why it is impossible in a Visitation to prevent the spreading of the Plague by the utmost human Vigilance. . . ." H. F.'s capacity for self-contradiction is particularly in evidence on this topic. Perhaps all we can finally do, he thinks, is to put our trust in God—except that, unfortunately, as we have heard H. F. concede, that does not always work either.

Pragmatically speaking, what seems to work best is self-reliance, since to depend on someone else requires exposure. The people least likely to contract the plague, H. F. suggests, are those who are "jealous of every Body," and he tells us that "a vast Number of People lock'd themselves up, so as not to come abroad into any Company at all, nor suffer any that had been abroad in promiscuous Company, to come into their Houses, or near them. . . ." It is for this reason, of course, that one of H. F.'s main items of advice, which he repeats and repeats, has to do with making due provision. Had the rich "been wise enough to have done" what "they ought to have done"—namely, "laid up Stores of Provisions . . . they had perhaps escaped the Disease better" (p. 97).

But H. F. invalidates this particular bit of advice even as he is issuing it, since the point he is making is that the very failure of the rich to provide in advance for themselves has been one of the chief things that have "contributed to prevent the Mob doing any Mischief" (p. 97). Had the rich had any provisions worth stealing, the mob would have "broken in." And in such an eventuality, the rich stood to lose not only their livelihood at the hands of robbers, but their very lives, as the result of exposure to the infected poor. It becomes, that is to say, pretty clearly a case of their being damned if they did and damned if they didn't.

The people in plague-stricken London who find themselves "the safest" are those who have had "Recourse to Ships for their Retreat . . . early, and with Prudence, furnishing themselves so with Provisions, that they had no need to go on Shore for Supplies, or suffer Boats to come on Board to bring them" (p. 114). On land the counterparts of these people are the Dutch merchants H. F. describes who "kept their Houses like little Garrisons besieged, suffering none to go in or out, or come near them" (p. 55) Such people do manage to survive, but only by effectually sealing themselves off from life in a sort of self-imposed quarantine.

There is a good deal of confusion in H. F.'s thinking as to whether confinement to a house constitutes a locking in or a locking out. If a person shuts himself voluntarily into his house, as H. F. thinks any rational person would want to do in order to escape infection, then he feels himself to be turning the key against a potential invading enemy and his house becomes for him a fortress. But inside he may also encounter a kind of death, for if the Londoner is involuntarily locked in so that he will not infect the world outside, his house becomes, instead, a prison. The effect of being shut off from life is the same in either case. And thus, in the *Journal*, confinement to a house effectively represents the basic dilemma that any human being faces.

Moreover, the man whose confinement is self-imposed feels himself no less confined than the one whom society locks up.[17] He shuts himself away to achieve freedom from death and finds his existence circumscribed, limited, unexpandable—that is, lifeless. And here H. F.'s own experience is a case in point. Like Crusoe, H. F. is never content within the limited environment he has mastered. Limitation is unendurable. And in his case it is again a matter of spatial expansion symbolizing expansion of knowledge. At times, it is true, he ventures forth from his safe retreat simply "for the Refreshment of a little Air" (p. 111)—to escape suffocation—but more often he leaves the security of his house in order to bring, or attempt to bring, under his rational control the thing that threatens him. It is the "great pit" in Aldgate—that "dreadful Gulph"—that, he tells us, "I could not resist my Curiosity to go and see . . ." (p. 59). Nor is one view of it enough, for at a later date he returns to the same spot: "my Curiosity led, or rather drove me to go and see this Pit again . . . and I was not content to see it in the Day-time . . . but I resolv'd to go in the Night and see some of [the bodies] thrown in" (p. 60).

He seems incapable of heeding the caution voiced by the sexton in the churchyard—that "good religious and sensible Man" who has "earnestly perswaded [him] not to go in" (p. 61). H. F. argues with himself that the pit will be "an Instructing Sight, that might not be without its Uses," and although he does hesitate at this juncture, he at last goes in. "I could not longer resist my Desire of seeing it," he says (p. 61). And still later he remarks; "tho' I generally came frighted and terrified Home, yet I could ot restrain; only that indeed, I did not do it so frequently as at first" (p. 80). There is something within him that defies caution. He *will* eat of the ree of knowledge though the consequence be death.

H. F.'s journal is itself, of course, an attempt to impose a rational order on rrational events. Not only does he include Bills of Mortality and statistical harts at frequent intervals, but—scientifically minded man that he is—he loggedly insists, as we have seen, on assigning to natural causes those phenomena which the less enlightened take to be supernatural signs and portents. He speaks with some condescension of "the Dreams of old Women" and of people who see in the clouds "Shapes and Figures, Representations and Appearances, which had nothing in them, but Air and Vapour." "I must be allowed to say of both," he remarks, ". . . that they heard Voices that never spake, and saw Sights that never appear'd, but the imagination of the People was really turn'd wayward and possess'd" (p. 22). Not for H. F. the disordered mind, the vaporings of the imagination. Whenever he cannot himself attest to the truth of something as the result of having seen it with his own eyes, he is careful to say so and either to cite his authority or to append some qualification or disclaimer.

All of this constitutes a mechanism of self-protection. H. F. refuses to allow himself to be imposed on and is quick to mistrust anything but an unvarnished tale. Thus he brands as "all Knavery and Collusion" the report from St. Giles's parish of fourteen plague victims, knowing it to be a falsification (p. 6). And thus he greets with skepticism the story of the nurse who "laid a wet Cloth upon the Face of a dying Patient, who she tended, and so put an End to his Life. . . . And another that smother'd a young Woman she was looking to. . . ." There were, he says, "two Marks of Suspicion . . . which caused me always to slight them, and to look on them as meer Stories, that people continually frighted one another with" (p. 84). He then proceeds to supply an eminently rational explanation for his disbelief.

If we look more closely at these two instances of H. F.'s skepticism, however, what we see are two different kinds of self-protection operating. Ostensibly, H. F. remains firmly committed to telling the truth about things. It is his self-appointed role to make us face the facts as he can bear witness to their actuality, since not to do so is dangerous. We must not, like the citizens of Wapping and Redliff, indulge in wishful thinking. We must not be lured by the published figures from St. Giles's parish into believing things are better than they are. If we don't know the truth, H. F. implies, we will be powerless to protect ourselves against it. We must look behind the facade of seeming soundness and recognize the putrefaction underneath. We must be on our guard.

Yet when H. F. is himself confronted with such stories of cruelty and inhumanity as those involving the nurses who murdered their patients, he protects himself by refusing to believe them. He does not want, for exam-

ple, to believe that "there was a seeming propensity, or a wicked Inclinatio
in those that were Infected to infect others" (p. 153). Therefore, rathe
than joining in the debate as to why people would behave in such a way, h
says flatly, "*I do not grant the Fact*" (p. 154), and then he offers a plausibl
reason why people might have been prompted to make up such stories. H
cannot tolerate the thought of such motiveless malignity, and so he reject
it, while at the same time neatly contriving a rational explanation as to wh
stories of the kind should have come into being. He finds a way to cope witl
his own fears by eliminating their cause.

Usually, as here, he is able to come up with excellent reasons for nc
believing certain kinds of horror stories, and it can be argued that the
things he refuses to believe are always those contingencies which, if true
would terrify him unendurably. He cannot—to cite an example related t
the one above—endure to contemplate the possibility that, in a world gov
erned by a divine intelligence, the "hellish, abominable Raillery" of whicl
the "dreadful Set of Fellows" in the tavern are guilty will go unpunished
Thus he concludes, we may remember, that "it could not but seem rea
sonable to believe, that God would not think fit to spare by his Mercy sucl
open declared Enemies, that should insult his Name and Being. . . ." Nc
wonder—given the "horror" and the "rage" he feels at such hellish rebel
lion against a heavenly father—that it pleases him to think of their being
"struck from Heaven" when they are "carried into the great Pit."

Like Moll Flanders, moreover, H. F. needs desperately to believe that he
will be comforted and protected in his helplessness. Why else would he
dwell at such length on and reject with such vehemence those "frightfu
Stories told us of Nurses and Watchmen, who looked after the dying People, *that is to say,* hir'd Nurses, who attended infected People, using them
barbarously, starving them, smothering them, or by other wicked Means
hastening their End . . ." (pp. 82, 83). "I must say," he states, "I believe
nothing of its being so common a Crime, as some have since been pleas'd tc
say, nor did it seem to be so rational, where the People were brought so lov
as not to be able to help themselves. . . ." He can acknowledge the possibility
of nurses having robbed their charges, but "as for murthers, I do not find
that there was ever any Proof of the Facts in the manner, as it has been
reported . . ." (pp. 83, 84).

There are times, of course, when facts whose truth H. F. is reluctant to
admit simply cannot be denied. In such cases, he often supplies a kind of
counterevidence. If there *were* infected people who ran about infecting
others—and he maintains that the report of their desiring to do so "was
really false"—he asserts that he "could give several Relations of good,
pious, and religious People, who, when they have had the Distemper, have
been so far from being forward to infect others, that they have forbid their
own Family to come near them . . ." (p. 70). And later, when he talks of
children having left infected parents to their fate, and parents their chil-

dren, he is quick to add: "there were many Instances of immovable Affection, Pity, and Duty in many, and some that came to my Knowledge; that is to say, by here-say. For I shall not take upon me to vouch the Truth of the Particulars" (p. 115). Here he may be unable to "vouch the Truth" but he chooses to believe it nonetheless. He hangs on to the reassuring thought that if he should be stricken, he would not be left alone to perish. That latter possibility is one his fears just will not allow him to face. Hence his mind, operating self-interestedly, rejects it.

As usual, however, the effort to have things the way he wants them does not always succeed. For all his attempts to see a meaningful pattern in the plague-stricken world he lives in—to give an account of events and to account for them—he has to admit that in "those terrible Times . . . the Amazement of the people encreas'd; and a thousand unaccountable Things they would do in the violence of their Fright, as others did the same in the Agonies of their Distemper . . ." (p. 103). The governing forces of London are as unsuccessful at imposing order as is the governing, controlling mind of Defoe's narrator. H. F. contrasts the behavior of the infected in the country—where "they ran about the streets with the distemper upon them without any control"—with the situation in London, where "every thing was managed with so much Care, and such excellent Order . . . that *London* may be a Pattern to all the Cities in the World for the good Government and the excellent Order that was every where kept . . ." (p. 155). And he has earlier set forth at considerable length the "orders of my Lord Mayor's" whereby order is to be maintained in the city.

Similarly, H. F. himself gives us an orderly account of things, duly supplying us with charts and making sure that each detail is set forth "in its order." Yet toward the end of his account, he writes: "when the violent Rage of the Distemper in September came upon us, it drove us out of all Measures: Men did then no more die by Tale and by Number . . . 'tis certain they died by Heaps, and were buried by Heaps, that is to say without Account" (p. 237).[18]

The Lord Mayor and sheriffs cannot, in fact, contain the plague, any more than H. F. can contain his own fears. The plague is a kind of madness. (H. F. often calls it a distemper.) It does not make sense. The government of London has no success at all in dealing with the "terrified . . . People, who were, as I may say, all out of their Wits already" (p. 25). As H. F. is constantly telling us, terror drives people to break out of any containment imposed upon them. Not only do people repeatedly escape from closed-up houses, but they break out of their own rational controls. H. F. cites, for example, the case of the mother who discovers that her daughter has contracted the plague, telling the story as proof of the fact that to his knowledge there were many people, during the plague year, who "*may well be call'd,* frighted to Death." And he continues, "there were great Numbers frighted to other Extreams, some frighted out of their Senses, some out of

their Memory and some out of their Understanding . . ." (p. 57). It is not
only people "in the rage of the distemper" who are to be seen "running
out of their own government." H. F. describes "some dying of meer Grief,
as a Passion, some of meer Fright and Surprize, without any Infection at all;
others frighted into Idiotism, and foolish Distractions, some into despair
and Lunacy; others into mellancholy Madness" (p. 81). And the picture
H. F. draws of London when the plague is at its height certainly calls into
question even more forcibly his protestations of "the good Government
and excellent Order that was every where kept."

Finally, it is despite his own incautious behavior that H. F. himself has
succeeded in staying out of the "great Pit"—"the common Grave of Mankind, as we may call it, for here was no Difference made, but Poor and Rich
went together . . ." (p. 62). Just how has he managed it? His is, he tells us,
one of the "wonderful deliverances from infection"; "I esteem my own
Deliverance to be one next to miraculous, and do record it with Thankfulness" (p. 193). And later he indulges in a bit of double talk to much the
same effect: "In that very Moment, when we might very well say, 'Vain was
the Help of Man' . . . it pleased God, with a most agreeable Surprize, to
cause the Fury of it to abate, even of it self . . ." (p. 237). Of what "use,"
then, has been all of H. F.'s cautionary advice? The *Journal* becomes a
mockery of itself—a mockery compounded by the concluding verse:

> A *dreadful Plague in* London *was*
> *In the Year Sixty Five*
> *Which swept an Hundred Thousand Souls*
> *Away; yet I alive!*

Just who is that "I"? We know only that he is (was?) a saddler whose initials
are (were?) H. F. and who survived the plague of 1665, thanks to divine
protection. He has not, in fact, preserved himself. God has preserved
someone we know as H. F. And ironically, we know something else about
him—namely, that he has not, after all, managed to stay out of "the common Grave of Mankind" into which "Poor and Rich went together." For just
beneath the passage in which H. F. tells us of one of the burial grounds for
plague victims—"a piece of Ground in Moorfields" (p. 233)—we find a
curious little note: "*N.B.* The Author of this Journal, lyes buried in that very
ground. . . ."

6

Colonel Jack

"the grief of one absent Comfort"

n the extended title of *Colonel Jack* two things are especially notable. One is
he fact of the hero's having been *Born a Gentleman*. The second is his being
characterized as *Truly Honourable*. Both these details suggest at once that
Colonel Jack possesses precisely that sense of himself as belonging to a class
and a tradition that is missing, for the most part, in Captain Singleton.
Whereas the young Bob is of a "thoughtless, unconcern'd Temper" and
keeps no journal—thus being ill-equipped to supply a meaningful "Account" of his own life—the young Jack prides himself on his superior
mental capacities. He may remain illiterate for a number of years, but
nonetheless he says of himself: "I was always upon the Inquiry, asking
Questions of things done in Publick as well as in Private, particularly, I
loved to talk with Seamen and Soldiers about the War. . . . By this means, as
young as I was, I was a kind of an Historian, and tho' I had read no Books,
and never had any Books to read, yet I cou'd give a tollerable Account of
what had been done, and of what was then a doing in the World. . . ."[1] In
relating his own *History*, Colonel Jack reveals an awareness of having a place
in a larger history. And he takes his rightful place in that history when he at
last becomes in actuality what he has made himself long before, a "Colonel
of a Regiment." In short, Jack is special. And he displays from the beginning a definite sense of that specialness.[2]

Indeed, his story takes on at times a markedly fairy-tale quality—a quality that will become even more insistent in *Roxana*. In both of these late
novels, the very unreality of many episodes constitutes, one might say, a
further undercutting on Defoe's part of the success-story motif, for to
devise episodes that strain credulity in the midst of what purport to be true
stories is surely to invite a skeptical response.

In the case of *Colonel Jack*, the fantasy element is present right from the
start. Young Jack—given the option of defining himself however he likes
("I was left to call myself Mr. Any-thing, what I pleas'd")—insists by right of
his parentage ("my Mother was a Gentlewoman . . . my Father was a Man of

121

Quality"), on promoting himself to a position of high rank without delay
As Robinson Crusoe is to the Spaniards and to Friday and Captain Singleton to the Portuguese and the Black Prince, so eight-year-old Colonel
Jack makes sure he is to the Major and the Captain—mental acumen, along
with social status, being the chief basis of distinction.[3] At first the nurse in
charge of the three Jacks presumes "to distinguish her own Son a little
from the rest" by calling him "Captain, because forsooth he was the eldest."
But our Jack soon sets things right, and in his subsequent description of
Captain Jack, his lesser qualifications (even in physical stature he is "lower")
are made abundantly clear. He has the manners of a boor; he is "sly, sullen
. . . brutish, bloody, and cruel in his Disposition"; he is not very bright; and
above all, he has no "Sense of being Honest" (pp. 5, 6). It is clear, from such
a characterization, that Captain Jack anticipates those Negroes "of a sence-
less, stupid, sordid Disposition" that, as Colonel Jack later says to his master
in Virginia, "may be found here and there" in the human race (p. 145).

Major Jack—who has come to that "Preferment by the Merit of his
Birth," his father being "a Major of the Guards"—stands predictably
higher on the scale of humanity than does the lowly Captain. He is witty,
courageous, and gentlemanly. But he too wants honesty.

As for Colonel Jack, if he is, as he says, "a poor unhappy tractable Dog,"
he is so not from lack of parts but from lack of education. He was, he
maintains, "willing enough, and capable too, to learn anything, if he had
had any but the Devil for his School-Master." Plainly, his mental alertness
puts him head and shoulders above his "Brother *Jacks*." His superior reasoning powers are manifest. ("I . . . defended my self by Argument, proving the Mistakes of my Accusers, and how they contradicted themselves. . . .
I had a natural Talent of Talking" [p. 7].) Much of what he tells us of himself
suggests unmistakably his kinship with Captain Singleton's Friend William:
"I shun'd Fighting as much as I could," he recalls, "tho' sometimes, I
ventur'd too, and came off well, being very strong made and nimble withal.
However, I many times brought myself off with my Tongue, where my
Hands would not have been sufficient. . . ." Moreover, when he goes on to
say, "I was wary and Dextrous at my Trade, and was not so often catch'd as
my Fellow Rogues," we are reminded of something Captain Singleton says
about William: "he had the better of us in this Part, that, if we were taken,
we were sure to be hang'd and he was sure to escape . . ." (*CS*, p. 144).

Taken together, the three Jacks appear to represent at once the social
hierarchy and, as brothers often seem to do in Defoe, a kind of composite
of human possibilities. In either context, the lower level is dependent on
the higher for survival. Thus Colonel Jack informs us: "the Captain . . .
would have starv'd if we had not kept him with us" (p. 10). We cannot but
be put in mind here both of Moll Flanders's preference for the elder of the
two Colchester brothers and, in a different way, of H. F.'s characterization
of the London poor in plague time, into whose heads "it was impossible to

eat any thing." In fact, Colonel Jack says of the Captain at one point,
there was no beating anything into his Head by Words . . ." (p. 98).

It is not only intellectual superiority, however, that puts Colonel Jack at
the top of the hierarchy. He has also been "born to better Things" (p. 80) by
virtue of possessing "a strange kind of uninstructed Conscience" (p. 55). "I
ad something in me," he says, "by what secret Influence I knew not, kept
the from the . . . general Wickedness of the rest of my Companions . . ."
(p. 60). He has "something that is Good at the Bottom; he has a Principle of
Honesty at Bottom . . ." (p. 86).

It is this characteristic of Colonel Jack's that has led some recent readers
to regard him as significantly different from Defoe's earlier protagonists—
and especially from Moll Flanders, with whom he is often compared.
Samuel Holt Monk even identifies him with Richard Steele's sentimental
hero young Bevil, and while conceding that Defoe was "no believer in the
natural goodness of man," has called this narrative "a sentimental novel in
embryo."[4]

Such a view, however, leaves out of account Jack's will to power of which
John Richetti talks so convincingly.[5] For if Colonel Jack wants to be a good
man, he also wants to be superman. We already have a hint of this in the
novel's subtitle, where we are told that he "is now abroad compleating a
Life of Wonders, and resolves to dye a General." And Jack himself remarks
near the beginning of his story, as he comments on the satisfaction he feels
at being elevated in rank above his older brother: "So universally is Ambition seated in the Minds of Men, that not a Beggar-boy but has his share of
it" (p. 5).

As a matter of fact, Jack's "strange rectitude of Principles" is intimately
tied in with his ambition. The urge to turn to God and repent evinced by a
Robinson Crusoe or a Moll Flanders is really no different from that urge to
be "Good at the Bottom" that motivates Colonel Jack. Both are gestures
toward conforming to the rules made by parent-figures—gestures made in
an effort to transcend the insignificant self by claiming *bona fide* member-
ship in a nourishing social stratum.

Self-transcendence by whatever means is invariably Jack's motive. His
superman ideal is that which he defines by the word *gentleman;* and his
aspirations amount to a desire to imitate his own father. It is easy to see,
then, why Colonel Jack behaves as he does in the scene in which he returns
to the "poor Woman" the money he has stolen from her: "Well, Dame,
come hither to me, *says I,* and with that I put my Hand in my Pocket, and
she came to me: Hold up your Hand, *said I,* which she did, and I told her
Nine half Crowns into her Hand; there Dame, *said I.* . . ." Jack is here
playing God as surely as do both Robinson Crusoe and Captain Singleton.
Making restitution in accordance with the rules of the social group to which

he aspires, he becomes in his own mind a member of that group. In beha*
ing in a way that is "truly honourable," he feels himself to be a "Benefa
tor"—a being whom others may one day address as "your Worship"—th
title by which he himself addresses his own later benefactor (p. 75).

Not long before this, he has been a participant in a memorable scene th;
clarifies for him what it means to be a gentleman and increases the "Fancy
he has of rising to that level. The scene begins as we witness a well-dresse
man, who has sworn "most horrid Oaths at every two or three Words
being roundly reproved by "an antient grave Gentleman." "It made th
Blood run Chill in my Veins," Jack says, to hear that "Swearing was only f
for such as we were"; and he goes on to comment: "when I began to grov
to an Age of understanding, and to know that I was a Thief, growing up i
all manner of Villany . . . it came often into my thoughts that I was goin;
wrong, that I was in the high Road to the Devil, and several times woul
stop short, and ask my self, if this was the Life of a Gentleman?" (pp. 6]
62).

Up to this point he has thought himself safely superior to "horrid Jack.
Whereas that Jack has "promis'd to be stout when grown up to be a Mar
but not to be tall," our Jack has been growing in stature as he grows i;
knowledge until, by the age of eighteen, he is, he says, "pretty Tall of m
Age."[6] Moreover, he has moved upward from sleeping on the ground or i;
the glass-house ashes to lodging with Will in "a little Garret fit for ou
Quality" (p. 45). He has moved from a condition of going "Naked, anc
Ragged" to ownership of "two Shirts, a Wastcoat, and a Great Coat" (p. 44)
And both these promotions have occurred because he has become "th
Scholar" of a "most exquisite Fellow, who," he recounts, was "above th
little Fellows, who went about stealing Trifles and Baubles . . . his aim was a
higher Things" (pp. 17, 18). His new friend, he goes on to say, "was a Thie
of Quality, and a Pick-pocket above the ordinary Rank, and that aim'c
higher abundantly than my Brother Jack" (p. 18). He "generally push'c
higher at such desperate Things as those, and he came off the cleanest, anc
with the greatest Success Imaginable" (p. 44). During this phase of hi;
career, Jack soon becomes rich—"so rich that I knew not what to do witl
my Money, or with myself" (p. 55), and he begins "to look higher" still.

It is not long, however, before he senses that the heights to which hi;
comrade Will aspires are not those toward which he himself is instinctively
drawn: "*Will* it seems understood that Word [gentleman] in a quite differ-
ing manner from me; for his Gentleman was nothing more or less than ;
Gentleman Thief, a Villain of a higher Degree than a Pick-pocket" (p. 62)
Thus, in choosing Will as his master (surely, Will is virtually an allegorica
figure here), Jack has, he knows in retrospect, chosen the wrong guide fo;
his conduct. He soon forgets, though, that he is "in the high Road to the
Devil": "these little things wore off . . . and I follow'd the old Trade again;
especially when *Will* came to prompt me . . . for he was a kind of a Guide tc

e in all these things, and I had by Custom and Application, together with
eing his way, learnt to be as acute a Workman as my Master" (p. 62).
A passage in Robinson Crusoe's *Serious Reflections* bears directly on what
efoe apparently regards as Jack's problem at this juncture: "There is an
considerate temper which reigns in our minds, that hurries us down the
ream of our affections by a kind of involuntary agency, and makes us do a
ousand things, in the doing of which we propose nothing to ourselves but
1 immediate *subjection to our will*, that is to say, our passion, even without
1e concurrence of our understandings, and of which we can give very little
count after 'tis done."[7]
Presumably, there is some importance in the fact that it is Will who calls
1ck brother and not the other way around, since Defoe has Jack dwell
1ther insistently on this point. "I knew nothing of Brother *Will, as he call'd*
1self," Jack reports at the time his comrade is fleeing for his life. And then
heard by great Accident that *Will*, who us'd to be seen with me, and who
1ll'd me Brother, was taken, and would be hang'd . . ." (p. 70). And when
1e Shoemaker collars Jack, he scolds him: "I hear bad News of you; they
y you are gotten into bad Company, and that this *Will*, calls you Brother."
'ill is Jack's "Master and Tutor in Wickedness" (p. 81), and when Jack is on
s way to make restitution to the poor woman and her maid, he reflects,
Vill, made me rob them" (p. 83). "I would advise you," says the
1oemaker to him, "to shift for yourself . . . I wont jest any more with you,
a thing of such a dangerous Consequence; I only advise you to keep the
:llow Company no more" (p. 71). To be led by Will is to be led downward
imprisonment and death—to succumb to one's own creatureliness. "I am
Dead Dog if I am taken," Will says (p. 72); and soon afterward Jack—
siting him at Newgate—finds him "in a sad Condition loaden with heavy
ons and [with] no prospect or hope of Escaping . . ." (p. 81).
Jack's own specialness is now becoming increasingly evident. When he is
prehended by a Constable, having been mistaken for Captain Jack, the
1dge asks the Constable, "are you sure this is the Person that is intended in
1ur Warrant?" Plainly, Jack is not, as is his brother, marked for early
:ath, and he refuses to divulge his name and thereby to accuse himself,
sisting "on the unreasonableness of it" (p. 79). Unlike the lowly brother
1th whom he has been confused, Colonel Jack knows how to use his brains
get himself off. "It is but Reason," the Justice says of the arguments he
'esents in his own defense.

Ironically, however (and it is an irony that is only beginning to develop at
1is point), Jack escapes death here—managing to convince the judge he is
1t the one "intended in [the] Warrant"—only by establishing himself not
somebody but as nobody ("the Men that took me knew nothing of me").
1ly by remaining nameless—by hiding—does he survive.

And despite his upward mobility, Jack has not yet managed to rise abov
or leave behind his low associations. The pattern of the first third of th
novel involves as many downs as ups. To be sure, the imagery of dirt an
ashes, which is repeatedly used to define the young Jack's low conditior
appears less and less often. Jack's dirtiness has been frequently mentione
early in the narrative, as has the fact that this is not the condition he is tru
born to: "As for my Person, while I was a dirty Glass-Bottle House Bo
sleeping in the Ashes, and dealing always in the Street Dirt, it cannot t
expected but that I look'd like what I was, and so we did all; that is to sa
like a *Black your Shoes your Honour,* a Beggar Boy, a Black-Guard Boy, c
what you please, despicable, and miserable, to the last Degree; and yet
remember, the People would say of me, that Boy has a good Face; if he wa
wash'd, and well dress'd, he would be a good pretty Boy . . ." (p. 7).

In these early days, however, Jack has relatively modest expectatior
when it comes to rising above this grimy state of things. Being in "utte
ignorance of greater Felicity," he thinks himself "exalted" when th
Major—who himself feels "elevated . . . to a strange Degree" (p. 14)-
shares with him the booty of his "devilish lucky Day" (p. 13). "I began to ca
to mind my being a Gentleman," Jack says when he obtains his first shoe
and stockings. "I thought with my self we began to live like Gentlemen," h
says when they eat their "luxurious" meal at "a boiling Cook's in Rosemar
Lane." And after remarking that "not the greatest Man on Earth could t
more happy in their own Imagination, and with less mixture of Grief, c
Reflexion," he sums up this adventure: "That Night the Major and
triumph'd in our new Enjoyment, and slept with an undisturb'd Repose i
the usual Place, surrounded with the warmth of the Glass-House Fire
above, which was a full amends for all the Ashes and Cinders which w
roll'd in below" (p. 16).

Jack's approach to the "Age of understanding" is marked, however, by
growing awareness that dirt and ashes are not his natural habitat. Thus, h
stands up for himself when a man at a broker's shop, after addressing hir
facetiously as "young Gentleman," comments that he looks as if he "be
long'd to the ragged Regiment," and he weeps when he hears a woma
there talk "of my being not Clean, and in Rags" (p. 27). But she too recog
nizes that he is "born to better Things" than are evidenced by his outwar
appearance: "the Boy is a pretty Boy, if he was clean and well dress'd," sh
says, echoing the earlier judgment of him, "and may be as good a Gentle
man's son for any thing we know, as any of those that are well dress'd
(p. 27). Another bystander in a subsequent scene also acknowledges hi
specialness: "This is a cleaver Boy . . . and yet very Ignorant and Honest, 'ti
pity some Care should not be taken of him, and something done fo
him. . . ." And when Jack confides to him that he has no home but lies at th
glass-house on the "Ground . . . and sometimes a little Straw, or upon th

varm Ashes," the observer states that "this poor Child is enough to make a Man Weep for the Miseries of humane Nature" (p. 37).

It is, of course, "the Miseries of humane Nature" that Jack seeks to rise above in his aspirations to become a gentleman. But he is soon to learn that to look like a gentleman is not necessarily to behave like one and is no guarantee that one has escaped from the dirty low world. This is the lesson being taught when, in the scene already alluded to, the "antient grave gentleman"—no doubt the representative of traditional values—chides a confrere for swearing:

> 'tis pity you that seem to be a fine Gentleman, well Bred and good Humour'd, should accustom your self to such an hateful Practice; why it is not like a Gentleman to swear, 'tis enough for my black Wretches that Work there at the Furnace, or for these ragged nak'd black Guard Boys, pointing at me, and some others of the dirty Crew that lay in the Ashes: 'tis bad enough for them, *says he,* and they ought to be corrected for it too; but for a Man of Breeding, Sir, *says he,* a Gentleman! it ought to be look'd upon as below them; Gentlemen know better, and are taught better, and it is plain you know better; I beseech you Sir, when you are tempted to swear, always ask yourself, is this like a Gentleman? does this become me as a Gentleman! do but ask your self that Question, and your Reason will prevail, you will soon leave it off. (P. 61)

In short, a man can all too easily allow himself to sink back into the dirt out of which he has raised himself. To be a gentleman is to behave morally, but moral behavior is a denial of animalism that can only be maintained if reason prevails. Thus, when, a few pages later, we see Will waylaying a coach in which are riding "a Gentleman and a Punk," and robbing the gentleman of his "Money, and his Watch, and his Silver hilted Sword," we cannot but be aware that the loss is a symbolic one, as was the case with the gentleman whom Moll Flanders robbed of his symbols of high status. To succumb to the lusts of the flesh leads to being reduced. Only in goodness is there hope of transcendence.

In all likelihood, it is Defoe's sense of this fact that leads to Jack's repeatedly associating stolen money with dirt. The earliest instance of this occurs when he wraps the four guineas given him by the major in "a dirty Linnen Rag," which he calls "a foul Clout" and which, displaying his instinct for cleanliness, he washes as best he can "in the Kennel" (p. 23). Later, he talks of Will's having "but Six-pence and a few dirty Farthings" (p. 28), and still later, he tells of Will's stolen pocketbook, "wrapt up in a Dirty peice of a Colour'd Handkerchief, as black as the Street could make it"—"a Dirty Rag" (p. 53). Money may be one of the outward signs of superior social status, but not dirty money—money dishonestly obtained. To be a "Gentleman Thief" is, Jack learns, to be no gentleman at all.

The sign of Jack's specialness, he discovers, is not the money he manages to pilfer; and in thinking that it is, he has been misguided by Will. The tru sign of a gentleman, and the one that even the young Jack often reveals, i an instinctive honesty (a word that he frequently uses to characterize hi own behavior). The implication seems to be, however, that while it is a trai that may be latent in man and may define his higher or better natur (Defoe was, apparently, far from sure), it is one that requires care if it is t develop properly: "'tis pity some Care should not be taken of him," say one gentleman of Jack. And Defoe says of him in the preface: "If he ha come into the World with the Advantage of Education, and been wel instructed how to improve the generous Principles he had in him, what Man might he not have been."

Implicit in Defoe's presentation of Jack's rise in the world is the recogni tion that the pursuit of goodness and the pursuit of wealth are alike i terms of motivation. And dirty money does not lead to promotion becaus a gain in one area becomes a loss in another, this being the difficulty Mol Flanders constantly faces and constantly has to get around. But if botl wealth and honesty are things to value as the means to power and statu and hence to safety and security, both require vigilance if they are to b maintained. And this need to take care brings cares along with it—care that the lower orders know nothing of. As long as young Jack has nothin and is nobody, he has nothing to lose. He feels the same safety an anima feels. But it is Jack's unhappy fate to grow to awareness of his own precari ous position in the world and then to seek to *have* something and *be* some body in order to give himself an illusion of security. And the mor "specialness" Jack or any other "gentleman" piles up in terms of eithe wealth or good behavior, the more he must "have a Care" to maintain it an hence the more cares he takes on and the more insecure and precarious h feels. Small wonder men see ignorance as bliss. In *Colonel Jack* Defoe has hi protagonist discuss explicitly what he has often suggested in his othe novels: that in the process of creating security for ourselves, we are simpl creating more insecurity: "now as I was full of Wealth," says Jack, "behold I was full of Care, for what to do to secure my Money I could not tell . . . ' (p. 23). Ironically, the only way to be secure is always to feel insecure an hence to be suspicious, wary, on one's guard. To see things clearly is to see potential enemy in every friend. Even nature in the form of that hollo tree proves untrustworthy. For an awful moment, it seems to have swal lowed up Jack's means of livelihood rather than keeping it safe for him.

To the extent that the account that Colonel Jack gives of his life consti tutes a success story in terms of achieved status, the first third of th narrative amounts to a kind of false start. Because care has not been taken because he has been abandoned by his real parents and must make his wa in the world unguided—a parable of the human condition as Defoe see it—Jack's higher nature, his reasonableness, is for some time in thrall to hi lower one, represented first by the two Jacks and then by Will. A "wicke idle Boy . . . left Desolate in the World" (p. 124), he comes to his senses an hus supposedly to a sense of his true self only after he goes through a series of stages, each of which entails some sort of escape motif. As was the case with Captain Singleton, Jack moves continually northward and upward in pursuit of freedom. With his repeated escapes through the London streets, however, as with Captain Singleton's repeated efforts to get away from Madagascar, there is a forward-and-back, or more accurately in his case, an up-and-down pattern, since he remains caught in the life of hieving and must attempt escapes again and again. Moreover, just as Captain Bob has lacked a clear sense of direction, so does young Colonel Jack. "I was Sick indeed of the wandering Life which I had led," he says of himself when he sets out to learn to read and write, "and was resolv'd to Thieve no more . . ." (pp. 102, 103). In fact, up to the time he arrives on board the transport ship bound for Virginia he has found himself no fewer than eight times confronted with situations that have led him to declare, "I knew not what to do with my self." And when Will at one point and Captain Jack at another look to him for advice, themselves not knowing "what to do," he can be of no assistance to either of them, for, as he says, "I knew nothing of the World" (p. 82).

One turning point in Jack's career comes in his making restitution to the poor woman whose means of livelihood he has stolen, since at this time he forswears the thieving life. In leaving London behind and moving northward toward Scotland, he enters a new stage in his pursuit of freedom. Yet he is still in the position of serving his lower nature in the person of Captain Jack and is still content to live off the Captain's ill-gotten gains. "I was loth to leave him," he says of his continuing association with his "suppos'd Brother" (p. 87); "it seems we were yet farther to take our Fate together" (p. 103). Indeed, after his first disastrous attempt to make an honest living, he finds himself "reduc'd . . . to the last Extremity" (p. 103)—"reduc'd almost as low, as my Captain," so that when the two brothers join the army they are "Rank'd together" (p. 104).

But by now he has again made restitution for a theft, in this case one having to do with a stolen horse; and as he begins his soldiering career, he has moved up a level from his earlier vulnerability: "I had a secret Satisfaction at being now under no Necessity of stealing, and living in fear of a Prison, and of the lash of the Hangman; a thing which from the time, I saw it in *Edinborough,* was so terrible to me, that I could not think of it without horror, and it was an inexpressible ease to my Mind, that I was now in a certain way of Living, which was honest, and which I could say, was not unbecoming a Gentleman" (p. 104). His contentment, unfortunately, is short-lived. Soon he must once more run away from a situation that threatens death. He may harbor ambitions of "being a Gentleman Officer, as well as a Gentleman Soldier," but he is, at this point, still a common soldier, and as such he knows well enough that to be sent into Flanders would be to become cannon fodder. In terms of survival power, soldiers are to officers what, in H. F.'s plague-stricken London, the poor are to the rich.

The sea voyage to Virginia is not, of course, one that Jack undertakes of his own volition. It is a passage from an old life to a new one that he passively undergoes, carried along by natural forces over which neither he nor anyone else has total control. But during the voyage he becomes clearly set apart from his brother, who reacts so violently and rebelliously to being transported that he is kept in irons below decks. From now on, the Captain's fate is, as Colonel Jack tells us, "no part of my own Story" (p. 116) Jack will hereafter follow the shoemaker's counsel and "shift for himself."

It is the next sequence of Colonel Jack's narrative that takes on an unmistakable aura of fairy tale or fantasy. Jack becomes the fairy prince in disguise—or a male Cinderella rising from the ashes. "I took up the air of what my Habit did not agree with," he says, and then recounts his having told the captain of the ship, "that [we] were not People to be sold for Slaves that tho' we had the Misfortune to be in a Circumstance that oblig'd us to conceal ourselves, having disguised ourselves to get out of the Army . . . yet that we were Men of Substance, and able to Discharge ourselves from the Service. . . ." Whipping out at this point his "Bill for 94 £.," he establishes that he is somebody, and the captain is satisfactorily "astonish'd": "lifting up his Hands, by what Witchcraft, *says* he, were you brought hither!" (p. 115).

The ship becomes a womb ("when I came there I was oblig'd to act in so narrow a Compass, that nothing very material could Present it self" (p. 110). And once arrived in Virginia, the prisoners are "deliver'd to the Merchants," and after being "carried up a small River or Creek," they are "delivered to the Head-man . . ." (p. 118). Jack is, as are the transported felons who arrive soon after he does, "just beginning the World again" (p. 120). He now enters a new course of life, which can only be seen a involving a wish-fulfillment or mythic scheme of things, in which he move steadily upward "from a Slave to a Head Officer, and Overseer of Slaves and from thence to a Master Planter" (pp. 151, 152).

The master whom Jack serves when he comes to Virginia in "this miserable Condition of being a Slave" becomes for him father, savior, ruler, and judge. He is that all-powerful, all-knowing authority figure to whom the child looks for protection in a world he finds overwhelming. Not only does Jack speak of him as "having been a Father to me" (p. 159), but he looks upon him as very nearly omniscient: "sometimes it came into my Head, that sure my Master was some extraordinary Man and that he knew all thing that ever I had done in my Life" (p. 121). Moreover, when Jack is called before him, the scene proceeds as follows:

> his Discourse . . . was in a large Hall, where he sat in a Seat like a Lord Judge upon the Bench, or a Petty King upon his Throne.
>   When I came in . . . he ordered his Man to withdraw, and I standing half naked, and bare-headed with my Haugh or Hoe in my Hand . .

near the Door, he bad me lay down my Hoe, and come nearer; then he began to look a little less Stern and Terrible, than I fancy'd him to look before. (P. 122)

It scarcely needs pointing out that this master represents to Colonel Jack what God represents to Robinson Crusoe and that Colonel Jack is, in turn, to the slave Mouchat what Crusoe is to Friday. And feelings of gratitude—the importance of which was one of Defoe's most fondly held convictions—become a central subject in this section of the narrative.

Moreover, in Jack's shifting points of view on this subject, we see especially clearly Defoe's awareness of human contradictoriness. At times the perspective is that of the servant to the master, as in Jack's gratitude to the master who becomes, in effect, his maker (he "made a Man of him" [p. 154]). It is the same sense of indebtedness he later feels toward King George.

Of his Virginia master Jack has said gratefully: "as I liv'd without any Personal Expence, but was maintain'd at my old Great Master's, *as we call'd him*, and at his Charge, with 30 £. a Year besides, so all my Gain was laid up for Encrease" (p. 158). And a little later, under the influence of his tutor, he at least pays lip service to yet another "giver of Life" (p. 168), arraigning himself for his ingratitude: "what a Creature am I, and what have I been doing? I that never once did this in all my Life! that never said so much, *God, I thank thee* for all that I have been sav'd from, or all that I have been brought to in this World; and yet my Life has been as full of Variety, and I have been as miraculously deliver'd from Dangers and Mischiefs, and as many of them, as ever he has; and if it has all been brought to pass by an invisible Hand in Mercy to me, what have I been doing, and where have I liv'd? that I only should be the most Thoughtless, and Unthankful of all God's Creatures!" (pp. 168, 169).

As Jack tells his story, however, neither God nor the "Great Master" becomes the recipient of his gratitude with anything like the insistence that he himself becomes the recipient of the gratitude of others. In fact, Jack would take no prizes for humility when it comes to his recollections of this phase of his life, although he is careful to do a little hedging in the matter. "I was not so Arrogant," he maintains, when telling of Mouchat's response to his mercy, "as to assume the Merit to myself; no, no, *said I*, I do not ask you to go, or run for me, you must do all that for our Great Master, for it will be from him entirely that you will be Pardon'd, if you are Pardon'd at all . . ." (p. 137).

But there is no denying the pleasure he derives from being the dispenser of favors and from having someone bow down in gratitude to *him*, however frequent his disclaimers may be:

I order'd him to be unty'd, gave him a Dram of Rum out of my Pocket-Bottle, and order'd them to give him some Victuals.
When the Fellow was let loose, he came to me, and kneel'd down to

me, and took hold of my Legs and of my Feet, and laid his Head upon
the Ground, and Sob'd, and Cry'd, like a Child that had been Corrected,
but could not speak for his Life; and thus he continu'd a long time: I
would have taken him up, but he would not Rise, but I cry'd as fast as he,
for I could not bear to see a poor Wretch lye on the Ground to me, that
was but a Servant the other Day like himself; at last, but not till a quarter
of an Hour, I made him get up, and then he spoke. *Me mucheé know good*
Great Master, mucheé good *you Master: No* Negro *unthankful, me* Dye *for*
them, do me so mucheé kind. (Pp. 139, 140)

In Mouchat's eyes, Colonel Jack possesses magical powers. Mouchat gazes
upon him, on one occasion, "as if he had been Thunderstruck, and stupid
. . . [and] then falls a Dancing about . . . as if he had been bewitch'd . . ."
(p. 142).

Nor is Mouchat the only one to feel beholden to Jack for favors rendered. Jack eventually establishes with another transported Englishman
exactly the relationship he himself has had with his Great Master. Just as
Jack has once stood before *his* master, hoe in hand, so now he finds "a clever
Fellow" standing before him. "I told him, a Book would become his Hands
better than a Hoe, and if he could promise to make me but understand
Latin enough to read it, and understand other Languages by it, I would
ease him of the Labour, which I was now oblig'd to put him to, especially, if
I was assur'd that he was fit to receive that Favour of a kind Master: In
short, I made him to me, what my Benefactor made me to him, and from
him I gain'd a Fund of Knowledge, infinitely more valuable than the Rate
of a Slave, which was what I paid for it . . ." (p. 158).

Jack has earlier served his own master in the role of teacher, and it is
becoming increasingly clear that gratitude is a matter of mutual back-
scratching. "My Master," says Jack, "shew'd the same Principle of Gratitude
to those that serv'd him, as he look'd for in those that he serv'd; and
particularly to me . . ." (p. 150) Jack has no illusions as to either giving or
receiving something for nothing. His master, he recalls, "promis'd to make
a Man of me and so he did, and in one Respect, *I may say,* I merited it of
him, for I brought his Plantation into such order, and the Government of
his Negroes, into such a Regulation, that if he had given 50 £. to have had it
done, he would have thought his Money well bestow'd . . ." (p. 159). We
come again to the Hobbesian connection between generous principles and
common sense, the first being a function of the second. It is easy to see why
Jack includes "Principles of natural Generosity" ("the Foundation of Gratitude") among the "Faculties of reasonable Creatures," since to treat people
with kindness and tenderness leads to receiving gratitude and service in
return and vice-versa. In arguing his case before his master, Jack repeatedly underlines the reasonableness of treating the Negro slaves kindly.
And he uses his wits when he responds as he does to his master's generosity
after his cargo of goods is lost: "I thank'd him, and did it with more

Ceremony and Respect than ever; because I thought my self more under
the Hatches than I was before" (p. 155). Like Moll, Jack knows that loyal
friends are money in the bank. "I had nothing of Stock," he reminisces of
his first coming to Virginia, "but I had a great Beginning, for I had such a
Man's Friendship, and Support in my Beginning, that indeed, I needed no
other Stock . . ." (p. 159). Jack describes his master as being "full of Tenderness" (p. 129), and later he characterizes himself as having "a Tenderness in my Nature" (p. 133), but in neither case is the trait valued for its
own sake.

Jack's behavior in this period of his life involves the walking of a tight
rope. And in recounting his response at the time of his master's death, he
plainly reveals the contradictory pulls he feels. Moreover, when Jack has
earlier been given his liberty, his response has suggested this same contradiction: "I Bow'd, and told him, that I was sure if I was my own Master, I
would be his Servant as long as he would accept of my Service . . ." (p. 149).
But the master speaks truer than he seems to know when, in reply to Jack's
vow to "serve him faithfully if he would accept of me as long as he liv'd," he
says, "So you shall . . . and serve your self too . . ." (p. 149). It is not long, as
it happens, before Jack is himself able to play the role of godlike deliverer
("I deliver'd my Tutor from his Bondage" [p. 173]).

Jack's sense of his own specialness receives reassuring confirmation during his sojourn in Virginia. One might say that he emerges as the chosen of
God. He experiences a steady upward rise from the time when, as he
relates, "my Master dismissing all the rest of us Servants, Pointed at me
saying] bring that young Fellow hither to me" (p. 122). And he is soon
call'd" again: "When I came to him, I came to be sure in the ordinary
Habit of a poor half naked Slave; Come hither young Man, *says he,* and give
me your Hoe, when I gave it him; well, *says he,* you are to Work no more in
the Plantation" (p. 126). Now occurs the transformation from frog to
prince: "here, *he says,* go in there a Slave, and come out a Gentleman . . .
which I did most willingly; and now you may believe that I began to hope
for something better than ordinary" (p. 127).

The fact is that Jack has for a long time hoped "for something better
than ordinary." And his movement toward becoming somebody in the
world is appropriately marked by images of growth, increase, self-
aggrandizement. But material increase is not the only kind he is aware of,
nor is it the most important. He begins to increase in self-respect as well.
Envisioning the possibility of becoming "something Considerable in time,"
he writes: "That original something, I knew not what, that . . . us'd to
Dictate to me when I was but a Child, that I was to be a Gentleman,
continued to operate upon me Now . . ." (pp. 155, 156). And this is only a
start. He senses that "tho' this was the Foundation of my new Life, yet that
this was not the Superstructure, and that I might still be born for greater
things than these; that it was Honesty, and Virtue alone that made Men

Rich and Great, and gave them a Fame, as well as a Figure in the World
and that therefore I was to lay my Foundation in these, and expect what
might follow in time" (p. 157).

   Now it is that his love of books commences, and what it leads to, ironically, is not satisfaction, but a renewed dissatisfaction. Like Robinson
Crusoe, he finds that he has not, after all, enlarged his domain, his sense of
control, sufficiently. His tutor, he recalls, "rais'd an unquenchable Thirst in
me, after seeing something that was doing in the World. . . . Now, I look'd
upon my self as one Buried alive, in a remote Part of the World, where I
could see nothing at all. . . ." In short, "this was not yet, the Life of a
Gentleman . . . this would not do, and I cou'd receive no Satisfaction in
it . . ." (p. 172). Thereafter, in the course of his "Life of infinite Variety"
(p. 263), he frequently recalls Virginia as a refuge; yet he continues to
regard it too as a place where he would, should he return, be "bury'd a-live"
(p. 233).
   Jack's sense of his own destiny involves that need for heroism, that need
to leave security behind and to push beyond known limits which is by now
thoroughly familiar. Like Crusoe, like Moll, like H. F., he can never rest
content. One might indeed say that at the time he leaves Virginia, he is in
precisely the situation that Robinson Crusoe occupied at the beginning of
his adventures. "That Original something" turns out to be the same thing
as Crusoe's "Original Sin." In wanting to become a gentleman, Jack really
wants to become God. He must reach out for more and more knowledge,
more and more wealth, more and more power, more and more life. But his
heavens on earth never prove to be heavens when he gets there. Always
something either within or outside himself makes his current position un-
tenable.
   No sooner does he gain command of a military company and become
"the savior of a city" (p. 209), than in the course of another battle he is
"knock'd down by a Gyant like a *German* soldier and is eventually found by
a rescue party "among the Dead . . . almost smothered with the dead
Germans . . ." (p. 220). What is more, all his firsthand experiences in "the
great War" do not satisfy that "unquenchable Thirst" of which he has
spoken, and he is still driven by wanderlust even after his military career
has come to an end: "I could not prevail with my self to live a private Life:
had got a wandring kind of Taste, and Knowledge of Things begat a Desire
of increasing it. . . . I could not live in the World, and not enquire what was
doing in it . . ." (p. 233).
   And this is not the only area in which he is unable to "prevail with [him-
self." He has by this time found himself driven by quite a different kind of
thirst or desire, the indulgence of which has led to his being "reduced" in
more ways than one. Like many a gentleman before him, he is "ensnared"

by "a Charm" for which all his accrued knowledge of the world has not prepared him: "I was a meer Boy in the Affair of Love . . . I had been till now as perfectly unacquainted with the Sex . . . as I was when I was ten Year old, and lay in a Heap of Ashes at the Glass-House" (p. 186). The association with young Jack's early life and his sleeping in the ashes is a fitting one, since our hero is now about to be reminded with a vengeance of his animality.

His sense of his own specialness is about to receive a severe shock. Jack is clearly aware of the irony of the situation when he recalls, concerning one of his early conversations with the new lady in his life: "she took a great many Occasions to rally the Men, and the weakness they were guilty of . . . he Women had out-witted us, and brought us upon our Knees, and made us whine after them, and lower our selves, so as we could never pretend to gain our equallity again" (p. 188). Jack is completely outwitted by his lady "she showed the abundance of her Wit, and I an abundant defficiency of mine . . ." [p. 192]), the result being that he is "almost ruined" (p. 186) and finds himself, at the end of his chaotic first marriage, "straitn'd, and re-luc'd" (p. 205). As he says, "the Extravagance of three Years with this Lady, had sunk me most effectually" (p. 199).

Not only is he reduced financially, but he is quite literally brought low in that he is "knocked . . . down" (p. 204) by some rogues in the employ of a gentleman friend of his wife's and receives wounds far more severe than those he will later receive on the battlefield. It would seem that in Defoe's view the human capacity for destructive violence is at least as likely to manifest itself in love as in war. In one way or another, each of Jack's first three marriages involves him in a "Life of Hellish Excess" (p. 241)—a phrase that he uses to describe the drunken debauchery into which his third wife sinks. Intemperance, leading as it does to lack of self-government, can, he declares, change "the most Virtuous, regular, well instructed, and well inclin'd Tempers into worse than Brutal" (p. 241). Clearly, Jack is a follower here of the Hobbes who equates drunkards with madmen.[8] Jack's "well bred Wife," he says, "grew a Beast, a Slave to Strong Liquor . . ." (p. 240). And he has earlier related that he himself became embroiled in his second marriage to a whore as a result of drink. Defoe seems always in his fictions and often in his essays to link liquor and lust and to see them as the most common causes of a gentleman's fall from grace; but in Jack's case it is not, it seems, his own lust but that of his wives which leads him in turn to unreasonable or brutal behavior. So frenzied does he become over the infidelities of his second wife that, as he says, "I had no Government of myself" (p. 225), and he actually thinks seriously of killing her. He has also had murderous thoughts in one of the scenes growing out of the unhappy events of his first marriage.

It may at first seem that Jack has regained control of his life when his first wife reappears on the scene in the posture of a supplicant: "falling down on her Knees just before me, O! Sir, *says she,* I see you don't know me, be merciful to me . . . 'tis righteous that God should bring me to your Foot, to ask you Pardon for all my brutish doings: Forgive me Sir, *said she,* I beseech you and let me be your Slave or Servant for it as long as I live . . ." (p. 255). Jack can now resume the role of godlike deliverer he has played so well with both his tutor and Mouchat. "I took her up," he says twice; and later he goes on to recount: "She . . . told me all she could claim of me, would be only to deliver her from her present Calamity, that . . . she was willing to do the meanest Offices in the World for me, and tho' she should rejoyce to hear that I would forgive her former Life, yet that she would not look any higher than to be my Servant . . ." (p. 257). Understandably, Jack cannot now resist the thought "of taking her into her first Station again . . ." (p. 259).

The master-servant relationship between Jack and his former wife turns out, however, to be a recapitulation of that earlier one between Jack himself as servant and his Great Master, in which Jack has risen to a position of power. Like her one-time husband before her, this woman, who has formerly "been in very good Circumstances and was bred very well," arrives in Virginia "almost naked," whereupon Jack arranges to "new Cloath her" in a manner more befitting her quality (p. 256). He then becomes her protector and supplies her with "a Servant to wait on her, and do everything for her" (p. 259), and eventually, while she vows "to assist and serve him on all Occasions" (p. 270), he in turn—acknowledging "the Goodness of her Judgment" in looking after his interests in a time of crisis—gives himself "chearfully up to her Management" (pp. 211, 212). In short, she becomes *his* protector and deliverer.

Not long after this episode—which has ended in Jack's restoring his wife "to a State of Ease and Plenty" (p. 261)—we find Jack himself fallen once more from high to low, the result of his ill-advised participation in the Jacobite rebellion. "I was now reduced," he recalls, "from a great Man, a Magistrate, a Governor, or Master of three great Plantations; and having three or four Hundred Servants at my Command, to be a poor self-condemned Rebel, and durst not shew my Face . . ." (p. 267). An "unseen Mine" has blown up all his "apparent Tranquility at once . . . and sent [him] a wandring into the World again; a Condition full of Hazards, and always attended with Circumstances dangerous to Mankind, while he is left to choose his own Fortunes, and be guided by his own short sighted Measures" (p. 264).

Overnight he has swung from a feeling of extra-specialness to one of almost total impotence and terror. And it is at this point that he, in desperation, looks to his wife for reassurance and salvation: "I was now going to put my Life into her Hands . . . it would be in her Power to deliver me up into the Hands of my Enemies. . . ." In some sense, Jack regresses here to an infantile state. For some three months his wife, having adopted the mother role, keeps him warm and cozy indoors with his legs wrapped in flannel. She is the source of both wise counsel ("pray do not want Government of yourself" [p. 269]) and comfort ("she perceiv'd my Disorder, and turn'd back, assuring me there was no Harm, desir'd me to be easie, and she would come back again presently . . ." [p. 269]). It was, he says, "by her Direction that I took every Step that follow'd for the extricating my self out of this Labrinth" (p. 268). And it is she, he acknowledges, who takes the final "Measures, for the Compleating my Deliverance" (p. 271).

The up-and-down pattern, "in Prison, and at Liberty," of which Jack's wife has spoken, continues to characterize Jack's own life to the end of his narrative. All his life Jack wanders in one labyrinth or another. "I knew not what to do" (p. 181), he says when taken prisoner by the French—and again "what to do I did not know" (p. 182). "I was extremely Melancholly and Heavy, and indeed, knew not what to do with my self," he says when he at last reaches London (p. 233); "I knew not what Course to take in the World," he says at the time of his fearful response to the transported Scots (p. 244); "the Question was, what I should do next?" he says after the narrow escape from the pirate ship (p. 275); "we were . . . confus'd . . . being not resolv'd what Course to take," he says during his ill-fated trading venture in the Gulf of Mexico (p. 298).

One way or another he repeatedly finds himself "a-wandring," whether driven, as Robinson Crusoe so often is, by his own curiosity ("I had got a wandring kind of Taste" [p. 233]) or by a need to escape the consequences of some previous action ("an unseen mine . . . sent me a wandring into the World again") or simply by a sense of lostness and aimlessness ("I had rambled up and down in a most discontented unsettled Posture . . . about a Year" [p. 244]). At last, having received word of the King's granting of a general pardon to the rebels, he declares, "I saw my Way open to return to my Wife, and to my Plantations, from which I promised my self never to wander any more" (p. 277).

But of course he breaks his promise, driven again by his need for expansion, his Hobbesian passion for accumulation. His career as a trader proves the culmination of a life that has been devoted to accumulating hedges against his own threatened destruction and basic helplessness. Judging the dishonestly acquired money of his thieving days well lost, he devotes his new life in Virginia to accumulating land and servants and learning and status, all of those things being reassuring indications to himself of his more legitimate power. He is constantly counting up his acreage and his slaves; and he has even piled up an impressive list of titles ("a great Man, a Magistrate, a Governor, or Master"). He also enumerates the titles of books he has read and later his triumphs in battle and later still his strategically placed friends.[9]

Jack finds a trading career irresistible. He is no longer the innocent boy of whom he has reminisced: "I had got Money, but I neither knew the

Value of it, or the Use of it; the Way of Living I had begun, was so natural to me, I had no Notion of bettering it . . ." (p. 40). He has long had definite notions of bettering his way of life, and the interest he has been able to accrue on his London savings account and the multiplying of acres and servants that he has set in motion are as nothing to the returns on his pounds that he sees he can achieve through trade. He once tells of a transaction involving, in all, a two-hundred-percent mark-up, and of another he writes: "taking a Cargo . . . of about five or six thousand Pound, I might easily make four of one . . ." (p. 290). Moreover, Jack's self-esteem is itself compounded in the course of such transactions as these. In one case he and his cohorts are "treated . . . like Princes" (p. 290), and in another he says of the reception given him: "my Patron the Merchant entertain'd me like a Prince, he made my safety his peculiar Care . . ." (p. 300). And he soon rises to such heights that he is calling this patron "Friend," just as has earlier happened with his Great Master. His sense of self-expansiveness seems at times to be bursting all bounds: *It is impossible to describe in the narrow Compass of this Work,* with what Exactness and Order, and yet, with how little Hurry, and not the least Confusion, everything was done; and how soon a Weight of Business of such Importance and Value, was negotiated and finish'd . . ." (p. 302, italics added).

The truth is, however, that all the time Jack is amassing his fortune, he is still, in actuality, running away from the demon of extinction. He is using money as a means of ransoming himself—of buying himself liberty—just as surely in these instances as he has used it to buy himself out of his Mexican captivity.

If there is any single image that dominates the narrative from first to last, it is surely the image of Jack in the postures of plotting and/or executing one escape or another. The need to escape is the story of his life. He runs away from the scenes of his crimes; he runs away from the perplexities in which his marriages land him; he runs away from military foes when retreat seems politic; he runs away from pursuing pirates. He might well concur with H. F.'s brother's pronouncement: "the best Physick against the Plague is to run away from it." It is thus fitting that he thinks of going "into my own Country" as constituting "a Retreat from the World" (p. 206), and that he says of the period in his life after he has remarried his first wife: "I began to think my Fortunes were settled for this World, and I had nothing before me, but to finish a Life of infinite Variety, such as mine had been with a comfortable Retreat . . ." (p. 263).

But what Jack learns is the familiar lesson that there is no such thing as feeling "settled for this World"—that one "retreat" in the sense of a safe abode only leads to another "retreat" in the more frequently meant sense of the word. Jack's wife urges him, once he has come "safe home" (p. 295) from his adventure-filled voyage to Antegoa, to "sit down satisfy'd," and Jack agrees as to the prudence of such a course: "Now was my time to have sat still contented with what I had got . . ." (p. 296). But whatever reason-ableness and a due sense of caution may dictate, Jack is still driven by dreams of glory; "so contrary to all moderate Measures, I push'd on for another Voyage. . . ."

We are surely not expected to condemn Jack for succumbing to the sin of avarice,[10] any more than we are to do in the case of Moll Flanders or Captain Singleton. Colonel Jack sees himself as having "a Door open . . . to immense Treasure"—as having "found the way to have a Stream of the Golden Rivers of *Mexico* flow into my Plantation of Virginia" (p. 296). There is a visionary quality to the imagery here that makes it necessary to acknowledge the presence in Jack of something beyond misguided mate-rialism. Perhaps he *can,* he thinks, at last make of Virginia the heaven and the haven of his dreams.

After all, Virginia has not, at this point, turned out to be a place where he could comfortably "live retired" (p 233). He has only recently learned by grim experience that his home in Virginia is not any safer a place to be than anywhere else: "I might with the same safety, or rather more," he says at the onset of that recent crisis, "have skulk'd about in *Lancashire,* where I was; or gone up to *London,* and conceal'd my self there, till things had been over; but now the Danger was come Home to me, even to my door, and I expected nothing but to be . . . taken up and sent to *England* in Irons . . ." (p. 267).

The fluctuations of Jack's life have, in fact, never been more than tem-porarily in abeyance. Time after time Jack finds himself in threatening situations from which he can only run away and hide. And as his narrative progresses, he becomes increasingly obsessed with self-concealment. "I had nothing to do now, but entirely to conceal myself, from all that had any knowledge of me before" (p. 184), he recalls of his first return to London from Virginia. And after his second return there from the war in France he states that he was "oblig'd to be very retir'd, and change my Name, letting no Body in the Nation know who I was except my Merchant . . . I was too afraid to go Abroad . . ." (p. 233). His need to hide becomes intensified by his having attacked his third wife's lover, and he soon flees London al-together: "I immediately remov'd my Family, and that I might be perfectly conceal'd, I went into the North of England . . . where I liv'd retir'd . . ." (p. 243). Later, when his first wife reenters his life in Virginia, he is bent on keeping their former association a secret ("I told her . . . her future good, or ill Fortune would depend upon her entire concealing it . . ." [p. 256]).

Jack is always reluctant to be known by his name, and here a clear ambivalence is once again to be seen. He wants at one and the same time to be somebody and to be nobody—to stand above the crowd and to be wrapped in anonymity. As one aspect of his upward rise in Virginia, he moves toward a respectable identity, and we are probably to regard his sense of himself as being complete at the time of his first return to London: "I Was now at the height of my good Fortune; indeed I was in very good Circumstances . . . particularly I had the Reputation of a very considerable Merchant . . . I began to be very well known." But he has taken care not to let any of his former comrades "so much as guess who I was," and having, as he explains, become known as "Colonel *Jacque*" during the year in France, "I pass'd for a Foreigner, and a *Frenchman*, and I was infinitely fond of having every Body take me for a *Frenchman* . . ." (pp. 185, 186). The same false identity again comes in handy on his second return to his own country: "I . . . resolv'd to settle somewhere in *England*, where I might know every Body, and no Body know me . . . So I went to *Canterbury*, call'd my self an *English* Man among the *French;* and a *French* Man among the *English;* and on that Score was the more perfectly concealed, going by the Name of Monsieur *Charnot*, with the *French*, was call'd Mr. *Charnock* among the *English*." Defoe himself seems to have become a little confused amidst all these changes of identity, but in any case, he has Jack go on to say: "Here, indeed, I liv'd perfectly *Incog* . . . and living retir'd and sober, was well enough receiv'd by all Sorts . . ." (p. 234). Even "at home" in Virginia, he remains incognito—a fact that affords him some comfort at the time of his Jacobite troubles ("they never knew my Name, but only I was call'd the *French* Colonel, or the *French* Officer, or the *French* Gentleman, by most, if not by all the People there . . ." [p. 267]).

Jack maintains this same dual identity on the title page of his *History*, and there the implications of the alias receive a certain expansion. It seems that the name "Colonel Jacque" stands, in Jack's own mind, for the gentleman of importance he has become during his lifetime (that identity having been completed during his year in France), while "Colonel Jack," being the name he is "commonly called," suggests that lower creature whose very existence he is so determined to conceal. David Blewett points out that one meaning of the word *Jack* in the eighteenth century was a "man of the common people; a lad, fellow, chap; esp. a low-bred or ill-mannered fellow, a knave."[11] We are reminded, in this connection, of Jack's insistence that in Virginia "every Desperate forlorn Creature" can achieve "a Reputation, that nothing past will have any Effect upon"—and that Jack has achieved "the Reputation of a very considerable Merchant." In wanting to conceal his name, Jack wants to hide his shameful past, his origins in the dirt and ashes of London. The guilty secret to be kept is that of his own creatureliness. Only by pretending to be someone else—someone higher and better—can he hope to be saved.

There is a certain irony operative in the fact that the name Colonel Jacque at once defines Jack's gentlemanly status and serves as a means of concealing his true identity. The name is a mark of his desire to stand out and to hide at the same time. Moreover, if his advice to his ex-wife regardng his tutor's proposal of marriage to her is any indication, Jack must ssume that this same desire is universal: "I reason'd with her upon her Circumstances, and how such a Marriage would restore her to a State of Case and Plenty, and none in the World might ever know or suspect who or what she had been . . ." (p. 261). (We may also note here that this woman prefers being Jack's slave to being the tutor's wife. Like Moll, she cannily prefers to cast her lot with the man possessed of superior status and power.)

Jack's secretiveness about himself has been in evidence as far back as his early days in Virginia. He has been content that his tutor should have quite other Notions of me, than I had of my self . . . 'twas no matter to any Body, what I had been, and as it was grown pretty much out of Memory, from what original disaster I came into the Country, or that I was ever a servant, otherwise than Voluntary, and that it was no Business of mine to expose myself; so I kept that Part close . . ." (p. 168). And with a due sense of fair play, Jack is generously willing to "excuse" his tutor from revealing his past: "to a Man under such Afflictions, one should always be Tender, and not put them upon relating any thing of themselves, which was griev-ous to them, or which they had rather was conceal'd" (p. 160). One thing about his tutor's past that he does learn, however, confirms for him the wisdom of his own habitual concealment of his true name. In telling Jack his story, the tutor talks of having been arrested "under a wrong Name." And he goes on to ask: "do you think that when I receiv'd the Grant of Transportation, I cou'd be insensible what a Miracle of Divine Goodness such a thing must be, to one who had so many ways deserv'd to be Hang'd, and must infallibly have Died if my true Name had been known? . . ." (p. 165).

There are times when Jack himself has felt that he "must infallibly have Died" not only if his real name were known but also if help had not come from someplace. Twice he refers to some deliverance he has experienced as "Life from the Dead," and both deliverances have been the result of another's care and generosity. Thus, although he may have been well coun-seled early in life "to shift for himself," he later learns that independence has its problems. When he feels, at the time of his Jacobite ordeal, "at a Loss how to Shift in such a distress'd Case as this," he turns, if not without some misgivings, to his wife ("I was now going to put my Life into her Hands"), and the relief he feels is immense: "A faithful Counsellor is Life from the Dead, gives courage where the Heart is sinking, and raises the Mind to a proper use of Means . . ." (pp. 267, 268).

In devising Jack's narrative, Defoe concedes once again that no human being is ever finally "Ransom'd from being a Vagabond" (p. 156) or "de-liver'd from Slavery"—that every man is always, in effect, "loaden with heavy Irons" as is Will in Newgate, and has "no prospect or hope of Escap-ing." No one can ever finally "live by [his] own Endeavours" (p. 156).

Hence, just as Robinson Crusoe ends his days in *Reflections* on his past actions, so Colonel Jack, as his adventures draw to an end, thinks of making "just Reflections" on "a long ill-spent Life." Jack's story becomes, like Moll's, a confession as well as an account of his own uniqueness. Looking back "with shame and blushes, upon such a Course of Wickedness, as I had gone through in the World," Jack has, he tells us, at last "leisure to reflect, and to repent, to call to mind things pass'd, and with a just Detestation, learn as *Job* says *to abhor my self in Dust and Ashes.*"[12] The truth is, however, that Jack has always, since coming to adult consciousness, abhorred himself "in Dust and Ashes." And no path he has pursued has given him any sure sense of offering a way out.

Jack defines Defoe's own perception of the human plight when he writes of his Mexican captivity (p. 307): "I had here now a most happy, and comfortable Retreat, tho' it was a kind of an Exile; here I enjoy'd every thing I could think of, that was agreeable and pleasant, except only a Liberty of going home, which for that Reason, perhaps was the only thing I desir'd in the World; for the grief of one absent Comfort is oftentimes capable of imbittering all the other Enjoyments in the World."

7

Roxana
"Apparitions of Devils and Monsters"

Some hundred pages into her *History* Roxana says something about her first husband that gives the whole show away. His was, she declares, "a most insignificant, unthinking Life." And she goes on to assert indignantly: "he was a meer motionless Animal, of no Consequence in the World; . . . tho' he was indeed alive, he had no manner of Business in Life, but to stay to be call'd out of it; . . . but saunter'd about, like one, that it was not two Livres Value whether he was dead or alive; that when he was gone, would leave no Remembrance behind him that ever he was here. . . . The Journal of his Life . . . was the least significant of any-thing of its Kind, that was ever seen . . . it was not important enough, so much as to make the Reader merry withal; and for that Reason I omit it."[1] Both in living *her* life and in writing it, Roxana is feverishly bent on imparting to it some meaning, some significance. And what constantly worries her is that the show will be exposed for the empty sham she fears it is. She is terrified of being reduced to the point where she will disappear altogether, leaving "no Remembrance behind that ever [she] was here." "I . . . knew little or nothing of what I was brought over hither for," says Roxana at the outset of her story; but she is determined to make something of herself—and not to "degenerate into such a useless thing" as was that first husband of hers (p. 96).

Much of what Roxana dwells on in the early part of her narrative has to do with what might be called wasting away. At the beginning of her adult life, she was, she tells us, by no means in want: "I wanted neither Wit, Beauty, or Money. In this Manner I set out into the World, having all the Advantages that any Young Woman cou'd desire, to recommend me to others, and form a Prospect of happy Living to myself" (p. 7). Owing to the "good Circumstances" of her father, she has already, at this point in her life, created a viable identity. "I had accomplish'd myself for the sociable Part of the World," she recalls, and goes on to recount that her acquiring "Intimates and Friends . . . forwarded very much the finishing me for Conversation and the World" (p. 6).

But thanks to her marrying—or rather being married to—an "eminent

Brewer" who proves to be every way a fool, this self that she has "accom
plish'd" quickly disintegrates. Wastrel that he is, her new husband proves t
be what she calls "the *Foundation of my Ruin*" (p. 7). Possessed of "no Geniu
to Business . . . no Knowledge of his Accounts" (p. 9), he soon finds "hi
Trade sunk, his Stock declin'd," and his "Money wasted" (pp. 10, 11), an
Roxana sees herself in a fair way "to be script at Home, and be turn'd out o
Doors with my Children" (p. 10). The family was, she says, "as it wer
starving, that little he had wasting, and . . . we were all bleeding t
Death . . ." (p. 14). Women who marry fools may, she concludes, expect th
worst: "once fall, and ever undone; once in the Ditch, and die in the Ditch
once poor, and sure to starve" (p. 96). Thus, far from finding herself with
secure base on which to "form a Prospect of Happy Living," Roxana find
the self she has constructed in danger of disappearing—just as her hus
band and his servants eventually disappear as "if the Ground had open'
and swallowed them all up, and no-body had known it . . ." (p. 12). It is th
old story: eat or be eaten.

Hereafter, the way to Roxana's heart will for a long time be through he
stomach. She must, as it were, start all over again in creating a self, an
what she asks first of any potential partner is sustenance of the mos
elementary kind. When the jeweler comes into her life and finds her with
out "anything to subsist with," he asks that she "give him leave to Trea
her"; and there is something almost primitive in the relish with which sh
talks of the "large very good Leg of Veal" and "the Piece of the Fore-Ribs o
Roasting Beef" (p. 25). "I had not eat a good Meal hardly in a Twelve
month, at least," she recalls. "I eat indeed very heartily, and so did he . . .
(p. 30). After the depths to which she has sunk, this was, she says, "like Life
from the Dead; . . . it was like recovering one Sick from the Brink of the
Grave . . ." (p. 30). And at a slightly later stage of this quickly developing
affair, the jeweler's arrival at Roxana's house is preceded by the arrival of a
"Basket-Woman, with a whole Load of good Things for the Mouth" (p. 41).
All of this, however, is a major step up from the downright barbarism, no
to say cannibalism, to which she has fallen, verbally at least, at the time
when, as she says, "all was Misery and Distress, the Face of Ruin was every
where to be seen; we had eaten up almost every thing, and little remain'd
unless, like one of the pitiful Women of Jerusalem, I should eat up my very
Children themselves" (p. 18).

Roxana's next affair moves her yet another step away from animalism,
since now her prince has come into her life. But the affair does start off a
the dinner table with "three roast Partriges, and a Quail"; and at the end of
the repast, the prince makes the pleasing gesture of pouring "Sweet-Meats
into my Lap . . ." (p. 63). Significantly, however, Roxana's attention is this
time more on the richness of the table setting than on the food. By now she
had begun to "value [herself] infinitely." She has again constructed a self
that amounts to something.

There is a fairy-tale appropriateness for Roxana in the coming of the prince (twice she calls our attention to her right to call him "my Prince"), since her experience heretofore has been that of Cinderella in reverse: "in Rags and Dirt, who was but a little before riding in my Coach, thin, and looking almost like one Starv'd, who was before fat and beautiful . . ." (p. 17). Nearly halfway through her narrative, Roxana is still dwelling obsessively on this miserable metamorphosis. Marriage, she declares to her importunate suitor the merchant, "takes from a Woman every thing that can be called *herself.* . . . she sinks or swims, as [her husband] is either Fool or wise Man; unhappy or prosperous; and in the middle of what she thinks is her Happiness and Prosperity, she is ingulph'd in Misery and Beggary . . ." (p. 149). In other words, she is swallowed up; she disappears.

Not for Roxana the sentimental twaddle about marriage as a merging of identities. The identity the two partners take on, she insists, is that of the man. The woman becomes a mere servant, and for Roxana as for Moll, to be a servant is to be nobody. Both women are outspoken advocates of women's liberation because they find the loss of what they regard as their independent selfhood appalling. As Roxana says to her merchant: "while a Woman was single, she was a Masculine in her politick Capacity; . . . she had then the full Command of what she had, and the full Direction of what she did; . . . she was a Man in her separated Capacity . . . while she was thus single, she was her own, and if she gave way that Power, she merited to be as miserable as it was possible that any Creature cou'd be" (pp. 148, 149).

Even in retrospect, Roxana seems incapable of recognizing how little she ever truly possessed "the full Command of what she had and the full Direction of what she did." She is determined to be her own person. She is adamant on the point that she will not take a husband and thereby give herself entirely away from herself" (p. 147). She has, she maintains on at least two occasions, been "born free" (pp. 147, 171). "I was at Liberty to go to any Part of the World, and take Care of my Money myself . . ." (p. 111), she asserts, in describing her situation after the death of her jeweler. "I liv'd a Life of absolute Liberty now; was free as I was born . . ." (p. 171), she says to Sir Robert Clayton a few years afterward. Yet she goes on to acknowledge two paragraphs later that what this free life of hers entails is, at present, a constant guarding against fortune-hunters, whose intention is to make a Prey of me and my Money"—that is to say, to eat her up. As with all Defoe's protagonists, to be free means, for Roxana, to be constantly on the defensive.

Roxana frequently sees herself as proudly independent, possessed of the Liberty of a Free Woman" (p. 171). Yet the story of her life is a building of defenses against annihilation. Once she is no longer concerned with putting on flesh, she turns her attention to putting on clothes or to furnish-

ing herself with suitable lodgings or to adding to her holdings of mone
and plate or to establishing a reputation.

The men in her life—those friends in high places—might also be put on
the list, except that they are not really ends in the same sense, but rathe
means to all of these other ends. And that, of course, is in itself an irony
For however self-congratulatory she may be as to the success of her machi
nations, the fact remains that Roxana has been wholly dependent on some
one else for the seed money. Just as Robinson Crusoe would almos
inevitably have perished had he been truly starting life on his island with
out any help from his friends—that is, without clothes or food or tools o
weapons—so Roxana could not have begun to build the defenses she doe
if she had had to begin her life as a free woman without any assistance a
all. She is able to play the satisfying role of fairy godmother to her ow
children only because she long before has had a fairy godfather of he
own.[2] Her prince would surely not have come had not the jeweler com
first to befriend her in her "stript" condition. She is able to deliver her so
from "the Fate of his Circumstances"—" all-dirty, and hard at-work
(pp. 190, 191)—and her daughters from their conditions of lowly servitud
only because she has herself over the years had more than one deliverer.

At no point in her life does she manage to exist for long without
protector. And during those few brief intervals when she does stand alon
in the world, she hardly sounds like a woman who has "full Direction o
what she" does. As is true of her predecessors, one of the laments we hea
from her most often is that she "knew not what to do" or "what Course t
take." (If nothing else, she is always in need of someone to guide an
befriend her in financial matters.) For all her "Amazonian language
(p. 171), she has almost as many father-figures in her life as she has men.

Behind her outraged condemnation of her fool of a first husband lies he
appalled awareness that she has hitched her wagon to a falling star.[3] H
does not use his head because he has no head to use: "when he came t
defend what he had said, by Argument and Reason, he would do it s
weakly, so emptily, and so nothing to the Purpose, that it was enough t
make any-body that heard him sick and asham'd of him" (p. 8). Indeec
"this Thing call'd a Husband" is little better than a dumb animal. He is "
weak, empty-headed, untaught Creature, as any Woman could ever desir
to be coupled with . . ." (p. 7).

Roxana's father, by contrast, while he may have had to flee for his lif
has remained, she takes pains to tell us, "in very good Circumstances
Once in London, he has established himself in a position of power—safel
superior to those "miserable objects of the poor starving Creatures, who a
that time fled hither for Shelter . . ." (p. 5). And Roxana's identificatio
with that power is only the first of many such identifications.

In this connection, the conflict that takes place between her brother-in
law and his wife, when Roxana looks to them to provide shelter for he

prood, may be seen as a dramatization of the fairy-tale struggle between the contradictory powers that parents represent to children (and God to man): the arbitrary, angry, punishing, destroying force and the reasonable, benevolent, loving, saving one. The aunt in this case is unmistakably the wicked stepmother. "Well, well, *says she,*" to her husband, "you must do what you will because you pretend to be Master; but if I had my Will, I would send them where they ought to be sent, I would send them from whence they came." Her husband, however, who has insisted on his ability "to spare a Mite for the Fatherless," does carry the day. "Could you hear these poor innocent Children cry at your Door for Hunger, and give them no Bread?" he demands (p. 23).

In him Roxana—identifying here with her own children—has found the second in a long series of benefactors who give her assurance that she will not be abandoned to "lie and perish in the Street" (p. 23). Characterized by "a charitable Tenderness," he is a guarantee that her children will be "well provided for, cloath'd, put to School," and Roxana declares that "he acted more like a Father to them, than an Uncle-in-Law" (p. 25).

Soon thereafter, Roxana conveniently encounters a protector of her own in the person of her landlord—that heaven-sent savior who provides *her* with bread and hence with "Life from the Dead." He is, she tells her maid Amy, "such a Friend as I have long wanted, and as I have as much Need of as any Creature in the world has or ever had" and she is "overcome with the Comfort of it." In justifying her first entry into whoredom, she presents him as the gentleman who "deliver'd me from Misery, from Poverty, and Rags; he had made me what I was, and put me into a Way to be even more than I ever was, namely, to live happy and pleas'd, and on his Bounty I depended . . ." (p. 35). How could she be expected to resist a man whose promise it is "to raise [her] again in the World"? (p. 33).

From this point on Roxana's rise in the world is, in fact, a steady if not an uninterrupted one. Her life may turn out to follow a pattern of being "reduced . . . to the utmost Misery and Distress; and rais'd again" (p. 42), but in terms of wealth and social status, each of her providers and protectors is a cut above the preceding one. And each raises her up to the level he occupies. When, for example, she protests to her first lover "that he was Rich, and I was Poor; that he was above the World, and I infinitely below it; that his Circumstances were very easie, mine miserable, and this was an Inequality the most essential that cou'd be imagin'd," he obligingly informs her that he has "taken such Measures as shall make an Equality still" (p. 42). And when a "dreadful Disaster" occurs, which, Roxana declares, "threw me back into the same state of Life that I was in before" (p. 51), the setback is no more than temporary. Ten pages later the prince appears, and we witness a scene very similar to the little one enacted before. As Roxana falls at the prince's feet and thanks him "for his Bounty and Goodness to a poor desolate Woman," he graciously responds, *"Levez vous donc";* and after Roxana has duly made a few more servile gestures, he insists, "let us talk together with the Freedom of Equals; my Quality sets me at a Distance from you, and makes you ceremonious; your Beauty exalts you to more than an Equality . . ." (pp. 62, 63). A mutual admiration society is in the making: "as the Prince was the only Deity I worshipp'd, so I was really his Idol . . .' (p. 70). And by the time this little affair has reached its climax, Roxana has come to feel that she lives "indeed like a Queen" ("for no Woman was ever more valued, or more caress'd by a Person of such Quality, only in the Station of a Mistress . . ." (p. 82).

By this time also, Roxana is well on the way toward regarding herself less often in comparative and more often in superlative terms. She is proclaimed "the most agreeable Creature on Earth" (p. 61) and "the *finest Woman* in France" (p. 62), and she has "the entire Possession of one of the most accomplish'd Princes in the World and of the politest, best bred Man . . ."—"no Amour of such a Kind, sure, was ever carry'd up so high" (p. 75).

Considerably later in the narrative she encounters and rejects "one of the honestest compleatest Gentleman upon Earth" (p. 158), who appears as yet another savior and deliverer. And he will mercifully stage a second coming in due course. At the time of his first appearance, however, she is not prepared to settle for anything less than the superlative of superlatives: "nothing less than the King himself was in my Eye" (p. 172). She can, in Hobbes's words, "relish nothing but what is eminent."[4] Hence, like Colonel Jack, who—at least according to the subtitle of his history—is finally unwilling to settle for anything short of the rank of general, Roxana is driven to what represents in her world the supremest self-expansion. And we are presumably to gather, amidst all her affirmations followed by denials and mystifications, that she does reach her goal.

One might think that after all this the merchant, whom she at last consents to marry, would represent a bit of a come-down. But by now she has a maturer view of her own ambitions. Or so she would have us believe. Yet it is only when the prospect of marrying her German prince and of being "call'd her Highness" falls through that she waxes eloquent on the madness, the lunacy of women who "fancy'd themselves Queens and Empresses" (p. 235). And there is no gainsaying the regret she feels at having "for-ever lost the Prospect of all the Gayety and Glory, that had made such an Impression upon my Imagination" (p. 236).

Still, as she tells her story, she makes it clear that the person she does succeed in becoming by marrying her merchant is a somebody to be reckoned with. She has carefully laid the groundwork for this claim in reporting to us a conversation she has had with Sir Robert Clayton even before she is launched on her heady London career. "Sir *Robert* and I agreed exactly in our Notions of a Merchant," she reports. "Sir *Robert* said, and I found it to be true, that a true-bred Merchant is the best Gentleman in the Nation; that in Knowledge, in Manners, in Judgment of things, the

Merchant out-did many of the Nobility; that having once master'd the World, and being above the Demand of Business, tho' no real Estate, they were then superiour to most Gentlemen, even in Estate. . . ." And she concludes: "The Upshot of all this was, to recommend to me, rather the bestowing my Fortune upon some eminent Merchant, who . . . wou'd at the first word, settle all my Fortune on myself and Children, and maintain me like a Queen" (p. 170). In the event, the Dutch merchant—who, incidentally, calls Roxana "his Princess"—is able to offer her a choice of titles and honor. With his wealth and connections he can have himself made either a baronet in England or a count on the Continent, and Roxana can choose to become either a lady or a countess. Amy offers irresistible advice on the subject: "which of them! *says she* . . . why not both of them: and then you will be really a *Princess;* for sure, to be a Lady in *English,* and a Countess in *Dutch,* may make a Princess in *High-Dutch* . . ." (p. 242). And with her merchant, Roxana has the added satisfaction of being cast in the role of romantic heroine—the object of a tireless quest by a modern-day knight-errant.[5] Although she protests, when Amy informs her that the merchant has "likely . . . come over now on purpose to seek Thee," that "Knight Errantry is over" (p. 218), her suitor himself later assures her he "cou'd not refrain the Knight-Errantry of coming to *England* again to seek me . . ." (p. 226).

To no other man in her life, moreover, does Roxana so insistently ascribe godlike attributes. He "sav'd my Life," she declares, "or at least, sav'd me from being expos'd and ruin'd" (p. 121). Through his powers, she is "pre-serv'd from Destruction." He is, she keeps reiterating, her "Deliverer." "I ow'd my Life to him" (p. 235), she says at the time she is putting him off after becoming "dazzled" by thoughts of her German prince. He seems to her on one occasion to be possessed of omniscience: "I cou'd not think it possible for any-one that had not dealt with the Devil, to write such a Letter," she says, when the merchant warns her of future ruin; "I was perswaded he had some more than humane Knowledge . . ." (p. 160).

The merchant has, in fact, amply demonstrated by this time his ability to deal successfully with the devil in the person of the Jew who has given Roxana such a fright. If her jeweler-husband has delivered her "out of the Devil's Clutches" after her abandonment by her husband (p. 37), the merchant does so at a time when her terrors of being reduced to nakedness are perhaps even greater. Giving her "Devil's Looks," the Jew has seemed, she says, "as if he wou'd devour me" (p. 113). The Jew threatens "to get the Jewels into his Hands" and thus, as she puts it, to send "me back as Naked to *England,* as I was a little before I left it" (p. 119). Again Roxana recognizes implicitly that to lose one's money is tantamount to losing one's very life.

Thus an important aspect of the salvation offered her by the merchant is that he helps her to preserve the value and hence the power she already possesses. But he also performs another service—a service she expects of all the men in her life—in that he makes a significant contribution to her reproductive capacities. Needless to say, Roxana, like Moll Flanders before her, is a good deal more interested in the potentials of seed money than in those of semen. One produces assets; the other, liabilities. If devils like the Jew threaten to eat up her substance, then the god- and father-figures in her life do not fulfill their proper role if they cannot be counted on to add to that substance very materially.

In relating the fact that she had five children by her first husband, Roxana comments that this is "the only Work (perhaps) that Fools are good for" (p. 10). Certainly, her landlord-lover promises better things: "he pull'd out a silk Purse, which had three-score Guineas in it, and threw them into my Lap, and concluded all the rest of his Discourse with Kisses, and Protestations of his Love; of which indeed, I had abundant Proof" (p. 42). This sexually suggestive little scene is obviously reminiscent of a similar scene in *Moll Flanders*. And so is a later scene in which Roxana's alter ego, Amy— here identified as her "Gentlewoman of the Bed-Chamber" (p. 177)—is involved. The incident occurs when, toward the end of one of Roxana's London parties, some of the gentlemen turn, at "two or three a-Clock in the Morning," to gambling. Amy, Roxana writes, "waited at the Room where they Play'd; sat up all-Night to attend them; and in the Morning, when they broke-up, they swept the Box into her Lap . . ." (p. 181).

The passion that the prince arouses in Roxana is yet another case in point. Not only does the "silk Purse" he puts into her hand recall the one given her by the landlord (except that this one contains "a hundred Pistoles"), but the "fine Necklace of Diamonds" which he later bestows on her during an intimate little scene enacted in "the darkest part of the Room" leads her to declare, "If I had an Ounce of Blood in me, that did not fly up into my Face, Neck, and Breasts, it must be from some Interruption in the Vessels; I was all on fire with the Sight, and began to wonder what it was that was coming to me" (p. 73).

While she is still in her childbearing years, Roxana generally emerges from each of her affairs with an additional offspring or two; but the breeding-powers of her body pale into insignificance beside those of her pounds and pistoles and jewels and plate. (Twice in one paragraph she talks about having left her "old Revenue . . . to grow" [p. 182]). Like Moll, she is given to taking stock of her assets at the end of every liaison, and the results of her weighing and measuring and counting are more and more gratifying. By the time she arrives in Holland after her ship has come to grief in the English Channel, she is already proclaiming: "Now I was become, from a Lady of Pleasure, a Woman of Business, and of great Business too I assure you" (p. 131). And being a hard-headed business woman, she makes of every love affair thereafter a business transaction that turns out to be a paying proposition of impressive proportions. In fact, when the English nobleman for whom she settles after her mysterious three-year "glorious Retreat" turns "his Discourse to the Subject of Love," she calls the gesture 'a Point so ridiculous to me, without the main thing, I mean the Money, hat I had no Patience to hear him make so long a Story of it" (p. 183).

But the kind of imagery she uses in describing herself at this stage of her career subtly emphasizes her essential dependency. After her "Time of Retreat," she says, "I did not come Abroad again with the same Lustre, or hine with so much Advantage as before. . . . I seem'd like an old Piece of Plate that had been hoarded up some Years, and comes out tarnish'd and discolour'd . . ." (pp. 181, 182). What she means by this, she indicates, is not hat she has been "at-all impair'd in Beauty" (p. 182), but that her value has been reduced, since she is now known to be, in effect, secondhand goods. The fact that she is valuing herself here as if she were a piece of plate surely indicates how precarious a sense she has of her own ground of being. And it serves to remind us that for all her pride in her own powers, she is, when it comes to the men in her life on whose favors she counts so heavily, not the chooser but the chosen. She may use some wiles with them and she may strike a pretty hard bargain, but she still depends for her identity and thus for her value on their seeking her out and on their approval of her beauty, their largess, their titles, their provision of well-furnished houses and elegant coaches and equipages. Her landlord is by no means the only man of whom she would have to acknowledge, "he had made me what I was."

How essentially Roxana looks for her identity to the well-furnished houses she occupies becomes clear very early in the narrative. One of the stories she concocts at the time she is abandoned by her husband and is trying to have her five children taken off her hands includes letting it be known that she has left her house and cannot be located. "I found all fast lock'd and bolted, and the House looking as if no-body was at Home," says one of her cohorts to the aunt onto whom four of the children have been foisted. "I knock'd at the Door, but no-body came, till at last some of the Neighbours' Servants call'd to me, and said, "There's no-body lives there, Mistress . . . What no-body live there! said I, what d'ye mean! Does not Mrs. _____ live there? The Answer was No, she is gone . . ." (p. 21). Later, the report is given out that there are workmen at the house, who are "fitting it up . . . for a new Tenant" (p. 89). This new tenant is, of course, the new Roxana, who has risen, like the phoenix, out of the ashes of the old distressed one—that pathetic nobody who has been discovered "sitting on the Ground, with a great Heap of old Rags, Linnen, and other things about" her. The image suggests the formless, amorphous, discarded refuse she feels herself to be at this moment. She bemoans "what a Condition I was in as to the House, and the Heaps of Things that were about me" (p. 17), and a few pages farther on she describes the garden, "which was, indeed, all in Disorder, and overrun with Weeds" (p. 29). The house, she tells us, "was now stript and naked" (p. 17).

Soon, however, her landlord kindly refurnishes it for her with what she defines as "the best of my former Furniture" (p. 32), hoping, she says, "to put me in a Condition to live in the World" (p. 30)—"to raise me again in the World" (p. 33). Not only does she now dress in a manner she calls "tight and clean," but, she affirms, "the House began to look in some tollerable Figure, and clean" and "the Garden . . . began to look something less like a Wilderness" (pp. 32, 33).

Moreover, in the double entendres that precede and follow this passage the identification of Roxana with her house is unmistakable.[6] Having declared, "I'll make you easie, if I can" (p. 27)—a resolve that he soon repeats ("He said . . . that he would make it his Business to make me compleatly Easie, first or last, if it lay in his Power" [p. 31])—the landlord now proposes that "the House being well furnish'd, you shall Let it out to Lodgings," and that "he would furnish one Chamber for himself, and would come and be one of my Lodgers, if I would give him Leave" (p. 32). Assuring him that he is "full Master of the whole House, and of me," Roxana then asks "if he wou'd come the next Day, and take a Night's Lodging with me" (p. 35). Lest we should miss the point of all this, Defoe has had Roxana helpfully underline it for us:

> after Dinner he took me by the Hand, Come, now Madam, says he, you must show me your House, (for he had a-Mind to see every thing over again) No, Sir, said I, but I'll go show you your House, if you please; so we went up thro' all the Rooms, and in the Room which was appointed for himself, *Amy* was doing something; Well, *Amy*, says he, I intend to Lye with you to Morrow-Night; *To Night, if you please Sir,* says *Amy* very innocently, *your Room is quite ready:* Well *Amy*, says *he,* I am glad you are so willing: No, says *Amy,* I mean your Chamber is ready to-Night, and away she run out of the Room asham'd enough. (P. 33)

Double entendres in which Roxana becomes one with her lodgings appear again at the time of her budding affair with her prince. The coy exchange begins with her relating that the prince "designed to visit me in the Evening; but desir'd to be admitted without Ceremony" (p. 61). He does indeed soon make his visit, with the expected result: "It now began to grow late, and he began to take Notice of it; but, *says he,* I cannot leave you, have you not a spare Lodging for one Night? I told him I had but a homely Lodging to Entertain such a Guest; he said something exceeding kind on that Head, but not fit to repeat . . ." (p. 64). Roxana now obligingly tells him: "I wou'd do myself the Honour to wait on him upon all Occasions," and changes into something more comfortable. ("It is only a loose Habit my Lord, *said I,* that I may the better wait on your Highness . . ." [p. 64].)

Roxana's houses become, it seems clear, symbols of her having achieved a "respectable" identity (she frequently tells us of the "respect" with which she is treated), but the pretense is as thin as is the pretentious, formalized anguage that barely covers over the basic animalism in such passages as those just quoted. In both cases, a high style serves as a defense mechanism—a means of falsifying the truth or of forcing it to remain unacknowledged. If the walls within which one lives seem to constitute an identity, what they actually do is serve to conceal from others (and from oneself) the vulnerable creature one really is; and as is also the case in *Robinson Crusoe* and *A Journal of the Plague Year,* "castles," once achieved, very quickly turn into either prisons or fortresses or both. Ironically, the higher Roxana rises in terms of wealth and status, the more vital it becomes to her to lock her doors against intruders—against people who might discover and disclose her true identity to the world. The more significant she becomes—or seems to become—the closer she approaches to suffering exactly that fate against which she has constructed walls around herself in the first place: the fate of disappearing.

As early as the time of her affair with her prince she is already finding it necessary to "be wholly within-Doors" (p. 67), and she is again, as in her days of abandonment, having it given out that there is nobody home ("I made the House be, as it were, shut up" [p. 67]). And she is experiencing that paranoia peculiar to Defoe's protagonists—the sense that the world is full of hostile forces (in this case, spies) bent on ferreting out one's guilty secret.[7] She makes, she says, "no Scruple of the Confinement" (p. 67) that her liaison with the prince imposes on her, and on one occasion he spends an entire fortnight with her: "he would learn," he tells her, "what it was to be a Prisoner" (p. 68). The irony becomes particularly heavy when, as the climax to her sparkling London career (those "shining masquerading Meetings"), she experiences "the most glorious Retreat . . . that ever Woman had"—and actually does disappear into obscurity for three years, calling the event "a Scene . . . which I must cover from humane Eyes or Ears" (p. 181).

Self-concealment in the interest of self-protection extends also to clothing; and in the course of her narrative, Roxana is far more often to be heard describing herself in the act of putting clothes on than taking them off. The phrase "in the act" is used here advisedly, for if there is one metaphor that dominates her history it is that of Roxana as an actress donning a costume and putting on a show. To be stripped is, for Roxana, to be nothing. Thus, in recalling her putting Amy to bed with her landlord over, she says, "I had stripp'd her, and prostituted her to the very Man that had been Naught with myself" (p. 126); and at the earlier time when her house is "stripp'd and naked" and she herself is in danger of being "stript at home," one of the first steps she takes to protect herself involves her dressing herself to appear as a gentlewoman: "I had dress'd me, as well as I could, for tho' I had good Linnen left still, yet I had but a poor Head-Dress and no Knots, but old Fragments, no Necklace, no Earrings; all those things were gone long ago for meer Bread" (p. 29). Amy also has her part to play in supporting the illusion: "*Amy* went up-Stairs, and put on her Best Clothes too, and came down dress'd like a Gentlewoman" (p. 31). Not for nothing does Roxana speak of herself at this juncture as "entring on a new Scene of Life" (p. 25).

During her life Roxana makes one impressive entrance after another and invariably she proves a consummate actress.[8] The clothes she wears, which she often describes in loving detail, are designed to support whatever role she is currently playing; and she takes on a new role and a new aspect of her identity each time she enters upon a new "Scene of Life." Perhaps those she lingers over with the most delight are the ones in which she most clearly holds center stage and hence the ones in which she has the most definite sense of being somebody. In the first of these—her affair with the prince—she sets the stage carefully ("I prepar'd not my Rooms only, but myself"), and we cannot but applaud the performance she puts on. "When he came into the Room, I fell down at his Feet before he could come to salute me, and with Words that I had prepar'd, full of Duty, and Respect thank'd him for his Bounty and Goodness to a poor desolate Woman oppress'd under the Weight of so terrible a Disaster, and refus'd to rise till he would allow me the Honour to kiss his Hand" (p. 61). The formalized diction, the extravagant gestures, the self-dramatization are magnificently carried off. And Roxana has taken pains to make the costuming contribute just the right touch: "I was dress'd in a kind of half-Mourning, had turn'd off my Weeds, and my Head, *tho' I had yet no Ribbands or Lace,* was so dress'd as fail'd not to set me out with Advantage enough, for I began to understand his Meaning; and the Prince profess'd, I was the most beautiful Creature on Earth" (p. 61).

As the affair moves from Act I to Act II, Roxana makes her entrance in a radically different kind of costume, but she is still playing much the same role and is still turning in an accomplished performance:

> I went away and dress'd me in the second Suit, brocaded with Silver, and return'd in full Dress, with a Suit of Lace upon my Head, which would have been worth in *England,* 200 £. Sterling; and I was every Way set out as well as *Amy* could dress me, who was a very gentile dresser too; In this Figure I came to him, out of my Dressing-Room, which open'd with Folding-Doors into his Bed-Chamber.
>
>   He sat as one astonish'd a good-while, looking at me, without speaking a Word, till I came quite up to him, kneel'd on one Knee to him, and almost whether he would or no, kiss'd his Hand; he took me up, and stood up himself, but was surpriz'd, when taking me in his Arms, he perceiv'd Tears to run down my Cheeks; My dear, *says he,* aloud, what mean these Tears? My Lord, *said I,* after some little Check, for I cou'd not

speak presently, I beseech you to believe me, they are not Tears of Sorrow, but Tears of Joy. (P. 71)

When Roxana breaks off at this point to remark, "It wou'd look a little too much like a Romance here, to repeat all the kind things he said to me on that Occasion," it becomes clear that she has indeed cast herself as a romantic heroine, even to describing her neck as "long and small" (p. 73) like those of the heroines of ballad.

Perhaps her favorite role, however, is the one she undertakes once she has her "handsome large Apartments in the *Pall-Mall.*" "I began to make a figure suitable to my Estate," she writes. And the supporting characters and the costuming this time are the most elaborately contrived of any in her long dramatic career: "I had a Coach, a Coachman, a Footman, my Woman, *Amy,* who I now dress'd like a Gentlewoman, and made her my Companion, and three Maids. . . . I dress'd to the height of every Mode; went extremely rich in Cloaths; and as for Jewels, I wanted none; I gave a very good Livery lac'd with Silver, and as rich as any-body below the Nobility, cou'd be seen with: And thus I appear'd, leaving the World to guess who or what I was, without offering to put myself forward." Her idea is to stage, as she says, "as gay a Show as I was able to do" (p. 165), and the results are undeniably spectacular. "I began to act in a new Sphere," she recalls; and her finest hour arrives when, to the gasps of an admiring crowd, she makes her entrance "dress'd in the Habit of a *Turkish Princess*"—a habit to whose magnificence she pays tribute by devoting paragraph after paragraph to its description. Never before or after does she have things so much her own way as in the performance she delivers at this time—unless it is at the return engagement she gives by popular request. On both occasions, she stands "in the middle of the Room," and no one could miss the satisfaction she feels in her dominance. Roxana's second performance proves even more gratifying than her first, since this time she triumphs over formidable competition. "I was Queen of the Day" (p. 179), she proclaims: "I had the Day of all the Ladies that appear'd at the Ball" (p. 180); "I was now in my Element" (p. 181).

At last Roxana has risen to the heights to which she has always aspired. And thus it is that the identity she is now given is the one to which she clings. "I had," she says, "the Name of *Roxana* presently fix'd upon me all over the Court End of Town, as effectually as if I had been Christen'd *Roxana* . . . the Name *Roxana* was the Toast at, and about the Court; no other Health was to be nam'd with it" (p. 176). The extent to which she fancies herself in the role is surely attested to by her giving yet another repeat performance many years later to a private audience.

Roxana seems, at certain times at least, to view the triumphs she experiences with the German prince and at the English court as belonging to her most essential self, since however elaborate her costuming may be, she i insistent, in both instances, on the fact that the face that she presents to the world is absolutely real: "*How my Lord!*" she reports having said to the prince, ". . . don't you know whether I am Painted, or not? *Pray let your Highness satisfie yourself, that you have no Cheats put upon you; for once let me be vain enough to say, I have not deceiv'd you with false Colours . . .*" (p. 72). "Nor was I," she adds a few paragraphs later, "a very indifferent Figure as to Shape . . ." (p. 23). And in recounting her huge success among the English courtiers, she avers, "I had no Mask, neither did I Paint . . ." (p. 180).

Late in the narrative, however, we hear an ironic echoing of Roxana's protestations to the prince when her Quaker friend tells her daughter Susan that "the Lady at her House was a Person above any Disguises . . . and therefore, seeing she had heard all she had said of the Lady Roxana and was so far from owning herself to be the Person, so she had censur'd that Sham-Lady as a Cheat, and a Common Woman; and that 'twas certain she cou'd never be brought to own a Name and Character she had so justly exposed" (p. 307). Of course, Roxana's censures at this time have themselves been all a cheat. She is exposing "Roxana" in order that she herself not be exposed for what she is behind the Quaker costume she has now put on.

What she *is* at this time, according to her Quaker friend, is "not a Sham-Lady, but the real Wife of a Knight Baronet; and that she knew to be honestly such, and far above such a Person as" that woman she has been taken for—namely, "a publick Mistress, or a Stage-Player" (pp. 307, 303). She has by now taken on a new identity, having decided, as she has told us, "to put myself into some Figure of Life, in which I might not be scandalous to my own Family, and be afraid to make myself known to my own Children who were my own Flesh and Blood" (p. 206). It is a "Figure of Life" that has required another change of both costume and setting. "Why *Amy*," she asks, "is it not possible for me to shift my Being, from this Part of the Town, and go and live in another Part of the City . . . and be as entirely conceal'd as if I had never been known?" To which Amy replies, "Yes . . . but then you must put off all your Equipages, and Servants, Coaches, and Horses; change your Liveries, nay, your own Cloaths, and if it was possible, your very Face" (p. 208). The upshot of the matter is that Roxana now opts for the plain style; and as usual she proves adept at learning her new part: "I had not only learn'd to dress like a Quaker, but so us'd myself to THEE and THOU, that I talk'd like a Quaker too, as readily and naturally as if I had been born among them . . ." (p. 213).

The obvious question here is whether this woman whom we still know only as Roxana has any more genuine an identity as "the real Wife of a Knight Baronet" than she has had as the mistress of a prince and a king. And the answer is plain. She is as much "an *Actress*, or a *French Stage-Player*" (p. 294) in one role as in the other.

Presumably, the real Roxana is that naked nonentity that lies underneath
whatever costume the actress is currently wearing and whatever manner of
speaking she is currently affecting. It is thus appropriate that the Quaker
disguise is a better "cover" than is the Turkish habit—the wearing of the
latter being, Roxana concedes, "but one Degree off from appearing in
one's Shift" (p. 247). The point at which Roxana, in her Quaker role, comes
the closest to being exposed by her daughter ("who was a sharp penetrating
Creature" [p. 284]) comes when she has appeared "in a kind of *Dishabille . . .*
. loose Robe, like a Morning Gown, but much after the *Italian* Way." "This
morning Vest or Robe," we are told, " . . . was more shap'd to the Body, than
we wear them since, showing the Body in its true Shape, and perhaps a
little too plainly . . ." (p. 283). The sight of Roxana in this costume at once
brings to daughter Susan's mind the famous Turkish habit, and the jig is
almost up.

Just as the formalized language in the scenes with the landlord-lover and
the prince throws only a thin veil of respectability over the sexual suggestiveness, so do the ritualized posturings and elaborations of setting in the
scenes with the prince only thinly disguise what is really going on. ("I found
the Fellow understood his Business very well, and his Lord's Business too,"
Roxana's matter-of-fact voice has interjected, as she is describing one occasion [p. 63].) And so do the clothes Roxana wears cover only thinly what she
in one instance refers to as "this Carcass of mine" (p. 74).

As Roxana moves from role to role, she seeks, of course, to achieve some
sort of identity, some measure of respectability. And the opposing roles
available to her involve a familiar dualism. In Roxana's case, it is given quite
explicit expression at the time she weighs the comparative advantages (and
disadvantages) of the roles of mistress and wife. Whatever her role, she
clearly wants both to stand out (to have an independent identity as
"princess" or "queen" or "lady" or "countess") and at the same time to be
protected and cared for and regarded as a good woman.

If we now seek to determine the naked truth behind all the parts Roxana
plays, the character to whom we must look is not Roxana herself but Amy.
Appropriately, Amy's prose differs markedly from that generally used by
her mistress. "Amy is earthy, pithy, often epigrammatic," says E. A. James.
While "Roxana is genteel, reserved . . . [Amy] is jestingly disrespectful,
vernacular in her diction, and sometimes slangy."[9] Apparently, it is Roxana's Amy-nature that reveals itself when we hear her using words like *slut*
and *jade* or arguing that to marry the man one has previously slept with "is
to befoul one's-self, and live always in the Smell of it" (p. 152) or saying to
Amy with reference to Susan, "I think the D——l is in that young Wench"
(p. 272), or to herself, "What the D——l is the matter" or "That's a damn'd
Lye" (p. 286). An anecdote that Defoe relates in a 1711 issue of his *Review*

supports the point. "I remember," he writes, "the late Duchess o
Portsmouth, in the time of King Charles II, gave a severe return to one tha
was praising Nell Gwynn, whom she hated. . . . They were talking of her wi
and beauty, and how she always diverted the King with her extraordinar
repartees; how she had a very fine mien, and appeared as much a lady o
quality as anybody. 'Yes, Madam,' said the Duchess, 'but anybody may knov
she had been an orange wench by her swearing.' "[10]

There has been in recent years general critical agreement that Amy—
whom Roxana describes as "always at my Elbow" (p. 238)—is an alter eg
for the heroine. It is Amy ("a cunning Wench, and faithful to me, as th
Skin to my Back" [p. 25]) who executes (and often inspires as well) the self
protective measures Roxana feels driven to take. "She would not leave me,'
Roxana says at the time of her "inexpressible Distress" (p. 16). Designatec
"half a Servant, half a Companion" (p. 209), she promises Roxana at on
point "that she wou'd do nothing but what shou'd be for my Interest'
(p. 215), and Roxana later calls her "my Privy-Counsellor" (p. 242). It i
frequently her function, moreover, to dress Roxana for the parts she plays.

What Amy seems to represent, then, is the essential self behind all th
parts that Roxana acts in her life.[11] Roxana is, we may recall, a French
woman by birth; hence it is fitting that Amy's name should suggest not onl
ami but *âme*. In one instance Roxana calls Amy "poor Soul" (p. 281), and ir
another Roxana's first husband says to her, "*what you are now*, whethe
Ghost or Substance, *I know not*" (p. 88). The French word *âme* is often usec
to refer not exclusively to one's immortal aspect but to one's informing
essence, the core of one's being—hence its particular applicability as a
name for Roxana's alter ego. She constitutes what we might call—in light of
one particular detail several times mentioned in the narrative—Roxana'
sleeping partner.[12] She is her "Chamber-Maid." That Roxana experience
some reluctance to acknowledge this side of herself is suggested by at leas
one passage—the one in which she is telling of her affair with her prince:

> I must mention something, as to *Amy*, and her Gentleman; I enquir'd o
> *Amy*, upon what Terms they came to be so intimate; but *Amy* seem'd
> backward to explain herself; I did not care to press her upon a Question
> of that Nature, knowing that she might have answer'd my Question with
> a Question, and have said, Why, how did I and the Prince come to be so
> intimate? so I left off farther inquiring into it, till after some time, she
> told it me freely, of her own Accord, which, to cut it short, amounted to
> no more than this, that *like* Mistress, *like* Maid; as they had many leisure
> Hours together below, while they waited respectively, when his Lord and
> I were together above; I say, they could hardly avoid the usual Question
> one to another, namely, Why might not they do the same thing below,
> that we did above? (P. 83)

One might say that Amy stands for the underside of Roxana, the earthbound side; and in this sense the above-below references here carry out the

high-and-low and pretense-and-reality pattern we have seen to be operating in this scene. Amy's liaison with her gentleman serves to remind us once again of what Roxana and her prince are really doing. Moreover, when Amy is left behind in Paris, there is a clear double meaning in Roxana's statement that "*Amy* was Madam, the Mistress of the House" (p. 100).

Amy is, in addition, closely associated in the narrative with one of Roxana's talents that Defoe seems to regard as sexually charged—namely, dancing. "Being *French* Born," Roxana tells us, " I danc'd, *as some say,* naturally, lov'd it extremely, and sung well also . . ." (p. 6).[13] In this instance, too, Amy functions as a part of the high-low pattern, which ties in here with the dressed-undressed or concealment-exposure pattern. Thus, shortly after she makes her appearance "dress'd like a Gentlewoman," we come upon the following passage: "*Amy* and I went to Bed that Night (for *Amy* lay with me) pretty early, but lay chatting almost all Night about it, and the Girl was so transported, that she got up two or three times in the Night, and danc'd about the Room in her Shift . . ." (pp. 31, 32). The scene anticipates a later one in which Roxana herself dances about a room in a dress that she describes as "unlac'd and open-breasted as if I had been in my Shift" (p. 181). In light of such details, Roxana's saying about her feelings at this time, "I was now in my Element," takes on a certain irony. Ostensibly she means that she has arrived at the height to which her ambitions have pointed, but there may be a hint that her element is, in reality, a considerably lower one than she is prepared to acknowledge. She admits that in the "easie and quiet" life she lives as a Quaker she "was like a Fish out of Water." Being "as gay and as young in my Disposition, as I was at five and twenty," she now feels quite out of her element (p. 214).

There can be little doubt that the last dance Roxana performs emphasizes again the high-low or concealment-exposure theme, for here she lays aside the "great-many rich Cloaths" she has acquired to accommodate her new title and dons again that costume which, she comments in a passage already quoted, was "not a decent Dress in this Country . . . for it was but one Degree off, from appearing in one's Shift" (p. 247). Her husband, she relates, "knew me . . . because I had prepar'd him . . . but he by no means knew Amy; for she had dress'd herself in the Habit of a *Turkish* Slave, being the Garb of my *little Turk,* which I had at *Naples, as I have said;* she had her Neck and Arms bare; was bare-headed, and her Hair breeded in a long Tossel hanging down her Back; but the Jade cou'd neither hold her Countenance, or her chattering Tongue, so as to be conceal'd long" (p. 247). Amy's costume does not conceal her any more effectively than the Turkish habit conceals Roxana. But probably the more important point here is that Amy becomes identified with that "young Turkish Slave" who gave Roxana the dress in the first place and by whose help she "learn'd how to dress in it" (p. 248). Keeping in mind Defoe's association of the pagan Turks with irrationality and lack of government, we must surely conclude that both Roxana's and Amy's costumes are less a concealment than a revelation of who Roxana really is underneath her civilized exterior. Her very name, which, as daughter Susan reemphasizes, is "a *Turkish* Name" (p. 289), becomes not a self-protective identity but a giveaway.

It is tempting to speculate, moreover, that the French associations of Amy's name (reinforced by her alias, Cherry) are intended to remind us of Roxana's French origins and thereby to supply an added hint as to her true nature. Given Defoe's response to Charles II's French court and his "Lazy Long, Lascivious Reign,"[14] his feelings about Roxana's French connection can scarcely have been entirely positive ones, whatever its associations with gentility. The many French words and phrases Roxana uses serve as constant reminders to us of her origins. And those, along with her insistence on being a "free Woman," can only have had for Defoe some associations with the libertine and the licentious.[15] Robinson Crusoe, in his *Farther Adventures,* refers to the French as "more volatile, more passionate, and more sprightly, and their Spirits more fluid, than in other Nations."[16] And Defoe himself writes in "The True-Born *Englishman*" that "Ungovern'd Passion settled first in France" and goes on to call the country "A *Dancing Nation,* Fickle and Untrue." Furthermore, Roxana has been given her Turkish costume while staying with her prince in Italy—a country where "Nature ever burns with hot Desires,/ Fann'd with Luxuriant Air from Subterranean Fires."[17]

It seems likely, then, that in Roxana's undressing of Amy and putting her to bed with her own lover, she is attempting to become dissociated from this aspect of herself—that is to say, from her own corruption.[18] Thus Amy is an externalized version of that same devil who appears in *Moll Flanders* as an inner voice prompting the heroine to her life of crime.[19] And she is like Moll's governess with Moll, reasoning Roxana out of her reason. "Had I now had my Sences about me," Roxana says, "and had my Reason not been overcome by the powerful Attraction of so kind, so beneficent a Friend; had I consulted Conscience and Virtue, I shou'd have repell'd this *Amy,* however faithful and honest to me in other things, as a Viper, and Engine of the Devil . . ." (p. 38). Roxana's Amy, in short, is that aspect of herself diametrically opposed to "Conscience and Virtue," and we witness at this juncture a lengthy see-saw battle between the contradictory voices within the heroine, each one offering a path to survival that contravenes the other:[20]

> I ought to have remembred that neither he or I, either by the Laws of God or Man, cou'd come together, upon any other Terms than that of notorious Adultery: The ignorant Jade's Argument, That he had brought me out of the Hands of the Devil, by which she meant the Devil of Poverty and Distress, shou'd have been a powerful Motive to me, not to plunge myself into the Jaws of Hell, and into the Power of the real Devil, in Recompence for that Deliverance . . .

Well, I know not what to do, *says I*, to *Amy*. Do! *says Amy*, Your Choice is fair and plain; here you may have a handsome, charming Gentleman, be rich, live pleasantly, and in Plenty; or refuse him, and want a Dinner, go in Rags, live in Tears; in short, beg and starve; you know this is the case, Madam, *says Amy*, I wonder how you can say you know not what to do.

Well, *Amy, says I*, the Case is as you say, and I think verily I must yield to him; but then, *said I, mov'd by Conscience*, don't talk any more of your Cant, of its being Lawful that I ought to Marry again, and that he ought to Marry again, and such Stuff as that; 'tis all Nonsense, *says I, Amy*, there's nothing in it, let me hear no more of that; for if I yield, 'tis in vain to mince the Matter, I am a Whore, *Amy*, neither better nor worse I assure you.

I don't think so, Madam, by no means, *says Amy* . . . Well, *Amy, said I*, come let us dispute no more, for the longer I enter into that Part, the greater my Scruples will be; but if I let it alone, the Necessity of my present Circumstances is such, that I believe I shall yield to him, if he should importune me much about it, but I should be glad he would not do it all, but leave me as I am. (Pp. 38–40)

Obviously, Roxana's mind is as agile at self-justification as is Moll's. But Roxana is far less easily self-deceived. In the middle of a later debate in which she talks herself into the "Lawful" nature of her affair with the Prince, she has a moment of truth: "It cannot be doubted," she says, "but that I was the easier to perswade myself of the Truth of such a Doctrine as this, when it was so much for my Ease, and for the Repose of my Mind, to have it be so . . ." (p. 68). It is such unwelcome clarity as this that will lead Roxana eventually to her fate. She finally comes to know that she cannot outrun herself.

Still, up to a point Roxana is successful at making her passionate, her rational self serve her aspirations. Characterized as "a Girl of Spirit and Wit," Amy not only supplies her mistress with convenient rationalizations but frequently becomes her emissary in the world. As Roxana says, "there was indeed, no great Difficulty to make *Amy* look like a *Lady*, for she was a very handsome well-shap'd Woman, and genteel enough" (p. 194). It is Amy who, in what Roxana calls "the dirty History of my Actings upon the Stage of Life" (p. 75), often does the dirty work. It is she—that "indefatigable Girl" (p. 7)—who dumps Roxana's children on their reluctant aunt; it is she who confronts Roxana's first husband and lies so ingeniously to him as to throw him safely off the track; it is she who makes a precautionary trip to Europe to check up on the various loose ends there and who, as a consequence of what she learns, plants in Roxana her hopes of becoming a *bona fide* princess; and it is she who acts as a kind of surrogate godmother when Roxana decides to take steps to improve her children's fortunes in the world.

As might be expected, though, Amy does not always govern herself as effectively as she might. On her trip to Versailles, she "foolishly" inquires for Roxana's husband by name (p. 67); and in her dealings with Susan it is her "false step" (her making an "unhappy discovery of herself" to the girl [p. 266]) that marks the beginning of Roxana's troubles in that quarter. We have, moreover, had ample evidence of Amy's ungovernable nature not long after the earlier of these two indiscretions when she and Roxana experience the terrible storm in the Channel. Roxana goes on for three pages in describing Amy's "Amazement and Horrour" and her "terrible Agony," and quotes her three times as saying "she was undone! she was undone! she shou'd be drown'd! they were all lost." She runs "about the Cabbin like a mad thing, and as perfectly out of her Senses, as any one in such a Case cou'd be suppos'd to be" (p. 124). The scene is a kind of reenactment of Roxana's encounter with the Jew immediately preceding it, with Amy's terror mirroring Roxana's on the earlier occasion. The Jew is described as putting "himself into a thousand Shapes, twisting his Body, and wringing his Face this Way, and that Way, in his Discourse; stamping with his Feet and throwing abroad his Hands, as if he was not in a Rage only, but in a meer Fury" (p. 113). And he talks in a language Roxana does not understand. He represents, it would seem, those chaotic, formless forces beyond rational comprehension and control which in our night-mares threaten to engulf us: "I thought I never saw any thing so frightful in my Life," Roxana declares; and soon she demands, "what makes him give me such Devil's Looks as he does? why he looks as if he wou'd devour me" (p. 113). Had this "ugly Business" succeeded, says Roxana, it "might have ruin'd me and sent me back as Naked to *England,* as I was before I left it" (p. 121).

Roxana moves, virtually without warning, from a position of power to one of near-powerlessness, and after her deliverance she thinks of thank-ing "the Power who had not only put such a Treasure into my Hand, but given me such an Escape from the Ruin that threaten'd me." Not having "any Religion," however, she settles for gratitude to an earthly father-figure. ("I had indeed, a grateful Sence upon my Mind of the generous Friendship of my Deliverer, the *Dutch* Merchant.") It is of some importance that Roxana begins this account with the statement, "And now *Amy* and I were at Leisure to look upon the Mischiefs we had escap'd . . ." (p. 121), for what Amy stands for here, as always, is that natural self which is the guid-ing spirit behind her actions.

Just when the threat to that self seems to be over, Roxana is forcibly reminded of the precariousness of her existence by the storm at sea. "I had never been in a Storm, and so had never seen the like, or heard it," she says, and the echo of her response to the Jew continues to sound as she goes on: "It struck me with such Horrour, the darkness, the fierceness of the Wind, the dreadful height of the Waves, and the Hurry the *Dutch* Sailors were in, whose Language I did not understand one Word of . . ." (p. 123). Confusion and disorder strike at Roxana's very being, for Amy is thrown "quite down," and hitting her head on the bulkhead, she lies for a space "as dead as a Stone, upon the Floor or Deck" (p. 123). Destruction and damnation become, this time around, prospects that seem all too real. "Here was no Help for me, or for poor *Amy*," Roxana laments, "and there she lay still so, and in such a Condition, that I did not know whether she was dead or alive; in this Fright I went to her and lifted her a little way up . . ." (p. 125).

As Roxana's earthbound self, Amy experiences in this scene a fall that brings her to an alarmed awareness of her low condition. "I go to Heaven!" she exclaims, when Roxana speaks to her of the possibility. "No, no, If I am drown'd, I am damn'd! *Don't you know what a wicked Creature I have been?* I have been a Whore to two Men, and have liv'd a wretched abominable Life of Vice and Wickedness for fourteen Years; *O Madam, you know it,* and GOD knows it; and now *I am to die; to be drown'd; O!* what will become of me? *I am undone for Ever!* ay, Madam, *for Ever! to all Eternity! O I am lost! I am lost! If I am drown'd, I am lost for Ever!*" (p. 125). And now Roxana in her turn cries, "*Poor Amy! what art thou, that I am not?* what hast thou been, that I have not been? Nay I am guilty of my own Sin, and thine too . . ." (p. 126).

Shortly after this, however, Roxana dissociates herself to some extent from Amy. For even when a "reviv'd" Amy sees land ahead, she still expresses some skepticism as to their prospects for salvation: "*O Madam,* says she, *there's the Land indeed, to be seen, it looks like a Ridge of Clouds, and may be all a Cloud, for ought I know, but if it be Land, 'tis a great Way off; and the Sea is in such a Combustion, we shall all perish before we can reach it; 'tis the dreadfullest Sight, to look at the Waves, that ever was seen; why, they are as high as Mountains; we shall certainly be all swallow'd up, for-all the Land is so near.*" If we take Amy's words as an allusion to the biblical smoke and fire of Exodus, then what Roxana says next suggests her sense of possessing a higher vision than Amy's: "I had conceiv'd some Hope, that if they saw Land, we should be deliver'd; and I told her, she did not understand things of that Nature . . ." (p. 127).

This statement surely explains what at first seems a peculiar parallel we are implicitly encouraged to draw between this storm scene and Roxana's encounter with the Jew. For if we are expected to identify "that hellish Fellow, the Jew" (p. 136) who has threatened to "put [Roxana] into the Hands of Justice" with the storm that promises to bring her to the same fate, we are, it seems, also expected to identify the Jew with Amy. The Jew's "mad fit" (p. 114) anticipates Amy's "swooning Fit" (p. 125) and her later falling "into Fits" (p. 130); and his "Agonies" (p. 113) find a parallel in her "terrible Agony" and in her subsequent calling "out aloud, like one in an Agony" (p. 126). Thus the picture that is drawn in the storm scene involves what amounts to a clash of two irrational natures—an inner and an outer, both of them "violent" and one threatening to destroy the other.

Read in this way, the scene can be said to foreshadow the clashing violences at the end of the novel. Ultimately it will not be any external violence that will bring Roxana down, but her own "black and horrid" crimes (p. 243) returning to haunt her. What she flies in terror from and what bids fair to "run [her] a-ground" (p. 289) is being stripped naked and thus exposed by her daughter Susan for the wicked creature she feels herself to be.[21]

Symbolically speaking, Roxana has produced two female offspring, representative of her higher and lower natures. The younger of the two, of whom we hear very little until the closing paragraphs of the narrative (she has, significantly, been harder to find), is a girl who behaves "sweetly and modestly" and whom Roxana describes as "the very Counterpart of myself, only much handsomer" (p. 329). This is the daughter Roxana "cou'd not hear-of, high nor low, for several years" (p. 207). But we must conclude that in Defoe's view it is her older daughter who is her essential self, since it is she who bears her mother's name. She stands for that self which insists on being acknowledged, that self whom she struggles in vain to deny and from whom she seeks in vain to escape—that is, that earthbound self of pride and passion to whom she always remains in thrall whatever veneer she may cover it with.

Regarded in this way, Susan is an inner voice that seeks to reelevate what we may call Roxana's Roxana identity—that past which the current Roxana, clad in modest Quaker dress and risen to the level of the respectable wife of a man of quality, looks upon as guilty and criminal and wants to deny ever existed.[22] Thus when the new Roxana puts down that past self of hers as "some French Comedian, *that is to say*, a Stage *Amazon*, that put on a counterfeit Dress to please the Company" (a statement that contains a good deal of truth), Susan responds by resurrecting and defending Roxana's earlier fictive identity: "No, indeed, Madam . . . my Lady was no Actress; she was a fine modest Lady, fit to be a Princess; everybody said, If she was a Mistress, she was fit to be a Mistress to none but the King" (p. 289). And a similar exchange takes place a few paragraphs later.

If we require other evidence for seeing Susan as "the very Counterpart" of Roxana's prideful, passionate self, it is not far to seek. It is clear, when she first enters the story, that she too wants to be Cinderella. "I have lost . . . all the Hopes of being any-thing, but a poor Servant all my Days," she complains, when the "Lady in a coach" has been unable to find her; and she describes this lady as having come "in a fine Coach and Horses, and I don't know how-many Footmen to attend her, and brought a great Bag of Gold" (p. 196). Roxana could be describing her own early experience all over again when she relates that the "Girl . . . was directed to put herself into a good Garb, take Lodgings, and entertain a Maid to wait upon her, and give herself some Breeding, that is to say, to learn to Dance, and fit herself to appear as a Gentlewoman" (p. 204). In the present Roxana's view, however, Susan has become, as a result of this rise in the world, "a little too much elevated . . . and dress'd herself very handsomely indeed" (p. 198), and an irritated Amy says to her: "Well, since you think you are so high-born, as to be my Lady *Roxana*'s Daughter, you may go to her and claim Kindred, can't you?" (p. 270). By this time Roxana has passed through that crisis of her middle years involving her own prideful ambitions of becoming a princess ("I had a strange Elevation upon my Mind"), and having taken up again what she apparently sees as a life of modesty and sobriety, she has had a good deal to say on the subject of the sin of pride.

That Susan symbolizes a past identity that Roxana seeks to bury in oblivion is further confirmed by the number of times the word *haunted* is used in some reference to her. Perhaps the most pointed example of this occurs at the time when Roxana complains: "I was safe no-where, no, not in *Holland* itself; so indeed, I did not know what to do with her: And thus I had a *Bitter* in all my *Sweet*, for I was continually perplex'd with this Hussy, and thought she haunted me like an Evil Spirit" (p. 310).

If we now turn to the question of where Amy fits into this particular scheme of things, we must first recognize that Roxana often uses the same denigrative terms in referring to her that she uses in talking of Susan. Where Amy has been called "the Slut," Susan is twice called "the young Slut." And where Amy has been repeatedly characterized as "ignorant Jade" and "Jade" and "devilish Jade," Susan is arraigned as "a sharp Jade." Moreover, Roxana has told us early in this concluding sequence that Susan "knew *Amy* as well as *Amy* knew me" (pp. 197, 198) and that "*Amy* and Susan . . . began an intimate Acquaintance together" (p. 205).

If Susan—"a passionate Wench" (p. 269)—symbolizes the past self that Roxana seeks to escape (Roxana relates that she "hunted me, as if, *like a Hound*, she had had a hot Scent" [p. 317]), then it is clear why Amy—still the "wild, gay, loose Wretch" she has always been—responds to this threat with the same ungoverned panic she has shown during the storm. Susan *is*, in effect, Amy; or to put it another way, Susan is right in thinking that she is Amy's offspring. Although it may seem that Roxana hides behind Amy, it is, in a deeper sense, the other way around. More than once during Susan's pursuit of her, Roxana tells us that she would have been exposed had Amy been in attendance. Amy is always behind whatever identity Roxana currently affects; and what Susan seems about to strip away is the Quaker dress behind which Roxana-Amy is concealed.[23]

Roxana has sought, as it were, to leave behind her flamboyant identity and to adopt a soberer one in its stead. And to the extent that she is successful, her Quaker friend, whose honesty she often extols, takes over the protective function that has heretofore been Amy's alone. (She would "do any-thing that was just and upright, to serve me, but nothing wicked, or dishonourable . . ." [p. 302].) That Roxana now identifies with her Quaker helper is made explicit when she acknowledges the reason for "giving my Bounty to her a Place in this Account": "I never look'd on her, and her Family, tho' she was not left so helpless and friendless as I had been, without remembring my own Condition" (p. 252). In raising the Quaker woman in the world, Roxana is making of her a surrogate self; and it is this self who now guards the door of the house in which she has taken refuge. She has been, says Roxana, not only a "true . . . Friend," but a "chearful Comforter to me, *ay, and Counsellor too*" (p. 244).

Still, Amy inevitably remains a part of her life, and there is no doubt some importance to her being identified toward the end as "now a Woman of Business, not a Servant" (p. 245). If she shows herself less often, that is presumably because Roxana's essential self is now farther from the surface than it has been before. She is, though, as subject to terrors as ever, and the panicked response she has to the relentlessly pursuing Susan parallels her response to the storm at sea. When she is "frighted . . . out of her Wits" (p. 268), she becomes again ungovernable. She is "mad . . . stark-mad" (p. 273); we are told that "she cry'd; she rav'd; she swore and curs'd like a Mad-thing" (p. 298) and that "she took up a mad Resolution" (p. 310). And when, Roxana relates, Susan "broke in upon our Measures . . . and by an Obstinacy never to be conquer'd or pacify'd, either with Threats or Perswasions, pursu'd her Search after me . . . till she brought me even to the Brink of Destruction, and wou'd, in all Probability, have trac'd me out at last," Amy "by the Violence of her Passion . . . put a Stop to her" (p. 328). It is fitting that Amy attempts to lure Susan ("this wild Thing" [p. 309]) into "the Wilderness . . . among the Woods and Trees" (p. 314) to dispose of her, for both figures belong to that wilderness side of Roxana which, as long ago as the time of her first illicit affair, she has managed to "put into a little order" (p. 29).

Roxana has experienced another passionate internal struggle when she turns down the merchant's original honorable proposal of marriage. She refers to herself, at that time, as "bewitch'd" and as having "form'd a thousand wild Notions in my Head":[24]

> Thus blinded by my own Vanity, I threw away the only Opportunity I then had, to have effectually settl'd my Fortunes, and secur'd them for this World; and I am a Memorial to all that shall read my Story; a standing Monument of the Madness and Distraction which Pride and Infatuations from Hell runs us into; how ill our Passions guide us; and how dangerously we act, when we follow the Dictates of an ambitious Mind. (P. 161)

The passage is a crucial one for understanding the closing pages of the novel, especially since Roxana then goes on to make use of sea and storm imagery in defining her predicament: "I call'd myself a thousand Fools, for casting myself upon a Life of Scandal and Hazard; when after the Ship-wreck of Virtue, Honour, and Principle, and sailing at the utmost Risque in the stormy Seas of Crime, and abominable Levity, I had a safe Harbour presented, and no Heart to cast-Anchor in it" (p. 162).

Ironically, the survival instinct that prompts Roxana to stay at home in "a safe Harbour" also prompts her to set out on the "stormy Seas of Crime," since those formless energies which threaten to reduce her to their level are in fact life itself. In killing Susan she has killed off the creative energies in herself (note the love-hate feelings that she expresses for Susan as well as for Amy[25]), and thus she has, in effect, opted for death.[26] And the "blast from Heaven" is actually a metaphor for the self-destructiveness her own fear-motivated violence has wrought.

In other words, Amy's killing of Susan is an externalization of Roxana's own violent controlling of her passions; she is acting out a declaration she makes that constitutes the story of her life: "I cou'd not conceal my Disorder without the utmost Difficulty; and yet upon my concealing it depended the whole of my Prosperity . . ." (p. 277). To conceal one's "Disorder"— one's wildness—requires either controlling it by hiding it behind some identity or, if it refuses to be controlled, eliminating it altogether. Neither is possible of course in the last analysis. In terms of short-run experience, however, Roxana's earlier identity could contain and control the chaotic self, while the Quaker identity—involving as it must both sobriety and modesty and representing "Conscience and Virtue"—requires its total repression. It is Roxana-Amy's repression of her passionate, ambitious self that leads to its asserting itself so forcibly, and it is her terror of losing that sober Quaker identity which she now regards as her "Prosperity" that prompts her to kill off Susan.

Roxana's "Amy nature" becomes, at the end of the narrative, so desperately bent on avoiding recognition and exposure that it is driven to strike out in terrified uncontrol. It must destroy in order that its "cover" not be destroyed; and thus it brings on itself the very "blast from Heaven" it has been running away from all along.

From all of this, it is now perhaps clearer just why we find echoes of the Jew in Roxana's description of Susan as well as Amy. When Susan was balked, we are told, "the passionate Creature flew out in a kind of Rage" (p. 270) and was "put . . . into Fits" (p. 268). And she becomes much the same kind of nightmarish figure the Jew has been earlier: "she haunted my Imagination, if she did not haunt the House; my Fancy show'd her me in a hundred Shapes and Postures . . ." (p. 325). Moreover, she is associated in Roxana's mind with snares laid by the devil ("I think the D---l is in that young Wench," says Amy, "she'll ruin us all and herself too, there's no quieting her . . ." [p. 272]). And Roxana finds herself "upon the Rack" (precisely the fate that the Jew has threatened) when confronting this "*Tormentor*" (pp. 278, 302).

Even when dead she refuses to go away. Like the Jew, she threatens to "put [Roxana] into the Hands of Justice." Roxana admits that she could not

avoid "Thoughts, of the Justice of Heaven, which I had reason to expect
would sometime or other still fall upon me or my Effects, for the dreadful
Life I had liv'd." And she goes on to say:

> And let no-body conclude from the strange Success I met with in all
> my wicked Doings, and the vast Estate which I had rais'd by it, that
> therefore I either was happy or easie: No, no, there was a Dart struck
> into the Liver; there was a secret Hell within, even all the while, when our
> Joy was at the highest; but more especially *now*, after it was all over, and
> when, according to all appearance, I was one of the happiest Women
> upon Earth; all this while, *I say*, I had such a constant Terror upon my
> Mind, as gave me every now and then very terrible Shocks, and which
> made me expect something very frightful upon every Accident of Life.
> *In a word*, it never Lightn'd or Thunder'd, but I expected the next
> Flash wou'd penetrate my Vitals, and melt the Sword *(Soul)* in this Scab-
> bord of Flesh; it never blew a Storm of Wind, but I expected the Fall of
> some Stack of Chimneys, or some Part of the House wou'd bury me in its
> Ruins. (P. 260)

The house that has represented Roxana's identity and her refuge now
threatens to bury her alive. She is never able to do what she says she has
done: to "put an End to all the intrieguing Part of my Life . . ." (p. 243). She
may think she has left behind those "grossest Crimes, which the more I
look'd-back upon, the more black and horrid they appeared." Indeed, she
talks of the "Satisfaction" she feels "in reflecting, that at length the Life of
Crime was over; and that I was like a Passenger coming back from the
Indies, who having, after many Years Fatigues and Hurry in Business, gotten a good Estate, with innumerable Difficulties and Hazards, is arriv'd safe
at *London* with all his Effects, and has the Pleasure of saying, he shall never
venture upon the Seas any-more" (p. 243). She later speaks of having come
"so smoothly out of the Arms of Hell, that I was not ingulph'd in Ruin,"
although she admits that she lacked "a Sence of Heaven's Goodness"—"a
Sense of being spar'd from being punish'd, and landed safe after a Storm"
(p. 261).

She has condemned herself to living in a nightmare world: "I grew sad,
heavy, pensive, and melancholly; slept little, and eat little; dream'd continually of the most frightful and terrible things imaginable; Nothing but Apparitions of Devils and Monsters; falling into Gulphs, and off from steep
and high Precipices, *and the like;* so that in the Morning, when I shou'd rise,
and be refresh'd with the Blessing of Rest, I was *Hag-ridden* with Frights,
and terrible things, form'd meerly in the Imagination; and was either tir'd,
and wanted Sleep, or over-run with Vapours, and not fit for conversing
with my Family, or any-one else" (p. 264).

Roxana has survived the alien forces *outside* herself (her first husband,
the Jew, the storm) only to be destroyed by an enemy within. Instead of the
"Nothing-doing Wretch" whom she "was obliged to watch and guard

against as the only thing that was capable of doing me Hurt in the World" and whom she was able to "shun . . . as we wou'd shun a Spectre, or even the Devil" (p. 96), she is confronted with a specter and a devil against whom no amount of spying can protect her. Amy's scouting expedition has produced reassuring news concerning both the Jew and her brewer-husband. One has fled; the other has "died of his Wounds." In short, both have obligingly disappeared. And the Jew has earlier suffered a kind of disintegration or reduction that Roxana finds entirely satisfactory. ("I laughed . . . most heartily" [p. 139].) He has had both ears cut off and been threatened with having "his Tongue [cut] out of his Head" (p. 134). But the stormy violence that Susan represents to Roxana's safe harbor is not so easily dealt with. Like the poor of H. F.'s London and like Captain Jack, she is not to "be beaten out of" her irrational rebelliousness against sober control (p. 272).[27] Not only is Roxana "run . . . a-ground," but she is "Thunder-struck" twice over (p. 268); she is "knock'd down . . . as with a Thunder-Clap" (p. 278) and is "all sunk, and dead-hearted" (p. 280); she complains, "the Clouds began to thicken about me" (p. 296); and she finds herself, she says, "struck . . . into the greatest confusion that ever I was in, in my Life" (p. 274).

Images of a disintegrating violence abound in the closing pages of the narrative: "had my Woman *Amy* gone with me on-board this Ship," Roxana relates, "it had certainly blown-up the whole Affair" (p. 280), and soon "another Accident had like to have blown us all up again" (p. 283). And before she experiences the "Blast of Heaven" of the last paragraph, she has expressed concern at bringing upon her husband "the Blast of a just Providence" (p. 260) and she has herself, upon learning of Amy's deed, been "struck as with a Blast from Heaven" (p. 323).

All that Roxana can do, in one last effort to bring form out of formlessness—to give herself some assurance of having had a meaningful existence—is to write a history that will make of the fragments of her life a coherent whole. Susan has, significantly, never been able to give more than "a broken Account of things." The story she has pieced together, Roxana says, "all consisted of broken Fragments of Stories" (p. 269). And the captain of the ship on which Roxana and her merchant-husband propose to sail to Holland has had relayed to him only "a broken Piece of News that he had heard by halves" (p. 299). Roxana cannot leave her story there. She cannot be like that first husband of hers who "when he was gone, would leave no Remembrance behind him that ever he was here; that if ever he did anything in the World to be talked of, it was, to get five Beggars and starve his Wife"—that husband whose journal "was the least significant of anything of its Kind."

But Roxana finds herself, at last, unable to bring her history to a satisfactory end. It is as if Susan's part of it insists on breaking through the bounds of form, just as Susan herself has broken in upon Roxana's sedate Quaker identity and just as Roxana's nightmares keep breaking in on her "regular contemplative Life" (p. 264). Fully a fifth of the narrative is given over to Susan's story: "I must now go back to another Scene," Roxana says abruptly, when she has, to all appearances, concluded her history, "and join it to this end of my Story . . ." (p. 265). "Fortunate Mistress" though she would like to appear, she cannot quiet her "bad" self—that finite self struggling to be its opposite. In vain she elevates her younger daughter—"the very Counterpart of myself"—who behaves "sweetly and modestly." Amy rejoins Roxana in Holland without being bidden, and together they suffer that "Blast of Heaven." The devil—the "secret Hell within"—will not be gainsaid. In fact, he has dominated the closing section of the book. Roxana has, much earlier, called herself "the Devil's agent" (p. 48) and "the Devil's instrument" in recounting her part in the debauching of Amy, and "the Devil's Hand" in defining her role as whore; and in the final episodes, it is not only Amy's and Susan's behavior that is marked by wildness and rage and madness. If they are devilish, Roxana is herself, by her own admission, "a She-Devil, whose whole Conversation for twenty-five Years had been black as Hell, a Complication of Crime" (p. 301).

And finally she is self-consumed. Her "Reflections," she says, "might be said to have gnaw'd a Hole in my Heart before; but now they made a Hole quite thro' it; now they eat into all my pleasant things . . ." (p. 264). Her narrative must leave us with a sense of incompleteness, since that is—after all her struggles for identity—her own sense of herself. Moll Flanders may have managed, after a lifetime of trying on different disguises, of taking different "Shapes," to settle on one that worked, however precariously. But not Roxana. Her true "Shape," which has been shadily visible through so many of her thin disguises and which she has once called "no despisable Shape" (p. 73), cannot truly be concealed and proves, for all her efforts at denial, subject to corruption. And what we are left with is a Roxana possessed, like the Susan of her recurring nightmares, of "a hundred Shapes and Postures." In *Roxana* Defoe has at last come face to face with the terrible irony that man is *driven* to deny his animal nature and that in denying it he denies the very life he is seeking to sustain. In trying to outwit death—to rise above his own earthboundness—he ultimately outwits himself.

8

Finis

"brought so low again"

Defoe published his first full-length fiction in 1718, his last in 1724. And the two dates mark a clear-cut beginning and end: for the "terrible Storm" that threatened Robinson Crusoe with destruction in the opening pages of his story has—in the formless fury of a "Blast from Heaven"—caught up with Roxana in the closing pages of hers. Irrationality has won out. And perhaps it is only in contemplating Defoe's fictional output in its entirety that we can fully appreciate what it has all along been most essentially about—namely, the lonely and futile search for a significant selfhood in an inhospitable and unsustaining world. We create a fiction of identity, David Hume insisted;[1] and in Defoe's six major fictions we catch six creators in the act. That is to say, we watch each of them carrying on the death-defying struggle to become a somebody who matters.

From Robinson Crusoe to Roxana we observe each of the protagonists engaged in that endeavor which occupies all of us at some points in the living of our lives. Faced with the formlessness and the pulsating energies of that natural world described with such relentless clarity by Hobbes, the human mind can never rest content with a cavalier "So what?" Always we are driven to "make something of it" and of our place in it. The precious "I" *must*, we maintain, count for something in the world. Hence Robinson Crusoe must continually seek new geographical worlds to conquer and must bring more and more people under his rule; Captain Singleton must command an army and a ship; Moll Flanders must become a gentlewoman and the thief of thieves; H. F. must outwit the plague that bids fair to lay him in a common grave; Colonel Jack must become both gentleman and general; Roxana must become a "Princess" and a "Queen." All of them must rise by virtue of their superior wit to positions of power and control.

In his *Tour through the Whole Island of Great Britain,* published in the same year as *Roxana,* Defoe as narrator closely resembles his own heroes in this regard. On one occasion, as he is traveling northward from Yarmouth, he comments on the surprise he experiences upon seeing so many buildings

constructed of the wrecks of ships, and he explains his surprise by observ-
ing that he "was not then fully master of the reason of these things."
Always seeking the sense of mastery that knowledge brings, he refers often
to being "led by curiosity" [p. 197]), and in one letter he tells his reader that
he is "resolved to see the very extremity of" Britain.³ And he sets out again
and again on new travels and piles letter upon letter to recount his dis-
coveries.

Moreover, the emphasis on prosperity and increase is everywhere. Pat
Rogers speaks of the "dogged accumulation of fact" (p. 27) that characterizes the *Tour*, and it might be remarked further that observations about
population growth, about flourishing markets and manufactures, and
about the numbers of ships and the number and size of buildings as well as
accounts of the wealth and splendor of the local gentry appear again and
again and again. Aesthetics runs a poor second to economics, and words
like *vast, prodigious,* and *inexhaustible* occur only slightly less often than such
words as *best, largest, greatest,* and *finest.* We hear of the "best and largest
oysters," "the neatest and finest" chapel, the "best mullets, and the largest,"
"the finest piles of building, and the best modelled houses," "the greatest
and best" cheddar cheese, the "most excellent good wines," "the best air,"
"the best and largest oxen," "the largest and richest town," and on and on.
For Defoe England was a land of superlatives. One is reminded once again
of Hobbes's view that "man, whose Joy consisteth in comparing himselfe
with other men, can relish nothing but what is eminent."

Yet it is not only in his preoccupation with competitive achievement that
Defoe's narrator here resembles his fictional protagonists, for as Rogers
goes on to say, "every image of growth, 'rising' towns or 'flourishing' country" has its "counter-image of exhaustion—barren land or broken remains.
Continually Defoe sets against his picture of health and plenty an idiom of
devastation. His *Tour* is pervaded by a sense of the fragility of human
contrivances . . ." (p. 30). Far more pervasive than Defoe's sense of the
ravages wrought by time, however, is his awareness of the terrors that the
English people have repeatedly experienced as a result of the dangers to
which they have been exposed. In the *Tour* we frequently have the feeling
that Defoe saw the English populace as being constantly reduced to a state
of fear and trembling.

We are struck, as in the fictions, by his sense of the predatory nature of
his world. Time is not the only "devourer of the works of men" (p. 371). He
speaks, to be sure, of Dunwich's "danger of being swallowed up" by time,
but he adds that it is being even more "manifestly decayed by the invasion
of the waters"; it is "as it were, eaten up by the sea . . ." (p. 79). Similarly, he
remarks of the people of Bredhemston that the sea "has by its continual
encroachments, so gained upon them, that in a little time more they might
reasonably expect it would eat up the whole town, above 100 houses having
been devoured by the water in a few years past . . ." (p. 145). And other

images of devouring abound, having to do either with the sea or with other appetitive forces. Talking, for example, of the wreckage of Spanish ships laden with bullion on the coast at Land's-End, he comments on "the voracious country people [who] scuffle and fight about the right to what they find," calling them "a fierce and ravenous people . . . so greedy and eager for the prey, that they are charged with strange, bloody, and cruel dealings . . . especially with poor distressed seamen . . . [who] find the rocks themselves not more merciless than the people who range about them for their prey" (p. 236). And this same region is in some places threatened by crows "of ravenous quality" (p. 238). Moreover, large cities can devour smaller ones, as London "has eaten . . . up" Southampton (p. 154).

Even more common than such images, though, are references to the awesomeness of nature and to the violence of natural forces. Defoe sees the mountains in South Wales as "horrid and frightful" (p. 376); he refers almost countless times to the "force and violence of the mighty ocean" (p. 237), to the "foaming furious sea" (p. 225), that "wild and dangerous road" (p. 137); at times he seems obsessed with thoughts of ships being dashed against rocks, towns being blown up by explosions or devastated by fires or plague, roads being inundated in the midst of violent tempests.[4] And in the same vein, one of the features of a town that he comments on frequently and describes in great detail is its fortification.

In the fictions, however, Defoe has dealt with the existential terrors of an irrational world at a far deeper level, for there the protagonists must cope not only with the chaotic energies outside themselves but with those making up their own lower natures. Small wonder, then, that all of them occupy themselves, as a part of their compulsive need to rise above their origins, with piling up money—high enough to reach the sky. But it is interesting to note that none of them, with the possible exception of H. F., actually *makes* the money he accumulates. For the most part, they all either steal it or find it or marry it. Or it multiplies upon itself. In short, it is not out of themselves that they have made value. They depend for their worth on the world outside the self. They are not, after all, self-made.

The fact is particularly ironic considering that in relating his life story, each of them is bent upon proving that he has "made it." All of them know the importance of making something of themselves. And of course that is what they are doing in telling their stories. They are making themselves up out of the available materials. Choosing a detail here and an event there, they perform the miracle of creation. But they are not truly self-made and self-sufficient in this sense either, for to define the self obviously requires the acknowledgment of another. What point is there to strutting if there is no one present to applaud? Robinson Crusoe needs, at the very least, a parrot to say his name. And what point is there in confessing one's sins, if there is no one to listen? For Moll, that's what friends are for.

Moreover, just as they can never make—or rather accumulate—enough money, enough value, enough power, they cannot seem to make enough of themselves to feel once and for all defined. One of the most fascinating things about the *Adventures of Robinson Crusoe* is that Defoe could not leave it at that. Crusoe makes more of himself and then more still. And the third volume is to the other two what Roxana's Quaker role is to her Roxana one and what Captain Singleton's William role is to his pirate one. We are left in each case with not one identity but two. There has been no integration of experience. Not order but disorder prevails.

What is more, the travelers among the protagonists almost invariably wind up back where they started. Leaving behind them the new worlds they have conquered in all their pride of power, they—or all but Roxana— come back to their fatherland and to God the Father—back to the home that beckons to them but that, as it proves, offers them no more sense of safety now than it ever did.

Roxana, of course, does not come home. She is unable to repent. She remains forever *ex patria*. Defoe's last novel is the most honest of his fictions—and the most terrible. For in it he actually confronts what has been only implicit in the earlier works. Nowhere else does he dwell so insistently on human physicality. Nowhere else does he concede so unblinkingly that the world, the flesh, and the devil are parts of a single inescapable fate.

That *Roxana* is also the most symbolic of Defoe's fictions perhaps testifies to the depths in its author from which it came. The concluding pages have the quality of nightmare. And Roxana learns at last that there is no hiding place anywhere. There is no identity that works. When she strikes down that devilish daughter who would expose who she really is in all her earthbound contingency, she strikes down life itself. In destroying the past, she destroys the future. No wonder that, after *Roxana*, Defoe was to write no more fictions.

Notes

CHAPTER 1. OUTWARD BOUND

1. *The Farther Adventures of Robinson Crusoe;* The Shakespeare Head Edition of the Novels and Selected Writings of Daniel Defoe (Oxford: Blackwell, 1927), 3:62.

2. Maximillian E. Novak, *Economics and the Fiction of Daniel Defoe* (Berkeley and Los Angeles: University of California Press, 1962), p. 70.

3. E. M. W. Tillyard seems to be talking about much this same aspect of puritanism, using different terms, when he says that in Defoe's time " 'trade' was no simple matter and suited more than one kind of temperament. It could lead to thrift, sobriety, and the stable domestic life or it could lead to enterprise, travel, hard competition, and even violence. The puritanism of the eighteenth century comprised both these sides of trade and sanctified them. . . ." *The Epic Strain in the English Novel* (London: Chatto & Windus, 1958), p. 27.

4. It is difficult to know what episodes John Robert Moore has in mind when he comments of Moll Flanders that she "never learns economy." He goes on to assert: "Even the caution which leads her to hold back part of her possessions provides for further luxuries rather than for future subsistence. . . . Moll could not thrive until she was on a remote plantation where there were no luxuries to buy." *Daniel Defoe: Citizen of the Modern World* (Chicago and London: University of Chicago Press, 1958), p. 245. Aside from the brief spending spree for which she blames her second husband, Moll spends as little money as do Defoe's other protagonists except when spending money becomes a matter of attaining either greater security or higher status. The one Defoe hero guilty of "luxurious" spending is Captain Singleton, and he soon learns the error of his ways.

5. For an incisive discussion of this period of historical ferment, see Paul Hazard, *The European Mind [1680–1715]* (Cleveland and New York: The World Publishing Company, 1963). Hazard defines the dominant spirit in England at the time as "a sturdy individualism, an earnest and courageous spirit of enquiry, complete independence in the realm of philosophical speculation" (p. 64). And he says in the opening paragraphs of his preface, speaking of those dramatic years: "Never was there a greater contrast, never a more sudden transition than this! An hierarchical system ensured by authority; life firmly based on dogmatic principle—such were the things held dear by the people of the seventeenth century; but these—controls, authority, dogmas and the like—were the very things that their immediate successors of the eighteenth held in cordial detestation. The former were upholders of Christianity; the latter were its foes. The former believed in the laws of God; the latter in the laws of Nature; the former lived contentedly enough in a world composed of unequal social grades; of the latter the one absorbing dream was Equality."

6. Maximillian E. Novak, *Defoe and the Nature of Man* (London: Oxford University Press, 1963), p. 136.

7. C. S. Lewis, "Addison," in *Eighteenth-Century English Literature: Modern Essays in Criticism,* ed. James L. Clifford (London, Oxford, New York: Oxford University Press, 1959), p. 155.

175

8. Louis I. Bredvold, "The Gloom of the Tory Satirists," in *Eighteenth-Century English Literature*, ed. Clifford, p. 4.

9. Novak, *Defoe and the Nature of Man*, p. 37.

10. Ibid., p. 64.

11. Thomas Hobbes, *Leviathan* (Everyman's Library. London: J. M. Dent and Sons Ltd. New York: E. P. Dutton and Co. Inc., 1947), p. 65. Novak could be describing the situation of *all* Defoe's protagonists, and not just that of Crusoe on his island when he writes: "Crusoe lives in a 'brutal solitude' and, like Pufendorf's natural man, leads a life of 'perpetual doubt and danger.' Pufendorf described such an existence as being worse than that of a beast. Nothing can be considered secure, and within the soul the passions rule instead of reason. Lacking the aid of his fellow man and forced to meet the enemy alone, the isolated natural man passes his life in continual expectation of destruction." *Defoe and the Nature of Man*, p. 34.

12. *Leviathan*, pp. 64, 65. "Whatsoever therefore is consequent to a time of Warre, where every man is Enemy to every man; the same is consequent to the time, wherein men live without other security, than what their own strength, and their own invention shall furnish them withall. In such condition, there is no place for Industry; because the fruit thereof is uncertain; and consequently no Culture of the Earth; no Navigation, nor use of the commodities that may be imported by Sea; no commodious Building; no Instruments of moving, and removing such things as require much force; no Knowledge of the face of the Earth; no account of Time; no Arts; no Letters; no Society; and which is worst of all, continuall feare, and danger of violent death; And the life of man, solitary, poore, nasty, brutish, and short." Novak quotes this passage in his *Defoe and the Nature of Man*, citing it as an apt description of Crusoe's experience in the state of nature.

13. In the review of Bohn's edition of Defoe in the *National Review* 3 (October 1856), the anonymous commentator writes of Defoe's heroes and heroines: "They are all single separate molecules, shifting to and fro in the wide sands of life—touching others, but never for a moment incorporated with them; they all live as using the world for themselves, and standing off from its binding influences; they grasp at others for a momentary assistance, but they never allow another's claim to interfere with their own liberty; they seize with the affections, but are never bound by them; they may cling to another life, but it is with a reserved power of disengagement, as a limpet clings to a rock; they never strike root in it, and grow from it like a plant."

14. Novak, *Defoe and the Nature of Man*, p. 19.

15. *Leviathan*, pp. 68, 78, 88.

16. Ibid., pp. 30, 49, 50.

17. Ibid., p. 35.

18. Ibid., p. 55.

19. Novak, *Defoe and the Nature of Man*, pp. 42, 45.

20. J. H. Plumb, "Reason and Unreason in the Eighteenth Century: The English Experience," in J. H. Plumb and Vinton A. Dearing, *Some Aspects of Eighteenth-Century England* (University of California, Los Angeles: William Andrews Clark Memorial Library, 1971), p. 18. Plumb, in making this citation, is noting the "thirst for knowledge" that characterized the eighteenth century.

21. Quoted in Ian Watt, *The Rise of the Novel: Studies in Defoe, Richardson and Fielding* (Berkeley and Los Angeles: University of California Press, 1957), p. 78.

22. This proves to be true even in Robinson Crusoe's *Vision of the Angelic World*, in which he is largely preoccupied with manifestations of the devil. The advice he gives is not of a kind that he himself always manages to follow: "I cannot but give a caution to all vapourish, melancholy people, whose imaginations run this way; I mean about seeing the devil, apparitions, and the like; namely, that they should never look behind them, and over their shoulders, as they go upstairs, or look into the corners and holes of rooms with a candle in their hands, or turn about to see who may be behind them in any walks or dark fields, lanes, or the like; for let such

know, they will see the devil whether he be there or no; nay, they will be so persuaded that they do see him, that their very imagination will be a devil to them wherever they go." *Serious Reflections during the Life and Surprising Adventures of Robinson Crusoe: With his Vision of the Angelic World,* ed. George A. Aitken (London: J. M. Dent, 1895), p. 247.

23. Quoted in Alan Dugald McKillop, *The Early Masters of English Fiction* (Lawrence and London: The University of Kansas Press, 1956), p. 4.

24. *Leviathan,* p. 1.

25. John McVeagh, "Rochester and Defoe: A Study in Influence," *Studies in English Literature* 14 (1974): 330, 332, 333. Novak does acknowledge that Defoe distrusted "human goodness as much as Rochester." *Defoe and the Nature of Man,* p. 18.

26. McVeagh, "Rochester and Defoe," pp. 334, 335. McVeagh continues: "Rochester says further that to be honest is foolish, that to defend themselves men are driven to knavery, and that virtue is the fair surface of cowardice; and this too, regarded as a description of what actually passes in the world, not as something one is being asked to approve of, Defoe accepts as broadly true. As we know, he disbelieved that a man's integrity could withstand trial. Man he regarded as a creature of prey. Far from being governed by a moral sense, he was not even equipped with one by nature. A sense of morality was an accretion. Hardship would dissolve it. 'Distress removes from the Soul, all Relation, Affection, Sense of Justice, and all the Obligations, either Moral or Religious, that secure Men against another' (*Review* 8:302). (Notice the *against* of the last line.)"

27. McVeagh, "Rochester and Defoe," p. 335.

CHAPTER 2. *ROBINSON CRUSOE*

1. *The Life and Strange Surprizing Adventures of Robinson Crusoe, of York, Mariner,* ed. J. Donald Crowley (London: Oxford University Press, 1972), p. 3. References to this edition will appear hereafter in parentheses within the text.

2. J. Paul Hunter defines Crusoe's action as "disobedience by reason of pride." *The Reluctant Pilgrim: Defoe's Emblematic Method and Quest for Form in Robinson Crusoe* (Baltimore, Md.: Johns Hopkins Press, 1966), p. 20.

3. John J. Richetti also uses the word *land-locked,* speaking of Crusoe's leaving home as an escape "from paternal restriction and the land-locked 'upper station of low life' . . ." *Defoe's Narratives: Situations and Structures* (Oxford: Oxford University Press, 1975), p. 32.

4. See Ian Watt, "Robinson Crusoe as Myth," in *Robinson Crusoe: An Authoritative Text, Backgrounds and Sources, Criticism,* ed. Michael Shinagel (New York: W. W. Norton & Co., 1975), pp. 311–32.

5. For an interesting discussion of the failure in our culture of traditional immortality symbols, see Ernest Becker, *Escape from Evil* (N.Y.: The Free Press, 1975), pp. 69–72.

6. Everett Zimmerman suggests much this same thing when he argues that in *Robinson Crusoe* "Providence often seems to be a method of interpretation, a theory rather than a force. And on several occasions, events suggest that it may be Crusoe's 'fancy.'" *Defoe and the Novel* (Berkeley and Los Angeles: University of California Press, 1975), p. 37.

7. *Serious Reflections,* pp. 178, 179.

8. In the *Farther Adventures* we learn that the Spaniard has similarly regarded Crusoe as divine. He tells Crusoe: "he was inexcusable, not to know that Face again, that he had once seen, as of an Angel from Heaven sent to save his Life" (3:147).

9. John Richetti, for example, writes of Crusoe: "He becomes at the moment of Friday's deliverance exactly like the deity who delivered him: suddenly visible, powerful, and obviously mysterious in that power." *Defoe's Narratives,* pp. 55–56. And Everett Zimmerman writes: "Christ is a role adopted by Crusoe but also sustained by Defoe (Defoe has things external to Crusoe also suggest that he is a savior)." *Defoe and the Novel,* p. 43.

10. This section of the book is particularly notable for its juxtapositions in this regard. Crusoe's thankfulness to his "great Creator" ("How can He sweeten the bitterest Providences, and give us Cause to praise him for Dungeons and Prisons. What a Table was here spread for me in a Wilderness, where I saw nothing at first but to perish for Hunger?") is not only succeeded by his own acting as god-king *vis-à-vis* his "Subjects," but it is immediately preceded by his account of his imprisoning and then feeding the goats: "I tethered the three Kids . . . and us'd them to feed as near me as possible to make them familiar; and very often I would go and carry them some Ears of Barley, or a handful of Rice, and feed them out of my Hand; so they would follow me up and down, bleating after me for a handful of Corn" (p. 147).

11. *Farther Adventures*, 3:6.

12. As E. Anthony James has pointed out, citing detailed evidence, there are in Crusoe's narrative "constant references to himself as savior and deliverer." *Daniel Defoe's Many Voices: A Rhetorical Study of Prose Style and Literary Method* (Amsterdam: Rodopi, 1972), p. 182.

13. Eric Berne, "The Psychological Structure of Space with Some Remarks on *Robinson Crusoe*," *Robinson Crusoe*, ed. Shinagel, pp. 332–33. Zimmerman comments, in this connection: "The most directly expressed of Crusoe's emotions are his fear of being devoured and his hatred of the wild men and beasts who devour. There is for him a fate worse than death— subsequently being eaten up: his body is his last barricade. The cannibals who visit the island produce extravagances of fear and hatred in him—intensities of emotion that are sustained for years." And he continues: "The ubiquitous references to being devoured point to a generalized fear: of being dematerialized—the reversal of the desire to accumulate. It is a fear shared by author and character; 'being devoured' is a way of conceiving of diverse fears." *Defoe and the Novel*, pp. 30, 32.

14. It is interesting to notice that Crusoe does not even consider an escape from the pirates until the time when the longboat is well supplied with provisions.

15. Zimmerman believes, similarly, that Crusoe's "enemy becomes both internal and external." *Defoe and the Novel*, p. 44. And Richetti writes: "This hysterical, formless, and naturally self-destructive aspect of Crusoe is only touched upon, although it is the threatening chaos implicit in his subsequent ordering of things." In a later passage, moreover, Richetti suggests that "the cannibals are an externalization of an anti-Crusoe, the natural man he has repressed by various means." *Defoe's Narratives*, pp. 38, 54.

16. Pat Rogers, "Crusoe's Home," *Essays in Criticism* 24 (1974): 388.

17. *Serious Reflections*, p. 242.

18. Berne, "The Psychological Structure of Space," p. 333.

19. Douglas Brooks, *Number and Pattern in the Eighteenth-Century Novel: Defoe, Fielding, Smollett, and Sterne* (London and Boston: Routledge & Kegan Paul, 1973), p. 25.

20. E. A. James points to a number of instances of Defoe's dramatizing his hero's "fluctuating moods and mental states," among which is his referring to himself alternately as a "helpless Prisoner" and "an absolute Monarch." "We are," says James, "given insight into the mentality of a character who is psychologically committed to making the best of things, and often indeed to making things better than they are, but a character who is not always capable of doing so." And among such instances of fluctuation James cites Crusoe's referring to his island dwelling as, on the one hand, "a Room or Cave" and "a Retreat" or "Cell," and on the other, a "Fortress" or "Fortification" or "Castle." *Defoe's Many Voices*, pp. 169–73.

21. Curt Hartog makes much this same point in his reading of *Robinson Crusoe* as "Defoe's best fictional example of the conflict between individual assertion of drives and the opposed demands of authority. . . . At the beginning of the novel, Crusoe's father describes the middle state in terms that demand not only submission . . . but virtually total passivity. . . . The passivity . . . is a kind of death. . . . to obey his father is to die metaphorically . . . But to disobey is to risk literal death." "Aggression, Femininity, and Irony in *Moll Flanders*," p. 123. On a similar note, Leo Braudy observes: "Part of Defoe's insight about the character in search of

security about his identity is his discovery of the similar anxieties of confinement and free-dom." "Daniel Defoe and the Anxieties of Autobiography," *Genre* 6 (1973): 82.

22. J. Glenn Gray, "The Problem of Death in Modern Philosophy," *The Modern Vision of Death*, ed. N. A. Scott (Richmond, VA: John Knox Press, 1968), p. 52.

23. Rogers, "Crusoe's Home," pp. 380, 384, 386, 390.

24. Ibid., p. 390.

25. This is a point on which a number of recent critics have dwelt. J. Paul Hunter, for example, writes of the episode involving the wolves in the Pyrenees: "Crusoe's final victory over bestiality culminates a pattern which had begun early in his life with encounters against a lion, a leopard, and a nameless beast on the coast of Africa." And he adds in a footnote: "The episode of the wolves also climaxes the motif of savagery which runs through the novel." *The Reluctant Pilgrim*, p. 198. John Richetti maintains that "the taming of the goats repeats Crusoe's own story; it is a reenactment of the conversion of his own unruly nature . . . by God, who catches Crusoe on the island and tames him the same way that Crusoe catches goats in a pit and tames them. Crusoe's entire career on the island as a bringer of order is, by extension, a taming of his externalized self." *Defoe's Narratives*, p. 50.

26. As Maximillian E. Novak says of Crusoe: "he is always afraid, always cautious, and always desirous of abandoning his isolated condition. . . ." And Novak continues, "Fear, Defoe was clearly saying, is the dominant passion of a man in Crusoe's condition. His isolation identifies him with the state of nature which precedes society, a condition in which man could live alone, not because he was godlike, but because he was bestial. . . . Pufendorf described such an existence as being worse than that of a beast. Nothing can be considered secure, and within the soul the passions rule instead of reason. Lacking the aid of his fellow man and forced to meet every enemy alone, the isolated natural man passes his life in continual expectation of destruction." Novak does not, however, seem to me to be justified in going on to maintain that "Crusoe is rescued from this condition by his tools, the symbols of learning, the arts, society, and that civilization which is the reverse of man's natural state." "Robinson Crusoe's Fear and the Search for Natural Man," *Modern Philology* 58 (1961): 238, 240, 244.

27. As Zimmerman says, "Although concealment is essential to Crusoe's defense, fortifications never figure in it. Crusoe fortifies to restore his psychic equilibrium; whenever he has brought his defenses to seeming perfection, he is again disturbed." *Defoe and the Novel*, p. 26.

28. Quoted in Ernest Becker, *The Denial of Death* (New York: The Free Press, 1973), pp. 53–54.

29. *Leviathan*, pp. 63, 64, 100.

30. *Farther Adventures*, 2:67; *Applebee's Original Weekly Journal*, Saturday, May 20, 1721. *Selected Poetry and Prose of Daniel Defoe*, ed. Michael F. Shugrue (New York: Holt, Rinehart, and Winston, 1968), p. 204.

31. *Farther Adventures*, 2:112; 3:110, 202, 208.

32. Ibid., 2:215.

33. *Serious Reflections*, p. 70:

> Tell us, ye men of notion, tell us why
> You seek for bliss and wild prosperity
> In storms and tempests, feuds and war—
> Is happiness to be expected there?
> Tell us what sort of happiness
> Can men in want of peace possess?
> . . . .
> Let heav'n, that unknown happiness,
> Be what it will, 'tis best described by peace.
> No storms without, or storms within;
> No fear, no danger there, because no sin:

Tis bright essential happiness,
Because He dwells within whose name is Peace.

34. David Blewett makes the connection between outer and inner storms explicit: "The storm scenes form part of an accumulating pattern of natural disasters and also dramatize Crusoe's mental state. There is an accompanying 'storm' in Crusoe's mind, a continual struggle between reason and passion, in which his good intentions are repeatedly overpowered by an irrational wilfulness." *Defoe's Art of Fiction: "Robinson Crusoe," "Moll Flanders," "Colonel Jack" and "Roxana"*(Toronto, Buffalo, London: University of Toronto Press, 1979), p. 32. And H. G. Hahn suggests the identification of Crusoe and Friday: "Through Crusoe Friday becomes the modern man, a seething savage beneath a veneer of civilization. He is both cannibal and Christian, a Caliban-Ariel on another Atlantic island. And Crusoe shapes in him what Crusoe really is." "An Approach to Character Development in Defoe's Narrative Prose," *Philological Quarterly* 51 (1972): 856.

35. William Bysshe Stein also emphasizes Crusoe's island apperance as a reflection of his animality. He calls "Crusoe's beard, the perfect accessory to the animalistic costume" and goes on to point out that "his reference to its Turkish model generates associations with the fabled savagery of these Asiatics." "Robinson Crusoe: The Trickster Tricked," *The Centennial Review* 9 (1965): 283.

36. *Serious Reflections*, pp. 100–101.

37. Ibid., p. 182.

38. Homer O. Brown has explored this whole question of the identity of Defoe's main characters (and of Robinson Crusoe in particular) in his article "The Displaced Self in the Novels of Daniel Defoe," *Journal of English Literary History* 38 (1971): 562–90.

CHAPTER 3. *CAPTAIN SINGLETON*

1. *The Life, Adventures, and Pyracies, of the Famous Captain Singleton*, ed. Shiv K. Kumar (London, Oxford, New York: Oxford University Press, 1973), p. 2. References to this edition will appear hereafter in parentheses within the text.

2. John Richetti comments: "Singleton remains a remarkably passive figure who simply has had to accommodate himself to the needs of the moment. His piracy, like his trek across Africa, is presented as an almost involuntary gesture of survival." *Popular Fiction Before Richardson* (Oxford: at the Clarendon Press, 1969), pp. 86–87.

3. Everett Zimmerman finds this the focal point of the novel: "The one element of psychological interest in *The King of the Pirates*—the pirates' desire to go home—is made the thematic center of *Captain Singleton*." *Defoe and the Novel*, p. 55.

4. John Robert Moore suggests that the gunner is to Singleton what Defoe's teacher, the Rev. Charles Morton, was to him. *Daniel Defoe*, p. 34.

5. *Farther Adventures*, 3:127.

6. *Leviathan*, see p. 106. "It is not," says Hobbes, ". . . the Victory, that giveth the right of Dominion over the Vanquished, but his own Covenant. Nor is he obliged because he is conquered; that is to say, beaten, and taken, or put to flight; but because he commeth in, and Submitteth to the Victor. . . ." And clearly, the conquered group in question here willingly submit.

7. Shiv K. Kumar does, in fact, maintain that it "follows the cycle of sin and redemption." Introduction to *Captain Singleton*, p. ix.

8. Zimmerman pursues this biblical reference still farther: "Defoe's narrative suggests the journey of the Israelites from Egypt to the Promised Land, a pattern used symbolically in many Puritan narratives to imply man's passage from his sinful origins to his final redemption.

Notes

181

Like the Israelites, Singleton's company finds salt water in the desert. Like Moses, the surgeon promises the disappointed men to 'make salt Water fresh.'" *Defoe and the Novel,* p. 71.

9. Another example of this same pattern reads as follows: "it was resolved to venture over for the Main; and venture we did, madly enough, indeed; for it was the wrong time of the Year to undertake such a Voyage in that Country; for, as the Winds hang Easterly all the Months from *September* to *March,* so they generally hang Westerly all the rest of the Year, and blew right in our Teeth, so that as soon as we had, with a kind of a Land Breeze, stretched over about 15 or 20 Leagues, and, as I may say, just enough to lose our selves, we found the Wind set in a steady fresh Gale or Breeze from the Sea, at West W. S. W. or S. W. by W. and never further from the West; so that, in a Word we could make nothing of it.

On the other Hand, the Vessel, such as we had would not lye close upon a Wind; if so, we might have stretched away N. N. W. and have met with a great many Islands in our Way, as we found afterwards; but we could make nothing of it, tho' we tried, and by the trying had almost undone us all; for, stretching away to the North, as near the Wind as we could, we had forgotten the Shape and Position of the Island of *Madagascar* it self; how that we came off at the Head of a Promontory or Point of Land that lies about the Middle of the Island, and that stretches out West a great way into the Sea; and that now being run a Matter of 40 Leagues to the North, the Shore of the Island fell off again above 200 Miles to the East, so that we were by this Time in the wide Ocean, between the Island and the Main, and almost 100 Leagues from both.

Indeed as the Winds blew fresh at West, as before, we had a smooth Sea, and we found it pretty good going before it, and so taking our smallest Canoe in Tow, we stood in for the Shore with all the Sail we could make. This was a terrible Adventure; for if the least Gust of Wind had come, we had been all lost, our Canoes being deep, and in no Condition to make Way in a high Sea" (pp. 36–37).

10. *Leviathan,* p. 10.

11. *Farther Adventures,* 3 : 102.

12. Maximillian Novak, for one, argues that in this scene the white man "reveals his avarice." "Robinson Crusoe and Economic Utopia," *Kenyon Review* 25 (1963): 485. And John Richetti says that "the Englishman's greed, suitably punished later we are told, preserves Bob's innocence and makes his accumulation by contrast a blameless aspect of survival." *Defoe's Narratives,* p. 87. Douglas Brooks, however, apparently sees the Englishman as a positive influence, calling him "the guide and leader of Singleton and his men." *Number and Pattern in the Eighteenth-century Novel,* p. 28.

13. It is tempting to see here an irony of which Defoe was, in all probability, unaware. The tone of superiority that Singleton adopts in his exclamation "an inestimable Treasure!" is the same we have often heard him use when talking about his dealings with the natives of Madagascar and Africa. He is mildly contemptuous of their simplicity in being willing to exchange such things as cows and goats and other provender (and even in some instances gold dust) for those "worthless" birds and dogs and fish which the Portuguese Cutler ("our Artist") creates out of various available metals, not all of them precious. The fact is, however, that gold is, after all, dust and that the value we give to it is as arbitrary as the value the natives give to "trinkets." As Norman O. Brown recognizes, "the value conferred on the useless object, and the prestige conferred on the owner, is magical, mystical, religious, and comes from the domain of the sacred." (*Life Against Death: The Psychoanalytical Meaning of History* [N.Y.: Random House, 1959], p. 245) There is, moreover, a further irony in Singleton's tone of condescension when the trade involves things like cows and goats, since while the white men are busy supplying their animal necessities, the natives are satisfying higher human needs.

14. Zimmerman condemns William out of hand. While arguing that he "sums up the contraries of the book," Zimmerman's subsequent description makes him sound remarkably all of a piece: "He is committed to systematic hypocrisy, and bare legality is enough to satisfy

any of his moral impulses. . . . William's practical attitude influences Singleton and the other pirates: he prevents many actions that are motivated by unthinking bloodlust. But having this rascally Quaker suggest repentance to Singleton compromises the moral tone of the ending—against Defoe's wishes, one assumes. It is difficult to believe in any integrity in William. . . . William is one of the few minor characters often mentioned by writers about Defoe. . . . Certainly he is one of the most totally corrupted." *Defoe and the Novel,* p. 60. Benjamin Boyce is almost, if not quite, as critical: "Perpetually eager for money, he either helps kill the natives whom his pirate-colleagues meet on land or he urges that they be spared, ostensibly according to proper moral principles but actually depending upon the likelihood of financial gain. . . . His advice to Bob Singleton, when at last Bob comes to repentance and shame for his ill-gotten wealth, is both superficially Christian and shrewdly selfish. Neither mere pirate nor true Christian nor real pacifist Friend nor mere hypocrite and certainly not a thoroughly evil man, he defies all simple categories." "The Shortest Way: Characteristic Defoe Fiction," *Quick Springs of Sense: Studies in the Eighteenth Century,* ed. Larry S. Champion (Athens: University of Georgia Press, 1974), pp. 9–10. H. G. Hahn occupies, perhaps, one step higher on the critical scale, but he largely invalidates his position at the outset by referring to William as "Will" (which, as far as I know, Singleton does not do at any point): "In Capt. Singleton's helper, Will Walters, the base and ideal impulses are fused, and because of this fusion he becomes a more provocative character than the hero himself. A Quaker, Will—and his name is delightfully ironic—is not only a moral conscience in his frequent warnings to Singleton to repent his life of wrong on the high seas but is also a force of intellect and volition when he advises the often rash hero in cautious and expedient solutions to the many predicaments he encounters." "An Approach to Character Development in Defoe's Narrative Prose," *Philological Quarterly* 51 (1972): 856. Both Manuel Schonhorn and John Richetti seem to regard William as a positive character, but both emphasize, rather questionably, his comic attributes. "Goodhumored, pleasant, agreeable William," Schonhorn says, ". . . modifies the nature of the expedition and makes of it a comic voyage." "Defoe's *Captain Singleton:* A Reassessment with Observations," *Papers on Language and Literature* 7 (1971): 45. Richetti is less certain: "It may be objected that William is merely a comic figure, a cunning Quaker whose smiling self-possession and excessively smooth casuistry provoke at once admiration and satirical laughter at his expense. William is more truly cunning, more effectively ruthless, and much more confident in his power than any of the other pirates, Bob included. But his wry power requires laughter, ours and his. . . . When power really emerges in Defoe's narratives, it must be treated as a joke; that seems to be a way of defusing its subversive accuracy." *Defoe's Narratives,* p. 91. Shiv Kumar seems almost unqualifiedly positive in his assessment. And so does James Walton, who writes: "the Quaker William Walters . . . combines the roles of leader and wise man and converts the hero from amoral flamboyance to spiritual moderation, from self-destructiveness to security." James Walton, "The Romance of Gentility: Defoe's Heroes and Heroines," *Literary Monographs* 4. (Madison, Milwaukee, and London: University of Wisconsin Press, 1971), p. 96.

    15. See John McVeagh, "Rochester and Defoe: A Study in Influence," pp. 327–41. "Of all the writers Defoe was brought up on," says McVeagh, "Rochester was his unquestioned favorite. Since Rochester was also a by word for irreligion and vice—the things Defoe most disapproved of—that should cause mild surprise; yet it is the case." McVeagh later goes on to say, "Of course Defoe did not condone the dissoluteness and profanity for which Rochester was so well known, though he thought him 'matchless' among profligates. He disapproved of them but he was fascinated nevertheless."

    16. Novak, *Defoe and the Nature of Man,* p. 137.

    17. Moore, *Daniel Defoe,* p. 73.

    18. In this connection, a few further observations may be in order as to William's identification with William III. For one thing, King William was characterized by Defoe as a "Praying and Fighting Monarch." (See Manuel Schonhorn, "Defoe: the Literature of Politics and the Politics of Some Fictions," *English Literature in the Age of Disguise,* ed. Maximillian E.

Novak (Berkeley, Los Angeles, London: University of California Press, 1977), p. 35. For another, Defoe calls King William repeatedly both in "The True-Born *Englishman*" and in various essays in the *Review,* England's "deliverer." For a third, he talks of William's having consented to come to England in consequence of "Our Call alone." For a fourth, he emphasizes in "The True-Born *Englishman*" William's gentleness and his peaceful nature—"Calmness was all his Temper, Peace his End"—hence, perhaps, Defoe's casting him as a Quaker. For a fifth, he also describes him in that same poem as having "Prompted the Laws their Vices to suppress." And finally, he speaks of him as follows in the *Review* (7 : 379, cited in Moore, *Daniel Defoe,* p. 78): "Has the King any more bounties to give, any more favors to bestow on me?—Any more smiles to animate me by?—no, no—but I abhor turning from point to point, and forgetting when he is dead the wisdom, the prudence, the anxiety which he exerted for us when alive." Obviously, Defoe saw William III as a "wise and wary Man."

19. "Defoe's perceptions of how madly people act," says McVeagh, ". . . are not far from Rochester's dispassionate removal of the entire ground from under the rationalist's and the moralist's feet." And he goes on to remark, "Defoe does not espouse sense and decry reason; quite the reverse. But he admits that reason is weaker than the appetites, that the latter are ineradicable, and that therefore any conflict between the two is bound to end in reason's defeat. Reason is thus dismissed as an incapable guide." "Rochester and Defoe," pp. 334, 338.

20. "His piratical adventures become a quest for some kind of spiritual anchorage: in a sense his entire career is a search for a spiritual father, and his encounter with William signifies the journey's end. Under William's beneficent influence he undergoes a moral metamorphosis, and all the disparate elements of his life are drawn into a meaningful pattern." Kumar, Introduction, p. xv.

21. Novak, *Defoe and the Nature of Man,* p. 78.

22. It seems pertinent here to cite Rochester's influence on Defoe one last time: "one's suspicion of a subconscious attachment to the kind of thing Rochester was saying . . . is strengthened," says McVeagh, ". . . by moments in his own work in which his allegiance to reason and religion jostles with a cynical perception . . . that all spiritual effort is worthless." And McVeagh asserts further that "Rochester . . . is partially responsible, responsible by proxy as it were, for those glimpses in Defoe's fiction and elsewhere of the fundamental insecurity of man in nature and society." "Rochester and Defoe," pp. 330, 341.

23. The Gunner pointedly makes a distinction between these natives and those met later: "he said it was his Opinion . . . that when we came among the Negroes in the North part of *Africa,* next the Sea, especially those who had seen and trafficked with the *Europeans,* such as *Dutch, English, Portuguese, Spaniards,* &c. that they had most of them been so ill used at some time or other, that they would certainly put all the Spight they could upon us in meer Revenge" (p. 108). Novak states that "Defoe frequently idealized the savage in order to satirize western society," but he adds that "in the majority of his writings he pictured the savage as an inferior being, condemned to a bestial life on earth and to eternal torment after death." *Defoe and the Nature of Man,* p. 42.

CHAPTER 4. *MOLL FLANDERS*

1. As Robert Alan Donovan puts it: "Moll is very much like Robinson Crusoe; both are centrally concerned with the elementary problem of survival, and beyond that with whatever material amenities a hostile environment can be made to provide." *The Shaping Vision: Imagination in the English Novel from Defoe to Dickens* (Ithaca, N.Y.: Cornell University Press, 1966), p. 36. Ian Watt implicitly acknowledges the elemental nature of Moll's experience when he writes, "few of the situations confronting Defoe's heroine call for any more complex discriminations than those of Pavlov's dog: Defoe makes us admire the speed and resolution of Moll's reactions to profit and danger; and if there are no detailed psychological analyses, it is because

they would be wholly superfluous." *Rise of the Novel*, p. 108. Mark Schorer largely concurs: "Strip *Moll Flanders* of its bland loquacity, its comic excess, its excitement, and we have the revelation of a savage life, a life that is motivated solely by economic need. . . ." *"Moll Flanders," Twentieth-Century Interpretations of Moll Flanders: A Collections of Critical Essays*, ed. Robert C. Elliott (Englewood Cliffs, N.J.: Prentice-Hall, Inc., 1970), p. 124. Both Watt and Schorer make use of this observation to accentuate the negative—that is, to argue the case for condemning Moll's materialism. Cesare Pavese, on the other hand, regards the elemental experience of Defoe's heroes and heroines as deserving of our sympathy: "The daily struggle of these people is not concerned with spiritual problems or with protoromantic ideals of passion. Defoe has reduced to its most elementary form the tragedy of existence: 'Give us this day our daily bread' is clearly the most insistent prayer that arises from every page of these autobiographies. It is less true that they also pray: 'Lead us not into temptation'; or, at least, the genuine piety that gushes from these hearts after the most tremendous trials is only a quite human reflection of their need for security and material sufficiency." "Preface to *Moll Flanders*," *Twentieth-Century Interpretations of Moll Flanders*, pp. 60–61.

2. John Richetti calls his chapter on *Moll Flanders* "The Dialectics of Power," but he sees the power game Moll plays as a winning one. He sees Moll's "skill and agility in the game of survival growing noticeably with each encounter" and later, in the same vein, he insists: "The imaginative center of *Moll Flanders* lies in its ratification of the possibility of private survival and even autonomy." And again: "Her resilience and infinite resourcefulness are far removed from any reasonable theory of personality or any possible set of normal social expectations. Her attractiveness stems from her function: to assert and enact the possibility of survival and prosperity in the face of impossibly limiting and even destructive circumstances. We respond as readers to her story because she enacts the delightful autonomy of the self without seeming to violate the equally autonomous facts of nature and society. She is an instrument for our delight in human survival, and towards that end she has to be more than human." *Defoe's Narratives*, pp. 117, 140, 144.

3. George Starr suggests in his introduction to the Oxford edition that Defoe's "narrative style . . . conveys well the sensations of bodies and minds in restless, obsessive motion—particularly the heroine's. . . ." *The Fortunes and Misfortunes of the Famous Moll Flanders, &c.*, ed. G. A. Starr (London, New York, Toronto: Oxford University Press, 1971), p. xx.

4. "The Luxury-Loving Middle Class," 1 [IX], no. 53 (Saturday, January 31, 1713), *The Best of Defoe's Review: An Anthology*, ed. William L. Payne (New York: Columbia University Press, 1951), p. 271.

5. *Moll Flanders*, ed. G. A. Starr, p. 5. References to this edition will appear hereafter in parentheses within the text.

6. Berne, "The Psychological Structure of Space," p. 334.

7. *Serious Reflections*, pp. 105–6.

8. McVeagh, "Rochester and Defoe: A Study in Influence," p. 332.

9. See James Sutherland, *Daniel Defoe: A Critical Study* (Cambridge: Harvard University Press, 1971), p. 185. Sutherland writes: "From what Moll says about herself and from what she does there emerges a character who is both warm-hearted and hard-headed: the warm heart remains in spite of the buffetings of life, the hard head was there from the first and has enabled her to survive." E. A. James seems more accurate: "the persistent denial of finer feelings for the sake of personal expediency does not simply reflect her conditioned belief that finer feelings are a luxury she can ill-afford in a rapacious world, a world in which, during her formative years, she received a stinging lesson to the effect that emotional indulgence and ethical concern merely weaken one's capacity for survival." His contention, however, that she is "far more passionate and loving than Roxana" and that she has a "natural impulse to be good" and "would generally prefer to be generous and virtuous"—that she "usually tries to behave decently"—seems to me questionable at best, as does his reference to "her sincere

emotional commitment to love and her sincere ethical commitment to marriage." *Defoe's Many Voices*, pp. 208–11.

10. Arnold Kettle points out that "to become a maid servant in that period meant the end of any possibility that could conceivably be subsumed under the words freedom or independence, any possibility therefore of individual human development or flowering." "In Defense of *Moll Flanders*," *Of Books and Human-Kind: Essays and Poems Presented to Bonamy Dobree*, ed. John Butt (London: Routledge and Kegan Paul, 1964), p. 63.

11. Curt Hartog concurs on this point: "The older brother and Lancashire Jemy seem more virile, more successful at exciting Moll's passions. . . . Besides being 'gentlemen,' both men are extremely aggressive. . . ." And he adds that "Moll seems to enjoy submitting to powerful men. . . ." "Aggression, Femininity, and Irony in *Moll Flanders*," pp. 131–32. James Walton makes the interesting observation that the "clerk personifies Crusoe's middle station in the same way that Jemy embodies her original dream of gentility. The former is 'a quiet, sensible, sober man, virtuous, modest, sincere, and in his business diligent and just'. . . . The latter is 'tall, well-shap'd' and 'had an extraordinary address. . . .'" "The Romance of Gentility," p. 117.

12. Richetti also recognizes the symbolic import of Newgate. "What matters about Newgate," he argues, "is not its concrete existence as a wretched habitation but its power to suppress and transform the self." For Richetti, however, Newgate is emblematic more in a sociological than a psychological sense: "The prison is a concrete embodiment of social restriction, unlike anything Moll has so far had to deal with in its effective concreteness, its real and effective exemplification of the control that society aspires to exercise over the self. . . . Newgate is primarily, therefore, irresistible social fact, the distilled compulsion that Moll escaped by instinct and luck as a child in Colchester and which now gathers its forces for one great assault on her extraordinary freedom." *Defoe's Narratives*, pp. 132–35.

13. Frederick R. Karl too regards Newgate as "the ultimate death symbol." "Moll's Many-Colored Coat: Veil and Disguise in the Fiction of Defoe," *Studies in the Novel, North Texas State* 5 (1973): 90; and David Blewett makes the point that "Newgate means for Moll not merely the misery and humiliation of that 'hellish' place, but the discovery of her identity, the place where the other thieves finally, and triumphantly, call her Mary Flanders." *Defoe's Art of Fiction*, p. 80.

14. *Farther Adventures*, 3:202.

15. In this connection, John Richetti says of Moll: "Like all of Defoe's characters, she learns to be more horrified by disorder than by evil. We can add that as characters in fiction they are justified in equating disorder and evil, for disorder precludes the order that constitutes being and freedom for a character." *Defoe's Narratives*, p. 109.

16. Ernest Becker, *Escape from Evil*, p. 81.

17. M. A. Goldberg supplies a beautifully succinct summary of the assumptions implicit in such passages as these: "Contrary to traditional allegory, evil is identified by Moll, not with the substantive world of things, but with poverty and a lack of substance, and virtue is identifiable with the world of material possessions—with commerce, luxury, wealth, and rank. . . . evil is the consequence of poverty in Moll's world, not its cause. And virtue does not bring about wealth; money is what opens the way to virtue." "*Moll Flanders*: Christian Allegory in a Hobbesian Mode," *University Review* 33 (1967): 275.

18. Norman O. Brown, *Life Against Death*, p. 251.

19. Afterword, Daniel Defoe, *The Fortunes and Misfortunes of the Famous Moll Flanders, &c.* (New York and Scarborough, Ontario: New American Library, 1964), p. 308.

20. Van Ghent, "On *Moll Flanders*," *Daniel Defoe*, ed. Byrd, p. 138.

21. *Life Against Death*, p. 287.

22. I am indebted for much of this to Terence Martin, "The Unity of *Moll Flanders*," *Modern Language Quarterly* 22 (1961): 117. Robert A. Erickson also underlines this aspect of Moll's thefts: "'the little Bundle wrapt in a white cloth' . . . is reminiscent of a newborn baby placed upon or near the itinerant midwife stool" and "the adjectives for describing babies and

watches in the novel are almost interchangeable ('pretty,' 'brave,' 'fine,' 'good,' 'charming'), both entities are small and delicate (possessing 'faces' and 'hands'). . . ." "Moll's Fate: 'Mother Midnight' and *Moll Flanders,*" *Studies in Philology* 76 (1979): 87, 91.

23. Becker, *Escape from Evil,* p. 83. Robert Alter recognizes the truth of this but continues to treat it ironically in the Van Ghent vein: "It is not surprising that, since the hell of *Moll Flanders* lies no deeper than the foundation stones of Newgate, there is one universally efficacious golden bough with which a soul can descend into 'all the horrors of that dismal place,' and return unscathed. For the literalist Defoe, of course, the golden bough is literally gold and nothing else. As long as a man possesses an adequate amount of cash, he need fear no evil. . . . If the characters in Defoe's novels never admit so frankly that money is their god, money is certainly the one sure sign for them that grace has been granted them by the God of the Christians. . . . And it is true, at least in one sense, that *Moll Flanders* is a fundamentally religious novel. If we adopt the broad definition of religion suggested by the modern existentialist theologians—an activity directed toward an ultimate concern—Moll can be described as a believer never remiss in her religious duties. In this respect, Defoe's novel looks . . . forward to the nineteenth century, to Balzac and the portrayal in the novel of the all-consuming quest for wealth." *Rogue's Progress: Studies in the Picaresque Novel* (Cambridge: Harvard University Press, 1964), pp. 75–77.

24. Van Ghent, "On *Moll Flanders,*" p. 128.

25. Becker, *Escape from Evil,* p. 83.

26. Arthur Sherbo comments at some length on "the recurrent theme of friendlessness and helplessness alternating with that of the acquisition of a friend and a renewed will to survive." He does not make much of the point, however, beyond remarking that the same is true in *Roxana* ("both Moll and Roxana are miserable when they are without somebody to lean on for help and advice") and that "Defoe himself expressed the same feeling about friends." "Moll's Friends," in Arthur Sherbo, *Studies in the Eighteenth Century English Novel* (East Lansing: Michigan State University Press, 1969), pp. 168–70.

27. *Leviathan,* p. 43.

28. As Lee Edwards says, "Man, in *Moll Flanders,* is most often brought to God by bounty." "Between the Real and the Moral: Problems in the Structure of *Moll Flanders,*" *Twentieth-Century Interpretations of Moll Flanders,* p. 104.

29. "The Defoe hero," says G. A. Starr, "yearns for a perfect community, more often represented in terms of parent-child than of husband-wife relationships. His dream of familial paradise comes true when he manages to find extraordinary exemplars of parental or filial loyalty, who echo God's assurance to Crusoe: 'I will never, never leave thee, nor forsake thee'." Introduction, p. x.

30. "seeing the Infant is first in the power of the Mother, so as she may either nourish or expose it; if she nourish it, it oweth its life to the Mother; and is therefore obliged to obey her, rather than any other; and by consequence the Dominion over it is hers. But if she expose it, and another find, and nourish it, the Dominion is in him that nourisheth it. For it ought to obey him by whom it is preserved; because preservation of life being the end, for which one man becomes subject to another, every man is supposed to promise obedience, to him, in whose power it is to save, or destroy him." *Leviathan,* p. 105.

31. Novak, "Defoe's 'Indifferent Monitor': The Complexity of *Moll Flanders,*" *Eighteenth-Century Studies* 3 (1973): 352.

32. As Maximillian E. Novak says, according to the dictates of natural law with which Defoe was familiar, "self-preservation is allowed to take precedence over parental love." "Conscious Irony in *Moll Flanders:* Facts and Problems," *Twentieth-Century Interpretations of Moll Flanders,* p. 44.

33. Novak, who, it seems to me, has written most persuasively and helpfully on the subject, assumes a conflict between conscience and necessity, between the Moll who is a Christian penitent and the Moll who "operates on a level of natural law"—between "moral principle or

. . . Christian virtue" and "the law of self-preservation." (See "The Problem of Necessity in Defoe's Fiction," *Philological Quarterly* 40 (1961): 513–24.) "When," says Novak elsewhere, "Moll blames herself for her crimes she judges herself from a standpoint of divine law and excuses herself on grounds of natural law." (See "Conscious Irony in *Moll Flanders*," p. 45.) And essentially Novak argues that the irony develops when, for Moll, "necessities" are no longer a problem and yet she is still falling back on that argument in her self-justifications: "Moll has no justifications for her actions after she has acquired wealth. Not only are we told that Moll is no longer in a state of necessity, but two false speeches on poverty are inserted ironically. . . . The difference between the perfunctory tone of these speeches and the conviction of the earlier utterances is unmistakable." "The Problem of Necessity," p. 522. Howard Koonce, who has also devoted an extensive article to the problem, sums his position up as follows: "On the one hand, we have a character compelled towards self-realization and able to act in a series of situations where real spiritual and moral awareness would be paralyzing. And on the other, we have that character's compulsion towards a moral and spiritual respectability which needs that awareness to be valid. It is the juxtaposition of these two forces that creates the real and sustaining conflict of the piece. And it is this conflict that Defoe resolves into the delightful muddle of *Moll Flanders*." "Moll's Muddle," *Twentieth-Century Interpretations of Moll Flanders*, p. 58. Lee Edwards takes exception to Koonce's basic position, and finds in *Moll Flanders* not "muddle" but "wobble." She points out that "the passages of moral evaluation [are] separated from the presentation of the incident itself" and concludes: "Far from being productive of a fruitful ironic tension, the opposition between the real and the moral in *Moll Flanders* is productive only of wobble." "Between the Real and the Moral," pp. 100, 97. Robert Donovan detects "two Molls," an "assumed self" and a "real self," the latter a "vegetable tropism that draws her to comfort and security," the former a false moral and religious identity. Ian Watt cites Donovan's argument approvingly and decides that there is a "pressing and yet finally unresolved conflict in *Moll Flanders* between spirit and matter, between salvation and ill-gotten gains, between love and egoism, between feeling and reason." "The Recent Critical Fortunes of *Moll Flanders*," *Eighteenth-Century Studies* 1 (1973): 125. And finally (although I do not mean to imply that this brief overview amounts to anything like an exhaustive summary) E. A. James follows this same general line of thinking in that he talks of one passage in Moll's narrative as involving a "glaring inconsistency between her preceding actions and subsequent protestations." *Defoe's Many Voices*, pp. 203–4.

34. Maximillian Novak "The Problem of Necessity in Defoe's Fiction," p. 517.

35. Maximillian Novak, "Conscious Irony in *Moll Flanders*," p. 43.

36. Ibid.

37. James, *Defoe's Many Voices*, p. 204.

38. Koonce, "Moll's Muddle: Defoe's Use of Irony in *Moll Flanders*," p. 50.

39. James, *Defoe's Many Voices*, pp. 210–11, 219.

40. *Serious Reflections*, p. 179.

CHAPTER 5. *A JOURNAL OF THE PLAGUE YEAR*

1. Defoe's account of the plague of 1665 in London has until relatively recently been regarded as closer to history than to fiction, and there can never, presumably, be any final word on that point with which everyone can be persuaded to agree. We now know, thanks to the patient efforts of a number of scholars, a good deal about Defoe's sources, and we know that the narrator who signs himself H. F. at the end of the *Journal* was Defoe's uncle Henry Foe, an unmarried saddler who lived in Aldgate at the time of the plague. (See F. Bastian, "Defoe's *Journal of the Plague Year* Reconsidered," *Review of English Studies* 16 (1965): 151–73.) The question here is the extent to which Defoe merely copied from sources. If the borrowing was extensive, then obviously any effort to "interpret" the *Journal* is rendered absurd.

On the subject of Defoe's borrowings, Bastian states categorically that "Henry Foe can have left nothing in the nature of a journal or diary, and that if he did leave any 'memorandums', they must have been scrappy in the extreme." And he goes on to argue: "To a large extent 'H. F.' was a convenient mask from behind which comes the voice of Defoe himself." But he still concludes that since there has been no imaginative "transmutation" of the factual, the *Journal* must be said to be "closer to our idea of history than to that of fiction."

It has often been argued, however, that whether we regard the *Journal* as a work of fiction or not, we must regard H. F. as, essentially, a fictitious character—as much a creation of Defoe's imagination as a Robinson Crusoe, a Moll Flanders or a Colonel Jack (all of whom have also been seen as projections of Defoe himself). Behind my own presentation here lies the conviction that H. F. is not Defoe but a typical Defoe character in a typical Defoe situation.

Maximillian Novak, while concurring on the question of the *Journal* as a fiction, sees it quite differently in terms of central focus: "the *Journal* focuses exclusively on London and its surroundings and is, in spite of considerable historical accuracy, fictional in its narrative viewpoint and overall structure. Neither the life of the time nor even the life of the plague went on in quite the way Defoe presented it. It is a novel with a collective hero—the London poor—and though it ends with the triumphant voice of the Saddler proclaiming his survival, it is the survival of London that matters." "Defoe and the Disordered City," *PMLA* 92 (1977): 243. Everett Zimmerman, on the other hand, maintains, "It is the intensity of the focus on the narrator that makes *A Journal of the Plague Year* something more like a novel than like either history or the seventeenth-century pious writings that lie in the background." And of the narrator Zimmerman has said earlier: "The disorienting forces of the plague expose the tensions within him, and we see his conflicts and mounting anxiety. The focus in Defoe is on the narrator; we are left with a character, not a lesson." "H. F.'s Meditations: *A Journal of the Plague Year*," *PMLA* 87 (1972): 417, 422.

2. *A Journal of the Plague Year: being Observations or Memorials of the most Remarkable Occurrences as well Publick as Private, which happened in London during the last Great Visitation in 1665*, ed. Louis Landa (Oxford, New York, Toronto: Oxford University Press, 1969), p. 236. References to this edition will appear hereafter in parentheses within the text.

3. My argument on this subject differs radically from those of both Michael Schonhorn ("Defoe's *Journal of the Plague Year*: Topography and Intention," *Review of English Studies* 19 (1968): 382–402) and Maximillian Novak in the article cited above. Schonhorn sees the *Journal* as "a song of praise to an older England." It is, he says, "a reminder of the prodigious charity and benevolence of the London citizenry in the past. And above all it is a clearly stated plea for sanity and tolerance in religious matters. . . . Everything has been seen in the best possible light" (pp. 397, 398). Similarly, Novak maintains that "the main impulse behind *A Journal of the Plague Year* was a demonstration of human pity and fellowship in the worst of disasters. . . . Defoe achieves his effect by showing a London in 1665 in which family love frequently triumphed over the drive for self-preservation" (p. 248). W. Austin Flanders seems to fall about halfway between these contentions and my own. He speaks of "Defoe's ambivalent feelings about his moral relationships. Where economic well-being and self-preservation are paramount, Defoe seems to anticipate modern attitudes of indifference toward our neighbors, especially obvious in the cities; on the other hand, when he asserts the duties of men to their fellows, he implies the view that responsibility for one's brother sufferers is a spiritual duty. . . ." I cannot at all agree with Flanders, however, when he argues that "the charitable frame of mind is shown to be essential to saving others from the plague; it is implied throughout that the refusal to give in to madness, hysteria, and hardness of heart preserves H. F. from the plague." "Defoe's *Journal of the Plague Year* and the Modern Urban Experience," *Daniel Defoe*, ed. Byrd, pp. 166–67.

4. Foreword to Daniel Defoe, *A Journal of the Plague Year* (New York and Scarborough, Ontario: New American Library, 1960), p. viii.

5. Zimmerman says, in citing this passage: "What has the most vivid effect upon H. F. is

not the repentance of the people but the almost total moral collapse brought by the plague. . . ." "H. F.'s Meditations," p. 419. In the passage in question, however, H. F. puts no emphasis at all, it seems to me, on what Zimmerman terms "moral collapse," and H. F.'s tone here seems to be one of acceptance rather than either horror or condemnation. In fact, it is questionable whether either he or Defoe would have regarded the situation as involving a moral collapse, since as Novak has shown, the natural law of self-preservation took precedence over the moral law in Defoe's scheme of things. It is certainly true, as Novak says in his article on the *Journal*, that H. F. tells stories "in which family love . . . triumphed over the drive for self-preservation." But most, if not all, the instances he cites of self-sacrifice have to do with parents sacrificing themselves for their children. H. F. makes no self-sacrificing efforts on behalf of his own little family (and does not condemn himself on that account). He does, it is true, make sure that they remain locked up, but then he cannot bring himself to do the same; hence, although he takes no note of it and in fact seems unaware of the danger to his family, he becomes a potential plague-carrier himself.

6. Zimmerman, in dealing with this passage as well as with what follows, argues that "H. F.'s confidence in his decision cannot be the reader's." The problem with such an argument is that it is the H. F. who is telling the story, not the one experiencing the indecision, who asks that we be "in such a case . . . directed what to do." "I mention this story," he says, using the present tense. As will shortly become clear, I concur entirely in Zimmerman's view that we have here an instance of "a man's choosing or accepting only that which is in accord with his own will"—hence the omitted passages from the biblical text—but I by no means agree with him when he says, "The *Journal* makes clear that H. F.'s decision to remain was wrong. The advice he finally gives is not to imitate his choice but to recognize his folly." "H. F.'s Meditations," p. 418. It seems to me that what Zimmerman repeatedly describes as H. F.'s "confusions" extends to this "particular" as well as to a number of other particulars in the *Journal*. Nor does it seem to me accurate to state that H. F. "reconsiders the implications of his choice and finally repents of it, seeing it as sinful presumption, not trust in God." I find no indication of any such conclusion on H. F.'s part. He himself never suggests that his repentance is anything but fear-inspired. He notes that the "lamentable Cries . . . would Pierce the very Heart to think of, especially when it was to be considered that the same dreadful Scourge might be expected every moment to seize upon our selves." And he does not seem thereafter to be talking about his repentance of his "sinful presumption" when he avers, "I cannot say, but that now I began to faint in my Resolutions, my Heart fail'd me very much, and sorely I repented of my Rashness" (p. 76).

7. Quoted in Becker, *Denial of Death,* p. 134.

8. It will be evident in the next few pages that I cannot regard Defoe's *Journal* as presenting London's poor primarily in a heroic light, as Novak would have it. Nor can I see H. F. as "a completely humane narrator whose all-pervading sympathy for human suffering extended to characters from the laboring poor." "Defoe and the Disordered City," p. 249. Elsewhere in his article, Novak points out that Defoe "thought mobs to be the very antithesis of government," and that, it seems to me, is precisely how H. F. views the poor in the *Journal*. Flanders characterizes H. F.'s attitude as one of "ambivalence," arguing that "Defoe perceptively records the struggle on the part of the bourgeois individualist between scorn and humanistic sympathy for the moral consequences of poverty." "Defoe's *Journal* . . . and the Modern Urban Experience," p. 165.

I do not, I should emphasize, maintain that H. F. shows no sympathy at all for the plight of the poor. What I do argue is that it is difficult, if not impossible, for anyone to experience compassion at a time when fear is his dominant emotion. And so I think it is with H. F. He does reveal sympathy and practice charity in the case of the waterman. But I hope I do not sound cynical in pointing out, with reference to this encounter, that first, he keeps a safe distance away during the conversation; second, not even H. F. himself suggests that anything in the nature of self-sacrifice is involved in his charity; third, he strikes up a conversation with the waterman just at the time when he is "musing how to satisfy [his] Curiosity" ("I had a great mind to see how things were managed in the River, and among the Ships; and as I had some Concern in Shipping, I had a Notion that it had been one of the best Ways of securing one's self from the Infection to have retir'd into a Ship . . ." [p. 106]) and he does indeed prevail on the waterman to carry him to Greenwich and back again.

I take more serious exception to Novak's argument in connection with the three fleeing Londoners: "though John argues for self-preservation at first, when he is stopped by a country Constable, he argues that self-preservation must come behind 'Compassion' (p. 145). The three Londoners use considerable ingenuity, but their survival depends on the charity of the countryside." I defer comment on the latter statement to a later point in this chapter, but on the former, I cannot forbear pointing out here that Novak fails to take into account the point of view. In John's first comment about self-preservation, he refers to his own rights in the matter and those of his friends. In the second instance, however, it is the Constable who pleads self-preservation. ("We wonder how you could be so unmerciful!" says John. To which the Constable rejoins, "Self-preservation obliges us." And it is at this point that John exclaims, "What! To shut up your Compassion in a Case of such Distress as this?" [p. 138].) In short, John is far from disinterestedly arguing, as Novak's summary suggests, that he himself would put compassion before self-preservation.

9. *Leviathan*, p. 1. The passage reads: "For by Art is created that great LEVIATHAN called a COMMON-WEALTH . . . which is but an Artificiall Man; though of greater stature and strength than the Naturall, for whose protection and defence it was intended; and in which, the *Soveraignty*, is an Artificiall *Soul*, as giving life and motion to the whole body; The *Magistrates*, and other *Officers* of Judicature and Execution, artificiall Joynts; *Reward* and *Punishment* . . . are the *Nerves*, that do the same in the Body Naturall; The *Wealth* and *Riches* of all the particular members, are the *Strength*; . . . *Equity* and *Laws*, an artificiall *Reason* and *Will*; *Concord, Health; Sedition, Sickness;* and *Civill war, Death.*"

10. *Leviathan*, pp. 21, 22. According to Hobbes, "though they have the use of Reasoning a little way, as in numbring to some degree; yet it serves them to little use in common life; in which they govern themselves, some better, some worse, according to their differences of experience, quicknesse of memory, and inclinations to several ends; but specially according to good or evil fortune, and the errors of one another. For as for *Science*, or certain rules of their actions, they are so farre from it, that they know not what it is."

11. *Leviathan*, p. 53.

12. When he speaks, toward the end, of "the merciful Part of this terrible Judgment" (p. 224), it is a little like the victim thanking his torturer for causing him pain because it feels so good when it stops.

13. Zimmerman, although arguing a rather different point, more than once emphasizes this fact. "As H. F. presents the multitude of details about the plague year," he writes, "we can see his confusion and anxiety reflected in his manner of narration." And again, "In his evaluations of people and policies, he is usually ambiguous and sometimes contradictory." And finally (although more questionably), "Although his faith in a moral scheme is confirmed, he continues to be baffled in his attempts to understand the complexities of divine justice." "H. F.'s Meditations," pp. 418–20.

14. See n. 1 above.

15. We may remember Hobbes's description of the state as being "of greater stature and strength than the Naturall, for whose protection and defence it was intended."

16. Zimmerman argues—in line with his contention that the entire *Journal* hangs on H. F.'s mistaken decision to remain in London and his subsequent repenting of that decision—that the story of the three men "is thematically relevant; the decision of these men to leave is the appropriate one and provides an indirect comment on H. F." "H. F.'s Meditations," p. 421. He fails to acknowledge, however, that the situation in which the three men find themselves is wholly unlike that of H. F. H. F. *wants* to stay in London to protect his "House, Shop, and

Warehouses fill'd with Goods" (p. 8), whereas the three men, although they too desire to stay, are faced, if they do so, with both homelessness and starvation.

17. Flanders makes much the same point: "we may understand that the isolation of the rich is no blessing either, for they are much limited under these circumstances; their isolation is preferable to death, but is in a sense its precursor—a *memento mori* prefiguring final entombment." "Defoe's *Journal* . . . and the Modern Urban Experience," p. 159.

18. It is interesting to note, apropos of this, that F. Bastian characterizes the Journal as "an uneasy compromise between a narrative and a commentary, an incoherent jumble which defies analysis." "Defoe's *Journal* . . . Reconsidered," p. 169.

CHAPTER 6. COLONEL JACK

1. *The History and Remarkable Life of the Truly Honourable Col. Jacque Commonly Call'd Col. Jack,* ed. Samuel Holt Monk (London, Oxford, New York: Oxford University Press, 1970), pp. 10, 11. References to this edition will appear hereafter in parentheses within the text.

2. So far as I know, John Richetti is the only recent critic to have pointed up this aspect of Colonel Jack. In fact he finds him Defoe's most triumphant hero: "Jack is consistently forced by necessity and circumstances to do things which seem destructive but which he converts by secret analysis into productive opportunities. It is the trick . . . that all Defoe's heroes aspire to master and among them Jack's performance is the most skilled and frequent." *Defoe's Narratives,* p. 166.

3. In his Introduction to the Oxford edition Samuel Holt Monk comments: "Defoe artfully introduces us to Jack, placed between the brutal and naturally criminal Captain . . . and the gay and careless Major . . ." (p. xv). But it seems to me important to emphasize that the three Jacks constitute a hierarchy in which the hero of the novel is placed not between but above the other two.

4. Introduction, pp. xiii, xv. James Sutherland, although commenting more on Jack's good fortune than on his goodness, reaches a similar conclusion: "It is all too good to be true: we are in the same world as that of Steele's sentimental drama." *Daniel Defoe: A Critical Study,* p. 202. And William H. McBurney sees Colonel Jack as "a creation very congenial with diluted Shaftesburyan ideas." "Colonel Jacque: Defoe's Definition of the Complete English Gentleman," *Studies in English Literature* 2 (1962): 327.

5. Richetti, *Defoe's Narratives,* p. 166.

6. When Jack goes into the Custom-House to return the stolen bills, he relates, "I went up and stood just at that Side of the writing Board, that goes up on that Side of the Room, and which I was but just Tall enough to lay my Arms upon" (p. 31).

7. *Serious Reflections,* p. 104 (italics added).

8. *Leviathan,* p. 37.

9. "More than any other of Defoe's heroes," says Richetti, "he is served by others who somehow recognize or discover his worthiness." *Defoe's Narratives,* p. 150.

10. S. H. Monk speaks of Jack's "disrupting the flow of gold froms the New World to the Old, merely to satisfy his own excessive avarice." Introduction, p. xviii. And Maximillian Novak, in spite of arguing that *Colonel Jack* "represents Defoe's closest approach to the novel as fictitious autobiography" ("Defoe's Theory of Fiction," *Studies in Philology* 61 [1964]: 656–57), insists elsewhere: "there is no doubt that avarice is Jack's ruling passion, and that eventually it carries him beyond the bounds of moderation." And he goes on to insist, with reference to Jack's Mexican venture, that "in violating the rule of mercantile morality he has committed a far worse crime than any of his petty thefts as a hungry young pickpocket on the streets of London." *Economics and the Fiction of Daniel Defoe,* pp. 122, 125. Zimmerman follows Novak's lead in this matter, concluding that "Jack is more aptly described as a greedy merchant than as a complete gentleman." *Defoe and the Novel,* p. 142. Zimmerman, however, goes considerably

beyond Novak in his negative view of Jack, finding virtually nothing to admire in him. John Robert Moore, on the other hand, seems not to see this Mexican episode as involving any moral problem at all. When, says Moore, Defoe "wrote with imaginative sympathy about a homeless wanderer like Robinson Crusoe, or a pirate like Captain Singleton, or merchant adventurers like Colonel Jack and the narrator of *A New Voyage Round the World*, he showed the clandestine trade of the English in Spanish America in its most favorable light." Moreover, earlier in his biography, Moore observes, talking specifically of *Colonel Jack:* "the theme of the interloping English merchant who braves the tyrannical restrictions of the Spanish rulers in America to trade with the planters had appeared two years before in *Captain Singleton*, and it was to recur three years later in *A New Voyage Round the World*." *Daniel Defoe*, pp. 297, 248.

11. Blewett, *Defoe's Art of Fiction*, p. 94. Blewett cites two other definitions, however, that seem to have a considerably more questionable applicability and that suggest he belongs to Zimmerman's camp as regards his view of Jack's character. One is " 'Jack-gentleman,' meaning 'a man of low birth or manners making pretensions to be a gentleman, an insolent fellow, an upstart.' " "This," says Blewett, "is precisely what Jack becomes when he returns to London and passes himself off as a French gentleman." The other is "Jack the Jacobite" (pp. 94, 95).

12. Not even George Starr can see such a statement as anything but a cursory lip service: "I do not think these passages give the work a predominantly religious orientation," he concedes. *Defoe and Casuistry* (Princeton, N.J.: Princeton University Press, 1971), p. 84. And S. H. Monk goes even farther: "neither Moll nor Jack is affected by Christianity" (Introduction, p. xvii).

CHAPTER 7. *ROXANA*

1. *Roxana: The Fortunate Mistress*, ed. Jane Jack (London, Oxford, New York: Oxford University Press, 1964), p. 96. References to this edition will appear hereafter in parentheses within the text.

2. James Walton has noted this fairy-tale aspect of the novel. "The Romance of Gentility," p. 133.

3. In the *Review* of October 4, 1707, Defoe anticipates Roxana in this: "the worst thing a sober woman can be married to is a FOOL. Of whom whoever has the lot, Lord have mercy, and a cross should be set on the door as of a house infected with the plague." *The Best of Defoe's Review: An Anthology*, compiled and edited by William L. Payne (New York: Columbia University Press, 1951), p. 133.

4. *Leviathan*, p. 88.

5. David Blewett maintains that in *Roxana* Defoe created "a novel that resembled a romance." *Defoe's Art of Fiction*, p. 122. And in his "The Romance of Gentility," James Walton comments in some detail on this aspect of the novel.

6. E. A. James has demonstrated that double entendres are to be found everywhere in *Roxana* and feels they are "meant to be seen as deliberate flourishes of naughty wit," on Roxana's part, "as would befit her character as a worldly courtesan." *Defoe's Many Voices*, p. 236. But just how conscious we are supposed to think Roxana is of the suggestive nature of such passages as those quoted here seems to me problematic. She is, I think, bent on concealing her lower nature from both herself and her readers, and it seems likely, therefore, that Defoe has her give herself away in a manner she does not intend.

7. ". . . you are to note," she says (p. 67), "that the People of *Paris*, especially the Women, are the most busie and impertinent Enquirers into the Conduct of their Neighbours, especially that of a Single Woman, that are in the World; tho' there are no greater Intriguers in the Universe than themselves; and perhaps that may be the Reason of it; for it is an old, but a sure Rule; that

When deep Intrigues are close and shy,
The GUILTY are the first that spy."

8. Roxana's associations with the Restoration and eighteenth-century stage have often been noted. Her calling herself a "Protestant Whore" has led to her being identified with Nell Gwynn. And J. R. Moore has stated that the "name Roxalana . . . had an intricate history on the English stage and in the intrigues of the court of Charles II, tracing back through the sultry oriental queens in Davenant's *The Siege of Rhodes* and Lee's *The Rival Queens* to its originals in the seraglio of the Turkish Empire." *Daniel Defoe*, p. 250.

9. James, *Defoe's Many Voices*, p. 252.

10. Defoe, *Review* 8, no. 61 (Tuesday, August 14, 1711); *Best of Defoe's Review*, ed. Payne, p. 262.

11. James Walton calls Amy "the personification of [Roxana's] fallen nature whose function it is to act out the basest impulses belonging to Roxana's situation," and later he defines her as "the agent of [Roxana's] own lawless propensities." "The Romance of Gentility," pp. 124, 131. H. G. Hahn says Amy speaks "for the baser impulses" of Roxana, and the Quaker for "the more ideal ones." "An Approach to Character Development in Defoe's Narrative Prose," p. 856.

12. Ralph E. Jenkins, for example, maintains that in the debate preceding Roxana's first illicit affair, "Amy plays the role of Body to Roxana's Soul. . . ." "The Structure of *Roxana*," *Studies in the Novel, North Texas State* 2 (1970): 147.

13. These are, in Defoe's view, the requisite accomplishments for a gentlewoman: Women "shou'd be taught all sorts of breeding suitable to both their Genius and their Quality; and in particular, *Musick* and *Dancing*, which it wou'd be cruelty to bar the Sex of, because they are their Darlings. . . ." "An Essay upon Projects," *Selected Poetry and Prose*, ed. Shugrue, p. 33. But in *Roxana* it seems that dancing becomes one more instance of a civilized veneer barely covering the "baser impulses."

14. Defoe, "The True-Born *Englishman*," *Selected Poetry and Prose*, ed. Shugrue, p. 51.

15. "Her French heritage," says James Walton, "consists of gifts of art and nature which qualify her as a budding *précieuse*. . . ." "The Romance of Gentility," p. 123. Rodney M. Baine argues, though, that it is George I's court, not that of Charles II, that is probably the real target of Defoe's satire. "Roxana's Georgian Setting," *Studies in English Literature* 15 (1975): 459–71. On this same point, David Blewett writes: "The special advantage to Defoe in creating a novel that resembled a romance was that, in addition to its immense contemporary popularity, the romance provided for an aristocratic setting and the revelation of aristocratic vices. And, more important, since many of the romances were set in the court of Charles II, Defoe was able to adopt the political expedient of criticizing the court of his own time under the cover of a description of the court of Charles II, and at the same time to suggest a moral comparison between the two." *Defoe's Art of Fiction*, p. 122.

16. *Farther Adventures*, 2 : 128.

17. *Selected Poetry and Prose*, ed. Shugrue, pp. 45–46.

18. At least two critics have said much this same thing about this celebrated scene. Stephen Cohan argues that "Roxana turns Amy into a whore in an attempt to legitimize her relationship with the Jeweler in his own mind." "Other Bodies: Roxana's Confession of Guilt," *Studies in the Novel, North Texas State* 8 (1976): 412. And John Richetti writes: "She forces Amy to act out her naturalism, that is, to become the true whore in their strange triangular relationship." *Defoe's Narratives*, p. 209. Terry J. Castle has recently made the interesting suggestion that Amy—"the secret sharer in Roxana's life"—functions as "a maternal persona." "'Amy, Who Knew My Disease': A Psycho-Sexual Pattern in Defoe's *Roxana*," *ELH* 46 (1979): 84, 89. Such a reading would lead one to see Defoe as emphasizing still more heavily Roxana's sense of herself as a helpless, dependent child, and it would also reinforce the idea of her desire to conceal from herself her own fallen nature.

19. According to James Walton, "she becomes, like that inner compulsion which leads Moll Flanders to crime, a type of Satan. . . ." "The Romance of Gentility," p. 125.

20. G. A. Starr suggests that Defoe himself may have experienced a similar dualism: "On

the one hand, there are signs throughout the book, which become unmistakable towards the end, that Defoe regards his heroine as a damned soul. On the other hand, his imaginative oneness with her often seems virtually complete, and at such times we too may be drawn into a kind of complicity with her. Defoe revels vicariously in Roxana's opulence, and chronicles her triumphs with evident relish; yet a contrary impulse to disavow any such involvement is increasingly powerful as the book proceeds." *Defoe and Casuistry*, p. 165.

21. "The pursuit by Susan too is a storm," says Zimmerman; and earlier in his discussion he has made a point closely related to this one: "Her hatred of her daughter Susan and her maid Amy's murder of the girl are the final and compelling testimonies to Roxana's identification with the malevolent world that she sees. The violence outside is also within. Susan is not only a daughter; it is Roxana's given name." *Defoe and the Novel*, pp. 173, 156.

22. David Blewett is thus right, I think, in stating that "Roxana is less a name than first a compliment and afterwards an accusation." *Defoe's Art of Fiction*, p. 23.

23. David Leon Higdon seems to be arguing essentially this point: "Roxana's life involves a constant struggle on her part to maintain a sense of self in the face of forces which conspire to strip it from her. . . . She mistakenly identifies self with money, things, and titles." And he goes on to insist, "Wealth and security are not at issue. . . . Her sense of self is at stake." "The Critical Fortunes and Misfortunes of Defoe's *Roxana*," *Bucknell Review* 20, no. 1 (1972): 79–80. It seems to me, however, that Higdon goes rather far off the track in identifying Susan with "compassion, emotion, and humanity."

24. In speaking of the pride that prompted her to thoughts of dropping the merchant in favor of the prince, Roxana uses similar descriptive words:

"I think verily, this rude Treatment of him, was for some time, the Effect of a violent Fermentation in my Blood; for the very Motion which the steddy Contemplation of my fancy'd Greatness had put my Spirits into, had thrown me into a kind of Fever, and I scarce knew what I did.

"I have wonder'd since, that it did not make me Mad; nor do I now think it strange, to hear of those, who have been quite *Lunatick* with their Pride; that fancy'd themselves Queens, and Empresses, and have made their Attendants serve them upon the Knee; given Visitors their Hand to kiss, *and the like;* for certainly, if Pride will not turn the Brain, nothing can" (p. 235).

25. "I cannot but take Notice here, that notwithstanding there was a secret Horror upon my Mind, and I was ready to sink when I came close to her, to salute her; yet it was a secret inconceivable Pleasure to me when I kiss'd her, to know that I kiss'd my own Child; my own Flesh and Blood, born of my Body; and who I had never kiss'd since I took the fatal Farewel of them all, with a Million of Tears, and a Heart almost dead with Grief, when *Amy* and the Good Woman took them all away, and went with them to *Spittle-Fields:* No Pen can describe, no Words can express, *I say,* the strange Impression which this thing made upon my Spirits; I felt something shoot thro' my Blood; my Heart flutter'd; my Head flash'd, and was dizzy, and all within me, *as I thought,* turn'd about, and much ado I had, not to abandon myself to an Excess of Passion at the first Sight of her, much more when my Lips touch'd her Face; I thought I must have taken her in my Arms, and kiss'd her again a thousand times, whether I wou'd or no.

"But I rous'd up my Judgment, and shook it off . . ." (p. 277). E. A. James notes that "Roxana's attitude toward her maid is extremely ambivalent," and he concludes by remarking that her "descriptions of Amy range from violently pejorative through fairly neutral to extremely honorific." *Defoe's Many Voices*, pp. 249–50.

26. In discussing the functions of Susan in the narrative, Terry J. Castle writes, "Part of the self [Susan] cannot be repressed without great damage to the whole." "'Amy, Who Knew My Disease' . . ." (p. 93).

27. "The poor Girl cry'd most lamentably, but wou'd not be beaten out of it still; but that which dumfounded *Amy* more than all the rest, was, that when she had rated the poor Girl a long time, and cou'd not beat her out of it, and had, *as I have observ'd*, threaten'd to leave her; the Girl kept to what she said before . . ." (p. 272).

CHAPTER 8. FINIS

1. See Hume's "Of the Sceptical and Other Systems of Philosophy," *The Philosophy of Hume,* ed. Herbert Austin Aikens (New York: Henry Holt and Company, 1893). At one point in this essay Hume writes: "were all my perceptions removed by death, and could I neither think, nor feel, nor see, nor love, nor hate after the dissolution of my body, I should be entirely annihilated, nor do I conceive what is farther requisite to make me a perfect nonentity. If any one, upon serious and unprejudiced reflection, thinks he has a different notion of *himself,* I must confess I can reason no longer with him. . . . He may, perhaps, perceive something simple and continued which he calls *himself;* though I am certain there is no such principle in me" (p. 170). And see also "Of Personal Identity," (Bk. 1, pt. 4, sec. 6) in *The Philosophy of David Hume,* ed. V. C. Chappel (New York: Random House, 1963), in which he writes: "The identity which we ascribe to the mind of man is only a fictitious one" (p. 180). For a more extended discussion of this whole question of identity as addressed in the eighteenth century by Locke, Hume, and others, see Zimmerman, *Defoe and the Novel,* pp. 5–12.

2. *A Tour of the Whole Island of Great Britain,* abridged and edited by Pat Rogers (Middlesex, England: Penguin Books, 1971), p. 94. References to this edition appear hereafter in parentheses within the text.

3. Defoe does show more prudence than Robinson Crusoe in at least one instance, for in this same letter he writes: "I had once, indeed, resolved to have coasted the whole circuit of Britain by sea, as 'tis said, Agricola the Roman general, did; and in this voyage I would have gone about every promontory, and into the bottom of every bay, and had provided myself a good yacht, and an able commander for the purpose; but I found it would be too hazardous an undertaking for any man to justify himself in the doing it upon the mere foundation of curiosity, and having no other business at all; so I gave it over" (p. 241).

4. Arthur Wellesley Secord remarks that "Powder explosions seem to have an unusual interest for Defoe," *Studies in the Narrative Method of Defoe, University of Illinois Studies in Language and Literature* 9 (Urbana: The University of Illinois Press, 1924), p. 158. And John Robert Moore observes: "Defoe's first reporting concerned a storm; he was always interested in storms, earthquakes, volcanoes, explosions, fires, and plagues. To the Puritan these were manifestations of God's power and his will; to the journalist they were always worth their space on the printed page." *Daniel Defoe,* p. 162. It is easy to see why one of the Delphic responses Robinson Crusoe cites (which he calls "the devil's oracles") has to do with storms:

Have I just cause the seas and storms to fear?
Echo—"Fear."

Serious Reflections, p. 276.

Select Bibliography

BOOKS

Becker, Ernest. *The Denial of Death*. New York: The Free Press, 1973.

———. *Escape from Evil*. New York: The Free Press, 1975.

Blewett, David. *Defoe's Art of Fiction: "Robinson Crusoe," "Moll Flanders," "Colonel Jack" & "Roxana."* Toronto, Buffalo, London: University of Toronto Press, 1979.

Brooks, Douglas. *Number and Pattern in the Eighteenth-Century Novel*. London and Boston: Routledge and Kegan Paul, 1973.

Brown, Norman O. *Life Against Death: The Psychoanalytical Meaning of History*. New York: Random House, 1959.

Byrd, Max, ed. *Daniel Defoe: A Collection of Critical Essays*. Englewood Cliffs, N.J.: Prentice-Hall, Inc., 1976.

Clifford, James M., ed. *Eighteenth-Century English Literature: Modern Essays in Criticism*. London, Oxford, New York: Oxford University Press, 1959.

Defoe, Daniel. *The Life and Strange Surprizing Adventures of Robinson Crusoe, of York, Mariner*. Edited by Donald Crowley. London: Oxford University Press, 1972.

———. *The Farther Adventures of Robinson Crusoe:* The Shakespeare Head Edition of the Novels and Selected Writings of Daniel Defoe, vol. 3. Oxford: Blackwell, 1927.

———. *Serious Reflections during the Life and Surprising Adventures of Robinson Crusoe: With his Vision of the Angelic World*. Edited by George A. Aitken. London: J. M. Dent, 1895.

———. *The Life, Adventures, and Pyracies, of the Famous Captain Singleton*. Edited by Shiv K. Kumar. London, Oxford, New York: Oxford University Press, 1973.

———. *The Fortunes and Misfortunes of the Famous Moll Flanders, &c.* Edited by G. A. Starr. London, New York, Toronto: Oxford University Press, 1971.

———. *A Journal of the Plague Year: being Observations or Memorials of the most Remarkable Occurrences as well Publick as Private, which happened in London during the last Great Visitation in 1665*. Edited by Louis Landa. Oxford, New York, Toronto: Oxford University Press, 1969.

———. *The History and Remarkable Life of the Truly Honourable Col. Jacque Commonly Call'd Col. Jack*. Edited by Samuel Holt Monk. London, Oxford, New York: Oxford University Press, 1970.

———. *Roxana: The Fortunate Mistress*. Edited by Jane Jack. London, Oxford, New York: Oxford University Press, 1964.

196

————. *A Tour of the Whole Island of Great Britain.* Abridged and edited by Pat Rogers. Middlesex, England: Penguin Books, 1971.

————. *The Best of Defoe's Review: An Anthology.* Edited by William L. Payne. New York: Columbia University Press, 1951.

————. *Selected Poetry and Prose of Daniel Defoe.* Edited by Michael F. Shugrue. New York: Holt, Rinehart, and Winston, 1968.

Donovan, Robert Alan. *The Shaping Vision: Imagination in the English Novel from Defoe to Dickens.* Ithaca, N.Y.: Cornell University Press, 1966.

Elliott, Robert C., ed. *Twentieth-Century Interpretations of "Moll Flanders": A Collection of Critical Essays.* Englewood Cliffs, N.J.: Prentice-Hall, Inc., 1970.

Ellis, Frank H., ed. *Twentieth-Century Interpretations of "Robinson Crusoe": A Collection of Critical Essays.* Englewood Cliffs, N.J.: Prentice-Hall, Inc., 1969.

Hazard, Paul. *The European Mind [1680–1715].* Cleveland and New York: The World Publishing Company, 1963.

Hobbes, Thomas. *Leviathan.* London: J. M. Dent and Sons Ltd. (Everyman's Library), 1947.

Hunter, J. Paul. *The Reluctant Pilgrim: Defoe's Emblematic Method and Quest for Form in "Robinson Crusoe."* Baltimore, Md.: Johns Hopkins Press, 1966.

James, E. Anthony. *Daniel Defoe's Many Voices: A Rhetorical Study of Prose Style and Literary Method.* Amsterdam: Rodopi, 1972.

McKillop, Alan Dugald. *The Early Masters of English Fiction.* Lawrence and London: The University of Kansas Press, 1956.

Moore, John Robert. *Daniel Defoe: Citizen of the Modern World.* Chicago and London: University of Chicago Press, 1958.

Novak, Maximillian E. *Economics and the Fiction of Daniel Defoe.* Berkeley and Los Angeles: University of California Press, 1962.

————. *Defoe and the Nature of Man.* London: Oxford University Press, 1963.

Richetti, John J. *Defoe's Narratives: Situations and Structures.* Oxford: Oxford University Press, 1975.

Secord, Arthur Wellesley. *Studies in the Narrative Method of Defoe* (University of Illinois Studies in Language and Literature 9). Urbana: The University of Illinois Press, 1924.

Starr, George A. *Defoe and Spiritual Autobiography.* Princeton, N.J.: Princeton University Press, 1965.

————. *Defoe and Casuistry.* Princeton, N.J.: Princeton University Press, 1971.

Sutherland, James. *Daniel Defoe: A Critical Study.* Cambridge: Harvard University Press, 1971.

Watt, Ian. *The Rise of the Novel: Studies in Defoe, Richardson and Fielding.* Berkeley and Los Angeles: University of California Press, 1957.

Zimmerman, Everett. *Defoe and the Novel.* Berkeley and Los Angeles: University of California Press, 1973.

ARTICLES

Baine, Rodney M. "Roxana's Georgian Setting." *Studies in English Literature* 15 (1975): 459–71.

Bastian, F. "Defoe's Journal of the Plague Year Reconsidered." *Review of English Studies* 16 (1965): 151–73.

Boyce, Benjamin. "The Shortest Way: Characteristic Defoe Fiction." In *Quick Springs of Sense: Studies in the Eighteenth Century*, edited by Larry S. Champion. Athens: University of Georgia Press, 1974. Pp. 1–13.

Braudy, Leo. "Daniel Defoe and the Anxieties of Autobiography." *Genre* 6 (1973): 76–97.

Brown, Homer O. "The Displaced Self in the Novels of Daniel Defoe." *ELH* 38 (1971): 562–90.

Castle, Terry J. "'Amy, Who Knew My Disease': A Psycho-Sexual Pattern in Defoe's *Roxana.*" *ELH* 46 (1979): 81–96.

Cohan, Stephen. "Other Bodies: Roxana's Confession of Guilt." *Studies in the Novel, North Texas State* 8 (1976): 406–18.

Erickson, Robert A. "Moll's Fate: 'Mother Midnight' and *Moll Flanders.*" *Studies in Philology* 76 (1979): 75–100.

Goldberg, M. A. "*Moll Flanders:* Christian Allegory in a Hobbesian Mode." *University Review* 33 (1967): 267–78.

Gray, J. Glenn. "The Problem of Death in Modern Philosophy." In *The Modern Vision of Death*, ed. N. A. Scott. Richmond, Va.: John Knox Press, 1968.

Hahn, H. G. "An Approach to Character Development in Defoe's Narrative Prose." *Philological Quarterly* 51 (1972): 845–58.

Hartog, Curt. "Aggression, Femininity, and Irony in *Moll Flanders.*" *Literature and Psychology* 22 (1972): 121–38.

Higdon, David Leon. "The Critical Fortunes and Misfortunes of Defoe's *Roxana.*" *Bucknell Review* 20 (1972): 67–82.

Jenkins, Ralph E. "The Structure of *Roxana.*" *Studies in the Novel, North Texas State* 2 (1970): 145–58.

Karl, Frederick R. "Moll's Many-Colored Coat: Veil and Disguise in the Fiction of Defoe." *Studies in the Novel, North Texas State* 5 (1973): 86–97.

McBurney, William H. "Colonel Jacque: Defoe's Definition of the Complete English Gentleman." *Studies in English Literature* 2 (1962): 321–36.

McVeagh, John. "Rochester and Defoe: A Study in Influence." *Studies in English Literature* 14 (1974): 327–41.

Martin, Terence. "The Unity of *Moll Flanders.*" *Modern Language Quarterly* 22 (1961): 115–24.

Novak, Maximillian E. "The Problem of Necessity in Defoe's Fiction." *Philological Quarterly* 40 (1961): 513–24.

———. "Defoe's Theory of Fiction." *Studies in Philology* 61 (1964): 650–68.

———. "Defoe and the Disordered City." *PMLA* 92 (1977): 241–52.

Rogers, Pat. "Crusoe's Home." *Essays in Criticism* 24 (1974): 375–90.

Schonhorn, Manuel. "Defoe's *Journal of the Plague Year:* Topography and Intention." *Review of English Studies* 19 (1968): 382–402.

———. "Defoe's *Captain Singleton:* A Reassessment with Observations." *Papers of Language and Literature* 7 (1971): 38–51.

Sherbo, Arthur. "Moll's Friends." In Sherbo, Arthur. *Studies in the Eighteenth Century English Novel.* East Lansing: Michigan State University Press, 1969.

Stein, William Bysshe. "Robinson Crusoe: The Trickster Tricked." *The Centennial Review* 9 (1965): 271–88.

Walton, James. "The Romance of Gentility: Defoe's Heroes and Heroines." *Literary Monographs* 4. Madison, Milwaukee, and London: University of Wisconsin Press, 1971. Pp. 89–135.

Watt, Ian. "The Recent Critical Fortunes of *Moll Flanders.*" *Eighteenth-Century Studies* 1 (1973): 109–26.

Zimmerman, Everett. "H. F.'s Meditations: *A Journal of the Plague Year.*" *PMLA* 87 (1972): 417–23.

Index

Addison, Joseph, 15–16
Alter, Robert, 186 n.23
Amy *(Roxana)*, 147, 149, 154. *See also Roxana*
Applebee's Journal, 46

Baine, Rodney M., 193 n.15
Bastian, F., 187–88 n.1, 191 n.18
Becker, Ernest, 84, 90
Berne, Eric, 34, 37, 39, 74
Biblical references, 58, 103, 104, 163, 180 n.8
Black Prince *(Captain Singleton)*, 55, 60, 122
Blewett, David: on *Colonel Jack*, 140, 192 n.11; on *Moll Flanders*, 185 n.13; on *Robinson Crusoe*, 180 n.34; on *Roxana*, 193 n.15, 194 n.22
Boyce, Benjamin, 182 n.14
Braudy, Leo, 178 n.21
Bredvold, Louis, 16–17
Brooks, Douglas, 38, 181 n.12
Brown, Homer O., 180 n.38
Brown, Norman O., 80, 81, 82, 83, 84, 95, 181 n.13

Camus, Albert, 101, 102
Cannibalism, 46, 47, 74, 144
Captain Singleton: appetitive (including sexual) references in, 50–51, 62–65; compared to *Robinson Crusoe*, 51; fire and heat imagery in, 57, 64, 65, 66, 67, 68; freedom-slavery theme in, 53, 55–56, 60–61; Friend William's role in, 63, 65–71, 181–82 n.14, 182–83 n.18; Gunner's role in, 52, 55, 58, 59, 60, 61, 62, 66, 180 n.4; guns and gunpowder in, 55–56, 67; hostile nature in, 56–61, 64, 181 n.9; identity question in, 70, 71; knowledge as power in, 52–57, 59–60, 61; money (gold) emphasis in, 62–63, 69, 70, 71, 181 n.13; navigation metaphor in, 52, 57–62; parent-figures in, 51–52, 70, 71; power of reason in, 53, 66–69, 70; Singleton as god-figure in, 55, 57; Singleton's mistrustfulness in, 69–72; Singleton's repentance in, 68, 69, 70; Singleton's search for home in, 50, 51, 56, 59–60, 71

Castle, Terry J., 193 n.18, 194 n.26
Charles II (king of England), 160
Clayton, Sir Robert, 148
Cohan, Stephen, 193 n.18
Colonel Jack: brutishness in, 122, 128, 135, 136; escape motif in, 129, 137, 138, 139, 141; fairy-tale quality of, 121–22, 130, 133; gratitude in, 131, 132, 133; honesty in, 123–24, 128, 129, 133–34; Jack as god-figure in, 123, 131–33, 136; Jack's accumulating tendencies in, 134, 137–38; Jack's hatred of dirt in, 126–27, 140, 142; Jack's reasoning powers in, 122–23, 125, 128–29; Jack's self-concealment in, 125, 139–41; Jack's sense of specialness in, 121–23, 125, 126, 127–28, 133, 135, 136, 191 n.2; Jack's upward social mobility in, 123–26, 128, 133, 138; money as power in, 127–28, 137–38; parent-figures in, 123, 130–31, 136–37, 141; up-and-down pattern in, 126, 129, 134, 135, 136–37; Will as allegorical figure in, 124–25, 128, 129, 141
Conscious Lovers, The (Steele), 16, 123
Crane, Stephen, 15, 17
Crusoe, Robinson: compared to Captain Singleton, 54, 56, 62, 67, 68; compared to Colonel Jack, 122, 123, 131, 134, 137, 141; compared to H. F., 104, 108, 110, 112, 113, 114, 116; compared to Moll Flanders, 73, 74, 75, 76, 79, 81, 85, 86, 90, 92, 100; compared to Roxana, 146

Defoe, Daniel: attitude toward drunkenness and lust, 135; attitude toward French, 160; belief in gratitude, 131; belief in natural law, 94–95; comparison with literary contemporaries, 15–18; Hobbes's influence on, 13–15; 17–23; as moralist, 15, 16, 93–94; resemblance to own protagonists, 171–73; Rochester's influence on, 21–23; as satirist, 21–22; tradesman mentality, 15
Descartes, René, 22
Donovan, Robert Alan, 183 n.1, 187 n.33

Doubles, 18, 66, 70. *See also Roxana* (Amy, Susan)
Dreiser, Theodore, 16
Dutch merchant *(Roxana)*, 145, 148–50, 62

Economic man (woman), 13, 14, 82
Edwards, Lee, 186 n.28, 187 n.33
Elliott, Robert C., 184 n.1
English captain *(Robinson Crusoe)*, 29, 32
Erickson, Robert A., 185–86 n.22

Fairy-tale motif, 23, 28. *See also Colonel Jack; Roxana*
Farther Adventures of Robinson Crusoe, 31, 46, 47–48, 60, 160, 177 n.8
Fielding, Henry, 18
Flanders, Moll: 175 n.4; compared to Captain Singleton, 50, 53, 56, 62, 68, 69; compared to Colonel Jack, 122, 123, 127, 128, 133, 139; compared to H. F., 107, 108, 111, 112, 114, 115, 118; compared to Roxana, 145, 150, 159, 160, 170
Flanders, W. Austin, 188 n.3, 189 n.8, 191 n.17
Freud, Sigmund, 80
Friday *(Robinson Crusoe)*, 29–30, 31, 32, 38, 46, 110, 122, 131, 180 n.34
Friend William *(Captain Singleton)*, 122. *See also Captain Singleton*
Fromm, Erich, 104

George III (king of England), 131, 132
German prince *(Roxana)*, 144–45, 147–48, 149, 150, 152–53, 154, 155, 156, 158
Goldberg, M. A., 185 n.17
Governess *(Moll Flanders)*, 87, 88–89, 90
Gratitude. *See Colonel Jack;* Defoe, Daniel; *Robinson Crusoe*
Great Master *(Colonel Jack)*, 130, 131, 132, 133, 136, 138
Gunner *(Captain Singleton)*, 180 n.4. *See also Captain Singleton*

Hahn, H. G., 180 n.34, 182 n.14, 193 n.11
Hartog, Curt, 178 n.21, 185 n.11
Hazard, Paul, 175 n.5
Heidegger, Martin, 44
H. F. *(A Journal of the Plague Year):* compared to Colonel Jack, 122, 129, 138
Higdon, David Leon, 194 n.23
Hobbes, Thomas: and Captain Singleton, 55, 60, 70; and Colonel Jack, 132, 137; and human "desire of Power," 19–20; and human reason, 21; and human self-centeredness, 19; as influence on Defoe, 13, 14, 15, 21, 23, 172; and irony in Defoe, 22; and *A Journal of the Plague Year*, 108, 110, 190 n.15; and Moll Flanders, 76, 77, 85, 87; and Robinson Crusoe, 24, 25, 29, 39, 40, 45;

and Roxana, 148; and state of nature, 18, 171
Home, Defoe protagonists' search for, 18, 174, 180 n.3. *See also Captain Singleton; Robinson Crusoe*
Hume, David, 171
Humphry *(Moll Flanders)*, 77, 83
Hunter, J. Paul, 177 n.2, 179 n.25

Identity question, 170, 173–74, 180 n.38. *See also Captain Singleton; Moll Flanders; Roxana*
Irony, 17, 19, 20, 21–22. *See also Moll Flanders*

Jack, Captain *(Colonel Jack)*, 122, 124, 125, 128, 129, 130, 169
Jack, Colonel: compared to Captain Singleton, 121, 122, 123, 129, 139; compared to Roxana, 148; desperation of, 22–23
Jack, Major *(Colonel Jack)*, 122, 126, 128
James, E. Anthony, 157, 178 nn. 12 and 20, 184–85 n.9, 187 n.33, 192 n.6, 194 n.25
Jemy *(Moll Flanders)*, 76, 77, 85, 89, 99–100
Jenkins, Ralph E., 193 n.12
Jew *(Roxana). See Roxana*
A Journal of the Plague Year: cautionary advice in, 102–4, 109, 111–12, 115, 120, 189 n.6; community survival in, 108–9, 111–14; helplessness in, 119–20; H. F.'s feelings of superiority in, 104–7, 109–11; history or fiction, 187–88 n.1; inferiority of the poor, 106–9, 110–11, 112, 189 n.8; mistrustfulness in, 115, 117–18; money as power in, 106–7; natural causes in, 110, 117; parent-figures in, 104, 111, 114, 118; rationality in, 105, 107–10, 113–14, 117–19; repentance in, 109–11; *Roxana* compared to, 153, 169; self-preservation in, 101–2, 117, 188 n.3, 188–89 n.5, 189–90 n.8
Jure Divino, 21

Karl, Frederick R., 185 n.13
Kettle, Arnold, 185 n.10
Knowledge, pursuit of, 19, 20, 116, 121. *See also Captain Singleton; Robinson Crusoe*
Knox, Robert *(Captain Singleton)*, 70
Koonce, Howard, 187 n.33
Kumar, Shiv K., 180 n.7, 182 n.14, 183 n.20

Lewis, C. S., 16
Locke, John, 22

McVeagh, John, 21, 22, 177 n.26, 182 n.15, 183 nn. 19 and 22
Martin, Terence, 185 n.22
Moll Flanders: compared to *A Journal of the Plague Year*, 102, 109; compared to *Roxana*, 150, 160; eat-or-be-eaten world in, 74–75, 81; identity question in, 90–92; ironic intention of author in, 81–82, 93–100, 186–

87 n.33; Moll's fear of exposure in, 89–92; Moll's friends in, 85–87; Moll's hatred of dirt in, 79, 80; Moll's mistrustfulness in, 75, 88–90; Moll's penitence in, 92–100; Moll's sexuality in, 82–83; money (gold) as power in, 76, 79–85, 186 n.23; Newgate as symbol in, 74, 78, 79, 80, 90, 91, 99, 185 nn. 12 and 13; parent-figures in, 86–88, 99, 186 n.29; power of reason in, 73, 77–79, 96–98; as psychological study, 15; self-indulgence in, 77, 94; service and self-service in, 75–77, 84; social status in, 76–77

Money, pursuit of, 14, 19, 20, 173–74. *See also Captain Singleton; Colonel Jack; A Journal of the Plague Year; Moll Flanders; Roxana*

Monk, Samuel Holt, 123, 191 nn. 3 and 10; 192 n.12

Moore, John Robert: on *Captain Singleton*, 180; on *Colonel Jack*, 192 n.10; on Defoe and storms, 195 n.4; on Defoe and William III, 66, 183 n.18; on Moll Flanders, 175 n.4; on *Roxana*, 193 n.8

Mother Midnight. *See* Governess *(Moll Flanders)*

Mouchat *(Colonel Jack)*, 131, 132, 136

Muscovite prince *(Farther Adventures)*, 47, 79

Naturalism, 21, 27

Naturalists (American), 15, 16, 17

Nature, alien, 20, 86, 173. *See also Captain Singleton; Robinson Crusoe*

Nature, state of, 13, 17, 18

Novak, Maximillan E.: on *Captain Singleton*, 181 n.12; on *Colonel Jack*, 191 n.10; on Defoe as moralist, 15; on Defoe and natural law, 94, 186 n.32; on Defoe and necessity, 69; on Defoe and passions, 65–66; on Defoe and Rochester, 21; on Defoe and self-love, 18; on Defoe and state of nature, 17, 19, 176 nn. 11 and 12, 183 n.23; on *A Journal of the Plague Year*, 112, 188 nn. 1 and 3, 189 n.5, 189–90 n.8; on *Moll Flanders*, 88, 95, 186–87 n.33; on *Robinson Crusoe*, 179 n.26

Older Colchester brother *(Moll Flanders)*, 75, 77, 78, 82, 85, 86, 122

Original Sin, 24, 26, 27, 134

Parent-figures, 14, 18. *See also Captain Singleton; Colonel Jack; A Journal of the Plague Year; Moll Flanders; Robinson Crusoe; Roxana*

Pavese, Cesare, 184 n.1

Plumb, J. H., 101

Pope, Alexander, 15

Portuguese pilot *(Captain Singleton)*, 51–53

Puritan, Defoe as, 15, 23

Puritanism, 23

Quaker Friend *(Roxana)*, 156, 165–66

Religious conversion, 13–14, 19–20, 23, 69, 142. *See also Robinson Crusoe*

Repentance, 69, 123, 142. *See also A Journal of the Plague Year; Moll Flanders*

Review, 46, 157–58, 183 n.18, 192 n.3

Rexroth, Kenneth, 81

Richardson, Samuel, 18

Richetti, John: on *Captain Singleton*, 180 n.2, 181 n.12, 182 n.14; on *Colonel Jack*, 123, 191 nn. 2 and 9; on *Moll Flanders*, 78, 184 n.2, 185 nn. 12 and 15; on *Robinson Crusoe*, 177 nn. 3 and 9, 178 n.15, 179 n.25; on *Roxana*, 193 n.18

Robinson Crusoe: circle imagery in, 41–42, 47; compared to *Roxana*, 153; Crusoe as god-figure in, 27, 29–33; Crusoe's attitude toward God and Providence in, 26–28, 37, 38, 48; Crusoe's feelings about home in, 13, 18, 25–27, 35, 39–41, 42, 47; Crusoe's rage for order in, 27, 28, 38, 45–46, 48; Crusoe's rebellion against limitation in, 24–26, 38, 41; Crusoe's religious conversion in, 25–26; gratitude in, 26, 27, 28, 29, 30, 31, 32; guns and gunpowder in, 30–33; hostile nature in, 23, 42–48; parent-figures in, 25, 26, 28, 39; powers of reason (ingenuity) in, 26, 27, 33–38, 48; pursuit of knowledge in, 28, 34, 36–38; state of nature in, 17

Rochester, Earl of, 21, 22, 26, 39, 65, 67, 75, 177 n.26, 182 n.15, 183 nn. 19 and 22

Rogers, Pat, 36, 40–41, 172

Roxana, 22–23, 174. *See also Roxana*

Roxana: Amy as alter-ego in, 150, 157–63, 165–70; fairy-tale motif in, 121, 145, 146, 147, 164; houses in, 151–53, 168; identity question in, 143–45, 147–49, 151–53, 155–70; money as power in, 149–51; parent-figures in, 146, 147, 148, 149, 150, 162; Roxana as actress in, 153–57, 159; Roxana's fear of disintegration and disappearance in, 143–45, 149, 151, 153, 162, 169–70; Roxana's self-concealment in, 153–57, 159, 160, 165–66; sexual references in, 152–53, 157, 159–60; symbolic significance of Jew in, 149, 150, 162, 163, 167–69; symbolic significance of Susan in, 164–70

Ruskin, John, 81

Satire in Defoe, 21–22

Schonhorn, Manuel, 182 n.14, 182–83 n.18, 188 n.2

Schorer, Mark, 184 n.1

Secord, Arthur Wellesley, 195 n.4

Serious Reflections of Robinson Crusoe, 27–28, 46, 48, 74, 99, 125

Shaftesbury, Earl of, 16

Sherbo, Arthur, 186 n.26
Smollett, Tobias, 18
Spiritual autobiography, 13, 49
Starr, George A., 184 n.3, 186 n.29, 192 n.12, 193–94 n.20
Steele, Richard, 15–16, 191 n.4. *See also The Conscious Lovers*
Stein, William Bysshe, 180 n.35
Susan *(Roxana)*, 160, 162. *See also Roxana*
Sutherland, James, 184 n.9, 191 n.4
Swift, Jonathan, 16–17, 80

Tillyard, E. M. W., 175 n.3
Tory satirists, 17
Tour through the Whole Island of Great Britain, 171–73
"The True-Born *Englishman*," 160, 183 n.18
Turkish references, 51, 110, 155, 157, 159–60, 180 n.35

Van Ghent, Dorothy, 81–82, 84

Vision of the Angelic World, 37, 176 n.22

Walters, William. *See* Friend William *(Captain Singleton)*
Walton, James, 182 n.14, 185 n.11, 192 n.2, 193 nn. 11, 15, and 19
Watt, Ian, 183–84 n.1, 187 n.33
Will *(Colonel Jack). See Colonel Jack*
William III (king of England), 65, 182–83 n.18
Wilmot, Captain *(Captain Singleton)*, 63, 65
Wilmot, John. *See* Rochester, Earl of

Xury *(Robinson Crusoe)*, 31, 37

Zimmerman, Everett: on *Captain Singleton*, 180–81 nn. 3 and 8, 181–82 n.14; on *Colonel Jack*, 191–92 n.10; on *A Journal of the Plague Year*, 188 n.1, 188–89 n.5, 189 n.6, 190 n.13, 190–91 n.16; on *Robinson Crusoe*, 177 nn. 6 and 9, 178 nn. 13 and 15; 179 n.27; on *Roxana*, 194 n.21